SEVE BALLESTEROS'S
Touch of Class

SEVE BALLESTEROS'S
Touch of Class

The 1984 Open Championship and the Meaning of Europe's Greatest Golfer

KENNY REID

Foreword by Andrew Cotter

pitch

First published by Pitch Publishing, 2024

Pitch Publishing
9 Donnington Park,
85 Birdham Road,
Chichester,
West Sussex,
PO20 7AJ
www.pitchpublishing.co.uk
info@pitchpublishing.co.uk

A CIP catalogue record is available for this book from the British Library.

ISBN 978 1 80150 886 5

Typesetting and origination by Pitch Publishing

Printed and bound in India by Thomson Press India Ltd.

Contents

In memory of my grandpa,

Graham Emmerson

Foreword
Andrew Cotter

Memories are not to be trusted

I WAS reminded of this recently when I was broadcasting and mentioned a one-club challenge involving both Severiano Ballesteros and Lee Trevino at St Andrews, which took place just a couple of days after the Old Course had staged the Open Championship in 1984. I always remembered (beyond any doubt, in my deeply untrustworthy mind) that Seve, using the 5-iron, which was his one club of choice, had hit a shot which so impressed Trevino that the American – one of the few players with the shot-making skills to rival Seve – had called out 'touch of class baby … touch of class' in admiration.

Of course, I was wrong, as I often am in my recollection of so-called facts. Not that the compliment hadn't been made by Trevino, but that the remark in question had actually been uttered during the third round of the Open Championship itself, after Seve hit his second shot into the par-5 5th hole.

The person who swiftly made me aware of my misbehaving memory was the author of this book and a friend going back to junior golfing days in Ayrshire.

Apart from being a richly gifted golfer himself – one of those deeply annoying people whose handicap obliges him to add shots on to his score at the end of a round – Kenny Reid is a lover of the game. And someone who has a passion for digging deep into the archives and into the minutiae of the great tournaments to bring them to life again.

What I do remember, without any doubt, is that 1984 is just about when my childish golf-mad enthusiasm was reaching its peak and St Andrews that year provided a near-perfect Open Championship for my needs. It had a Scottish first-round leader in Bill Longmuir, it had an elegant young rising talent in Ian Baker-Finch. It had a mustering of some of the biggest names in the game in Norman, Langer, Faldo and Trevino. But above all, it came down to the last couple of holes and to my two favourite golfers in Tom Watson and Seve.

I idolised Watson because he was the greatest of the modern Open Championship players. I had watched him up close in my home town of Troon as he won two years before. How incredible now that he should have been going for three Claret Jugs in a row and his sixth within the span of nine years. And then, of course, there was Seve ... Who could not be won over by the magical Spaniard?

His looks and his personality held you in their thrall – we felt all of his emotions as he put them so obviously on display for us. He painted a round of golf with beautiful and often abstract strokes.

As I remember it, I was actually disappointed when Watson nestled his second shot close to the wall on the Road Hole, but then quickly lost all those feelings of deflation in Seve's beaming smile when his birdie putt curled and fell with its final roll on the 18th green.

Not only are memories untrustworthy, but when it comes to sport they tend to be short. People wax lyrical about the current stars and believe that progress is endless and that all things now must surely be better. We have a habit of forgetting just how talented past generations were and how they captivated us. And we certainly forget the finer detail.

Which is why books like this are so wonderful to read. To remind us of the facts and to revive the very precise feelings from four decades ago. To place us there again rather than floating in unreliable memory.

One other thing I do recall, nearly 40 years on from that Open Championship at St Andrews, is that during the second round I found myself in possession of one of Seve's own tee pegs, fresh from having balanced Seve's own ball and having been flicked by a flash of his gleaming persimmon driver and sent spinning back, nearly landing in my lap as I crouched by the second tee. It was light green in colour and had his own name running down the wood in stylish black writing. I cherished it for about a week until it went missing. Possibly put into a bin by mistake. Perhaps one of my brothers took it and used it themselves – we never did get to the truth of the matter.

Of course, it might have been during the first round. And now that I think about it, it might actually have been his drive on the third hole. Or maybe none of this happened at all. I will have to check with Kenny.

But I enjoyed returning to St Andrews in 1984 and hope you do as well.

PRACTICE ROUND

'Everything you can imagine is real.'

Pablo Picasso

1983: The Masters Tournament

Battles at Augusta National – A Dramatic Charge – Tension in 1980 – A Chip-and-Run

SEVE GESTURED the American should go first. Tom Watson motioned for the Spaniard to play, Ballesteros stoic as he glared, focused on his approach to Augusta National's alluring but dangerous par-five 15th. Into a strong breeze, with Watson hooking his drive, both players had laid up and faced testing wedges to a pin cut front left, silvery waters beckoning a mishit or undercooked third shot. Was Watson being polite, wondered Seve. Maybe it was politeness cloaked in an effort to disconcert him? On the angle, it was Ballesteros to play. He took the pin out of the equation, knocking his ball to the back of the putting surface. Watson learned nothing, and the European's four-shot lead was intact.

The 1983 Masters Tournament was once again within Severiano Ballesteros's gift, but for 90 minutes it had been in the balance. A Monday finish was the result of rain wiping out Friday's play, and on this bright spring day in Georgia, as the rest of the planet went about its daily toil, Ballesteros had seemingly tried to erase his own lead. Playing in the penultimate group with Watson, one stroke behind the leaders Ray Floyd and defending champion Craig Stadler, the Spanish two-time major winner had left the starting grid with all cylinders firing.

Dressed in his favourite final-day blue – a paler shade courtesy of Lacoste when in the US – in contrast to the sombre brown and fawn of Watson, and with American Nick DePaul hefting his Sounder bag around the course of Bob Jones's dreams, Seve immediately attacked Alister MacKenzie's masterpiece. He striped a 7-iron through the breeze into eight feet at the 400-yard 1st. Birdie. At the downhill, boomerang-shaped 555-yard 2nd the Spanish *experto* smacked a drive 300 yards, flushed a 4-wood on to the green and canned the 15-foot eagle putt: this was met with barely a change in demeanour, a subtle smile acknowledging the second gain of the day. A par followed at the 360-yard 3rd after almost holing a 20-footer for another birdie. Then Seve stiffed his 2-iron at the tricky par-three 4th. Two feet. Seve was four under par through four holes and had vaporised the leaders' slim advantage: three, three, four, two saw him accelerating away from Watson, overtaking Floyd and Stadler at speed, beating the field average for those holes by more than four shots. He was two ahead of Floyd, three in front of Watson and Tom Kite. Kite remarked that while the rest of the field were Chevrolets, Seve had started like a Ferrari. Then, like a finely tuned, high-end sports car, Seve began to misfire.

> 'Tall, dark, and handsome, Ballesteros had blossomed into an exceptional golfer and a major box-office attraction. He hit glorious long irons and could shoot like Wyatt Earp – he was deadly.'
>
> **Robert Sommers**, *The US Open: Golf's Ultimate Challenge*

A front nine of 31 cemented his position, but at the often-treacherous short 12th, Golden Bell, he overshot the green, perhaps a subconscious pull as a reaction to the threat of missing short right and ending in Rae's Creek. The tee shot landed in the shrubbery, but trickled back towards the short stuff. Earlier,

Scott Simpson had taken a treble bogey from the vegetation. Ballesteros settled for a four. At Azalea, the par-five 13th, Seve hooked his drive into the woods left of the stream, fortunately found his ball, hacked out on to the fairway and then took on the pin with his next, a 6-iron. Crazy or confident, he whipped it through the breeze, right at the stick, the pin cut towards the water. The ball stuck on the front of the green, 15 feet from the pin, 15 feet from the creek. In a later Masters video compilation, Jim Kelly, the US commentator, would say, 'Oh my, goodness gracious, where does a man get the moxie to pull off a shot like that, at a moment like this?' Severiano Ballesteros was no stranger to moxie.

Seve burned the right side of the hole, narrowly missing his birdie. They would say Ballesteros was lucky finding his tee shot, and getting it back into play with his second. He resolved to complete the final four holes in par; he'd been in this position before. Almost. On winning the Masters in 1980, he faced similar dilemmas. Entering round four he was 13 under par and seven shots ahead of American Ed Fiori, bidding to become the second overseas winner after Gary Player, three green jackets in his wardrobe. Player's most recent had been the 1978 instalment when he shot seven birdies in the last ten holes, a 64, and defeated, among others, the defending champ Tom Watson into second place. Seve told his early biographer, Dudley Doust, 'I think Player maybe likes to think people are against him so he can fight harder. I'm like that. The more against you are the crowd, the more you want to prove something.' This brand of negative reinforcement would become a salve to Seve Ballesteros. Great sportsmen and women use all manner of methods to galvanise themselves. To the fan he was artist and noble warrior; to others, invader and pillager. By the time Seve entered the back nine in 1980 he'd mentally gone through winning the tournament, but had these visualisations truly considered a lead of ten shots with nine to play after he engineered a flawless 33 on the front side? The lowest winning total was there for the taking. A back nine of 34 would hand Seve the first Masters trophy won by a European, from the biggest-ever 54-hole lead, in a total of 270 blows. Then he faltered severely, as if he stopped focusing, and it became, for a while, a contagion. He three-putted the 10th, double-bogeyed the 12th, and bogeyed the 13th as his nearest challengers made advances. At one stage his lead was cut to four. Was this in Seve's mind in 1983? Possibly. It's likely it was in Tom Watson's. Maybe there was a score to settle. In 1980 Seve eventually won his first green jacket; in 1981 he missed the cut and, as defender, measured up Tom Watson for his second. In 1983 the Spaniard pulled himself together, made four more pars and came to the last with a four-shot lead as Stadler endeavoured to make birdies behind him.

On the final tee, sweater illuminated by the dying sun, Ballesteros's tee shot was slightly pushed, his backswing almost perfectly reaching the horizontal but pointing a fraction towards the pines. Tom Watson watched, as did Seve, the Spaniard listing to the left, cosmically encouraging his ball to do likewise. As the hole breaks to the right at the top of the steep rise, then about 250 yards from the tee, the ball clattered into the timber but pinged back to the side of the fairway. Lucky in anyone's book. Seve tramped up the rise looking relaxed, right hand raised, acknowledging the polite near-victory applause from the patrons. His Hollywood features were radiant in the dusky sunlight, shadows amplifying his good looks, belying the pressure of the last few hours. As the shadows grew, and fuelled by the near-certainty of a second win in Georgia and a breeze at his back, Seve's approach overshot the green by some 15 yards, beyond the flag by 20. He was faced with a chip back over short grass before reaching a fast green, the pin, and then the slope to the bottom tier.

'I was four shots clear. I wasn't worried at all,' Ballesteros would say.

He eyed up the chip for a couple of minutes, hands on hips, arms moving back and forth, imagining the shot, how the ball would react. As he took his stance, he realised he had to move some of the gallery back, including a Pinkerton guard who'd get a mouthful of wedge if he remained stationary. Tom Watson and his caddy, Bruce Edwards, watched from the back right of the green. Some in the US media would say the Spaniard fluffed his chip, but in truth he struck a delicate shot that stuck to the short grass a fraction more than expected, finishing a yard shy of the putting surface. At Augusta, another ounce of power or a fractional change in one of the ball's hops could've delivered it to a matter of feet. Seve gave a wry smile. He walked to caddy DePaul, handed his iron back, surveyed his lie and the remaining few feet to the green: a shot that would gather pace on a green as slick as a billiard table. As Ballesteros contemplated the proposition, Stadler missed birdie at the 17th and the Spaniard's lead remained intact. Seve did not know this. Yet. CBS commentator Ken Venturi suggested the safe shot would be a putter, 'guiding it down as close as he can'; however, the player had already pulled an iron. He got over the ball, feet close together, body fractionally open, clubhead just ahead of the heel of his left golf shoe. His strong, slender hands looked relaxed and at home on the grip. With a short swing and fluid cock of the wrists the ball was smoothly chipped on to the putting surface.

'Go in!' came the high-pitched tone of a southern belle. The ball smoothly rolled straight into the heart of the hole. Ballesteros straightened up, looked around and gave a gentle fist pump followed by a shake of the arm. He'd won his second Masters in three years. He saluted the crowd and walked to the hole. CBS declared it destiny; but also focused on an alternative.

'That ball was not going very slow,' declared Venturi.

'If he hadn't hit the pin, he might have gone down that slope,' Pat Summerall figured.

Venturi continued, 'It hit the pin, it went in the hole, it was meant to be.'

CBS seemed to think he was lucky – Tom Watson was later reported to have concurred – even though the ball ran into the cup like a well-paced putt. It was dramatic, great for the fans and global television. Seve had won in the USA. Again.

Ballesteros resented the tag of being lucky. He'd been crowned the 'Car Park Champion' at Royal Lytham in 1979 on winning his first Open. Hale Irwin declared him fortunate on a number of occasions that week. Seve had attacked the Lancashire links from the outset, recognising the further up a hole one got, the less intense the rough. At Augusta National, some of the media and players focused on luck and chance, but the numbers didn't lie. In the heat of battle, the Spaniard shot the second-lowest round of the day, only Ben Crenshaw had beaten him, with a classy 68. Watson, Floyd and Stadler shot 73, 75 and 76. Their Chevys had piled up on the first lap, fenders crumpled, engines smoking, co-driving caddies dazed and confused. Even if Seve hadn't chipped in he could've two-putted and won by two. He could've lost more shots on the back nine, but he didn't. 'The greats' like Palmer, Nicklaus and Player all recognised the wisdom of luck, that it appeared often when one was in full flight, when all the hard work had been put in elsewhere and in preparation, and now it was time for a gentle break. But often a gentle break can be golf's Grim Reaper in disguise, toying with a player's mind, a suggestion of time running out or that one's reserves have been depleted. Quality players refocus and charge on, taking good fortune as a sign of what now must be done, not entertaining the threat of future shots being met with no luck or, worse, bad luck. Later in 1983, when Seve chipped in to force World Match Play extra holes against Arnold Palmer, Palmer was asked if the Spaniard was lucky: 'No, not lucky. When I was young and making those, I used to like to think they were just good shots.'

Watson and Ballesteros did not directly get on, and while there was never hostility, there was also no sense of *genuine warmth*. There was, however, the respect one must give to one's hunter. Perhaps Watson was not conscious of his own luck and how, as so often in the way of golf, great players make that happen. In the 1977 Open Championship's 'Duel in the Sun', on the 15th hole of the final round at Turnberry, Watson pulled his 4-iron to the short hole, landed inches beyond the bunker guarding the left and came to rest five yards from the putting surface in some scraggly grass. He faced a putt of 60 feet: after leaving the putter face the ball jumped slightly, but landed back on Watson's intended line. With at least ten feet of pace too much the ball rattled the pin and dropped. It was a massive dent in Nicklaus's expectations. Jack was 12 feet from the hole but did not come close to making birdie. The rest, in 1977, is history. In 1982 Watson chipped in at Pebble Beach's 17th, helping him win his only US Open. Watson predicted that chip in, telling his caddy he'd make it, but later admitted it may have been a once-in-a-lifetime shot. To utilise luck you have to be in position, playing well, with a crystal-clear mind. Seve was now the luckiest player in golf. He was three days into his 26th year, had won three majors, two of them in the USA.

In summing up the 1983 Masters Tournament, Herbert Warren Wind wrote in *The New Yorker*:

> On [sic] the last round of the Masters, after taking command with that glorious surge in the first four holes, he kept his emotions well in check and played his way home with the blend of assertiveness and prudence the

> situation called for. If he sets his mind to it, there is no limit to what Ballesteros can accomplish in the years ahead.

Tom Watson would tell *The New York Times* that during the early holes of that final 18 he felt like a boxer being floored twice in the first round. In Seve's opinion, the first four holes in the last round were the best he ever played.

1984: The Open Championship, St Andrews

Ballesteros Senses His Chance – Tom Watson Pursues

SEVE HAD played 274 shots since lunchtime on Thursday. It was now late afternoon, minutes before six o'clock on Open Championship Sunday. The delirium of the crowds was founded on intense expectation. For Ballesteros a few more shots would be the difference between a win and a loss, four majors and three majors. Another Claret Jug was within reach. Or perhaps Tom Watson, as he eyed up his second to the 17th hole on the Old Course, could already taste the full-blooded Bordeaux as it glugged into his sixth jug.

The Spaniard walked tall and upright across the Swilcan Bridge, his long arms and big hands relaxed at his side, a confidence in his step. The calm seemed to belie the opportunity he faced. Opportunity also faced the American: winning an Open Championship on the Old Course at St Andrews, golf's primal playing field. As they marched up the 18th towards his tee shot, Seve told caddy Nick DePaul that if they made birdie, the championship would be theirs. Ballesteros sensed *el destino. Everything you can imagine is real.*

2012: Somo Beach, Cantabria

Arriving in Santander – The Start of a Journey

I THROW my bags on to the bed and walk to the window, its frame rattling in the wind, overlooking the bay. I draw back the curtain. Palm trees mark the bottom of the panorama, mottled skies the top, and the multicoloured sails of kitesurfers sweep up and down the channel where the Bay of Santander dissolves into the Bay of Biscay. Away and to my left I see a long crescent of sand in the near distance; it's maybe half a mile long, shaped like the tip of Aladdin's lamp, the right-most end curling like a spout. Immediately I recognise it as a place where another harnessed the power of sorcery. It was the sweep of the beach at Somo, where many a Seve photoshoot took place, mimicking his early boyhood golfing days on the beach by the golf club.

Across the channel I recognise Real Golf de Pedreña and the holes stretching towards the water, clubhouse tucked in the trees. I spot Seve's house, that area's highest property looking down to the small fishing port. The hotel room is a gift, the entire vista familiar from a BBC documentary. 'For non-fiction projects, ideas are everywhere. They just go by in a ceaseless stream,' wrote John McPhee, master of the form in both *The New Yorker* and his own books.

I am faced by the genesis of European golf's greatest years. From this small, seaside place in one of Europe's highest countries a boy grew and became a man. A golfer who put no stock in reputations, who sought to redefine those and in so doing defined the sport for the generations who saw him play. I looked out and over the Bay of Biscay, its surface fractured with glints in a seascape of grey and black, the sky above a darkish blue punctuated with autumnal blotches. Beyond the horizon lay the 'New World', literal new worlds for the young Seve. In what better place could a young Ballesteros live, dream and anticipate the sting of sporting battle? Room 114 had delivered me to the source of his ceaseless stream.

2000: San Roque, Andalusia

Encountering Seve – Memories of Greatness – Pain and Loss

EARLY MORNING, December 2000. The sun struggled to appear on a typically brisk Andalusian start to a winter's day. A sharp wind licked the coast, bristling the cork oaks around the estate. The land had been pounded by rain and many golf courses were closed, leaving a few thousand tourists and residents bereft of the chance to play as the year drew to a close. A few venues remained open, including The San Roque Club, set in the former family home of Ernest Hemingway's favourite sherry producers, Domecq, between Marbella and Cadiz. I was standing on the putting green, half protecting myself from the dawn chill. A nice glass of Amontillado would have been a useful winter warmer. As each putt rolled, the ball caressed the morning dew and spat it up and out like a small but violent Catherine wheel, ball after ball charting dark-green lines on the silvery putting surface, left, then right of the hole, and occasionally into the heart of it, these successes ending in a pleasing rattle in the otherwise silent morning. A few golfers and some staff milled around.

'Good morning, Sir,' said the young greenkeeper, his friendliness belying the dank look of his green uniform, and his command of English emphasising the course was at the heart of Spanish golf tourism, something that barely existed 25 years before.

'Morning. A bit cold, but at least we're getting golf,' I replied, happy for the interruption.

'Yes, it's been very wet. Bai-esteros is on the tee.'

'Really, which one?' thinking Manuel or Vicente.

'Sebby. Seberiano Bai-esteros.'

I looked up, gauging if he was serious. I was due off in 15 minutes. I picked up the balls, grabbed my bag and made for the 1st tee. When I arrived, there, dressed in a familiar Sunderland rain jacket, keeping the chill at bay, Seve was taking an occasional practice swing while chatting with brother Vicente and two young pros. I couldn't quite believe it. A handful of people had gathered, and an older couple asked for Seve's autograph.

'No, sorry, I am on the course now, it is my work,' Seve replied graciously, a look of mild apology in his dark eyes.

I took in the scene. Vicente, Seve's immediate older brother, stood by the golf cart, ready to take the helm. I studied him – tall, slender, receding hairline – and cast my mind back to 1986 when Seve cruised a 6-iron into eight feet at Augusta National's 13th and Vicente held his brother's arm aloft proclaiming, 'Fantastica! Fantastica!' He wasn't wrong, the 1980s were Seve's greatest days. I was star-struck. Nine months prior, my brother had played in the Madeira Island Open and stood on the practice ground next to Seve, hitting shots. Alan spoke of Seve's penumbra of greatness, and what a thrill it was just to have that experience. At San Roque, the prospect of stepping on the same stage was priceless. It came time for Ballesteros to play. He teed up, stepped back and surveyed the challenge, a pleasant par four of medium length. From the elevated tee the player can see all: a fairway bunker down the left and then another further up the right, jutting towards the centre, warning the aggressive and long player that danger lurks. Seve took a couple of graceful practice swings, his action as fluid and pleasing to the common eye as ever, including some of the familiar cues. He took his position over the shot, gave a slight tug of adjustment to his left trouser leg and swung, making clean contact with the ball. It flew right; a push, over the wall and out of bounds.

His star shone brightly, now in a different orbit. His game was fragile, but still he was the greatest I had seen play, a man who revelled in *total golf*, who made his way around a golf course like a heavyweight boxer down on points won a title fight. He was still the Severiano Ballesteros I loved as a teenager. That second shot into the 13th in the 1986 Masters final round is – for me – the greatest swing: Seve's poise, angles, balance, grace, power. Few could exhibit fluidity combined with such intent. That day at San Roque was but three years since Ballesteros had been in the fray at the 1997 Ryder Cup. Valderrama, the venue, was just across the valley. His manic captaincy and fervent support for the European cause ruffled a few feathers, but it was the stamp of the man. The mercurial Spaniard could be as quick to temper as a ball exploding off a clubface, but he could be as gracious and kind as a gentle bounce towards the hole. He ribbed and worked the crowd sometimes, and then shot glaring, laser stares the next. One minute a control freak, the next devil-may-care. He described the European Tour head honchos as a type of mafia (while at a tournament in Italy), and fought tooth and nail against Deane Beman and the PGA Tour commitment to a minimum number of events for membership. He was a beacon for all European golfers, yet was sometimes petulant and childlike when he didn't get his own way, *or what he felt was the right way.* Passionate, that's what Severiano Ballesteros was. He could woo US crowds just as he totally detested some of their players. He shared all our flaws both on and off the golf course, but it all seemed to come from the heart.

He won five majors in a career littered with over 90 victories – counting Ryder Cups and where his winning started, the Pedreña caddy championships – accolades and adulation. In the UK he was feted as an ideal the country's own golfers were far from achieving. From his looks to homegrown technique, to skill, to his simple, elegant style: men, women and children swooned. No one matched his strength, grace or his derring-do. His thumping drives, long irons and majestic touch captivated millions. We hung on his every shot, his every gesture and golfing nuance. He fascinated and infuriated by turn. He caused elation and heartache. Seve was human. These qualities drew his many fans. He was capable of the shots of every golfer's dreams. And many shots no one had dared imagine. Ballesteros was a divine wind of golfing greatness who, at times, seemed to harness elemental forces. At the 1978 Hennessy Cup he became the first to drive the 10th green at The Belfry, then a 310-yard par four that *demanded* a lay-up with an iron followed by a wedge to the green, the risk–reward being the further up the left a player went, to get closer to the pin, the narrower the tee shot target. Ballesteros didn't like demands. Or other people's ideas. The faraway target was protected by water that ran along its front and entire left flank, but Seve pounded a driver on to the green. The shot was a literal embodiment of Isaac Newton's Third Law of Motion: *For every action, there is an equal and opposite reaction.* Seve crashed into the golf ball, drove through the shot to the top of his follow-through then rocked back on his feet, as if reeling from the recoil of an artillery gun, fighting against his own power. With a persimmon driver. And a balata ball. With might and determination, not crude strength and hope.

* * *

Ten years after San Roque, late April 2011, I was out with a friend who works in golf, for a major winner. He'd heard that

Seve was most unwell, probably on his 'way out'. This was a shock, as we admired his extreme determination to reappear on the golfing stage, but part fateful; it had been clear he was caught in a struggle for life. On Saturday, 7 May, Seve Ballesteros passed away. Social and traditional media were awash with tributes and memories. Postings of golf clips and photos inundated personal and golf pages on Facebook. It felt as if I read every single post, watched every video clip. At home I flicked through some books of pictorial essays, and in *Severiano Ballesteros* by Dave Cannon, the Spaniard said of Tom Watson, 'He is one of my biggest rivals.' I recalled the great moments and how I felt when watching him in person or on TV: Open Championships, the Masters, Ryder Cup dramas. The photographs brought his charisma alive. Even Seve's darker moments burn in my psyche. Thirty minutes or so after his towering iron into the 13th at Augusta in 1986 he dumped an horrific 4-iron into the pond at the 15th, a rotten non-hit. We had all done *that*. If only he'd smashed a 5-iron. Despite that pain and the failure to victoriously commemorate the death of his father that year, the 1987 Masters saw Ballesteros into a play-off with Greg Norman and Larry Mize.

The final round was the evening before the start of the Scottish Boys' Championship at Dunbar, near Edinburgh and I had played a practice round and found myself hitting the ball well, going through a phase of holes where I seemed to be knocking the pins out. The father of the boy practising in front complimented my iron play. I thanked him, but didn't let on. My game was worse than streaky, it was bitty. I could flag hunt for six holes, struggle to hit greens for another six, then spend the rest in the golfing boondocks. Sometimes a round felt like more than 18 holes. I was at Dunbar to make up the numbers but my first-round draw gave me an early start on the Tuesday, allowing a guilt-free Sunday night of TV from the comfort of my guesthouse. I cowered underneath my bedding, peeking at Seve playing the last few holes, the tournament in the balance as Larry Mize had finished at three under par and Seve and Greg Norman were still battling on the course to win, or to tie the native Georgian. Robert Green recounts it in his biography of Ballesteros, and for me, too, the 72nd hole is one of Seve's great unsung moments.

I was emotionally rapt as Seve came up the fairway, I *could not bear* to see him make bogey, to miss a possible play-off, although Greg Norman could still win outright. I was invested fully in the outcome, every good, every bad shot, mine. I felt the protagonists' pain but could only match some of their pleasure. Wearing his hair a bit longer than 1986, and perhaps with the strain and desire to win etched across his face, Seve looked to have aged more than a year. At the 15th he'd almost holed a long-range putt, and he also just missed for birdie at 16, his hands raised to his sides, crucified by disgust. But at the 17th he rolled in a testy, delightful five-footer for birdie, his putting stroke sure. Coming up the last, he had matched Mize's score and his drive found the right side of the fairway. Once again dressed in final-day blue, this time a lighter, more vibrant, electric tinge, Seve turned out of his approach iron a tad early, leaving it right, pin high. In the bunker. This did not help my disposition. *I did not want to witness him fail.* He eyed the lie and the shot intently; the roll up to, and the position of, the pin. The quick green would carry the ball towards the hole without much momentum, but penalise a heavy-handed shot. He took his stance, weight favouring his left side, knees bent to allow him to glide the club through the sand, under the ball. He swung gently, wafting the ball two yards on to the putting surface and it rolled up three feet shy of the hole. Exquisite. His hands had looked so relaxed on the club, as if he was putting. The bunker shot was deft, near faultless, belying the pressure and tension

Ballesteros *must* have felt, *desperate* to expunge the memory of the previous year. After giving the three-foot putt the necessary respect and attention, Seve, his hands on the putter grip like a violinist's on his bow, stroked it sweetly into the hole. He paused, thoughtfully, crouched in his putting position, rose to his full height, raised his left hand and his index finger. He smiled contentedly and walked off the green, looking back down the fairway for Greg Norman, the only man who could now defeat him and Mize. I was delighted, not ecstatic, gripped still by fear of failure. Major golf unfolded in a heightened sense of real time, and Seve had brought the seconds to a crawl. It was great sport but uncomfortable viewing.

Around 45 minutes later Seve three-putted the first extra hole, the 10th, and traipsed up the fairway, refusing a buggy, wanting space to consider the implications of this otherwise common, simple mistake. Apparently, he wept. I had a lump in my throat, I felt sick for the man, physically sick. This was an integral part of being a Seve fan: the heartache, the loss, the fallibility. We'd all done it, three-putted at a crucial point and, looking back, unable to fathom how or why, knowing that if we dropped 50 balls in that spot, we'd be unlucky if we repeated the error.

Watching Ballesteros, we invested our hearts and minds in the firebrand and shared his joys and his sorrows. The zenith of this was his passing allied with the joy of looking back on his career; the highs and the lows, the crazy shots, the bad shots, the wondrous shots. For my generation, Seve was golf writ large on the scoreboard of life. I didn't travel to see him at every opportunity. To have done so would have taken me to the root of the word 'fan': the fanatic. In his ESPN.com essay, 'Sports can distract, but they don't heal', the late David Halberstam was wary of putting too much stock in the powers of sport: 'I am made uneasy by those who seem to need sports too much, these crazed superfans who bring such obsessive behaviour to games where complete strangers compete. There is an equation at work here: The more obsessive they are as fans, the emptier I suspect their real lives are.'

Halberstam saw sport as a complement to our lives, not a reason to get up in the morning. I followed Seve through thick and thin in the papers, magazines and on TV. There was a lot more golf on terrestrial TV then, although televised tournaments were thin on the fairway. But Halberstam starts to get to the nub of why Seve was adored. He didn't feel like a complete stranger, he felt like one of us. Growing up playing golf between the mid-1970s and mid-1980s Seve from afar encouraged me and my pals to take on the big shot, to enjoy the challenge, to attempt the improbable, to dream the impossible. I could perhaps blame him for my inconsistency, my streaky play, my inability to put a score together often enough to be a truly good player, but his encouragement to enjoy the challenge also brought the best out at certain moments – looking at all options for a shot, sometimes going up the wrong hole to advance one's ball; the look of shock on an opponent's face when the daring attempt comes off. These moments didn't build a player in me, but thinking of them evokes fond memories of a distant schooling. In a golfing life of searing mediocrity, I enjoyed my moments when I dared to pull off the ridiculous shot. With Ballesteros as an icon, we could all become imagineers.

* * *

This book is a journey, using the 1984 Open Championship as its locus. I wanted to understand my own thoughts about Seve and why people took to him so easily and so passionately. And why he endures. The book is a portrait, a perspective of Ballesteros and his golf and a view of his influences; snapshots, accounts and reimaginings of how Seve rocked the firmament, attacked courses, reputations and received wisdom, often all at once. He battled with the Americans, Tom Watson in particular, but in many ways all these players had more in common than not. Severiano Ballesteros was classed as an artist, a magician, a matador, a conquistador and much more – what did all that really mean?

For years I have been thinking about the Spaniard. For long periods this meant almost every day, and I would see him everywhere. Books and articles on the most obscure subjects generated ideas and notions that seemed to encapsulate Seve. Even songs allowed me to relive in my mind, over and over, his greatest moments; and his weakest ones. Almost all of it cemented why he was so popular and beloved throughout Great Britain and Ireland, across Europe and by many in the USA. Ballesteros represented the idea that the unattainable could be achievable, that the impossible could be attempted and brought off. Seve took the art of play to new levels for the men, women, boys and girls walking their own fairways. I hope, during the course of this journey, I serve the reality and the memories of Severiano Ballesteros well. For those who never saw Seve, I hope I conjure up a small piece of his flamboyant, dramatic golf.

At San Roque it turned out we weren't playing directly behind my hero. Instead, a German couple in their 50s (ages and handicaps) were between us. I doubt the German gent finished a single hole in less than nine: it was like a golfing Stalingrad as he struggled to reach each cup. He was a lefty but otherwise had the same action as Spalding, the spoiled nephew in *Caddyshack*. We witnessed the Teutonic southpaw attack the golf ball the way one imagines a stern 19th-century Prussian would repeatedly beat a recalcitrant child. Imagine being just about to tackle Lionel Messi and in slides a shambling wreck of a Sunday pub footballer, taking your feet away. Or you're about to receive a Superbowl-winning pass from Peyton Manning and being spear-tackled. Still, in what other sport can one legitimately be on the same playing surface as an icon, playing the same game, almost? So, we – my playing partner, Murray and I – watched Seve from afar. It wasn't usually a pretty sight, but up the 5th it was a bonus. Playing the hardest hole on the course, the 6th, Ballesteros had sniped his tee shot towards our fairway, just as we were coming up it. It was a thrill to be at close quarters with the man, despite his recent playing struggles. We stopped and watched him play his shot up to the green. He was focused, and seeing him politely refuse an autograph earlier meant we knew not to invade his space. On the par-five 9th the Germans let us through and as we caught up with Seve by hitting our seconds up near the green, Vicente disappeared with the cart and Ballesteros sauntered towards the clubhouse, finished. To miss playing directly behind Seve stung, but it merely emphasised how great he was. To experience moments with your heroes was the point of sporting fandom, as well as the desire to emulate, to ascend briefly into their sphere of capabilities. Just to have been in Seve's proximity was enough to evoke a slew of priceless memories.

ROUND ONE

'Travelers, there is no path, paths are made by walking.'

Antonio Machado

No.1

American Might – No.2 at Augusta National, Pink Dogwood

SINCE 1966 Mark McCormack had been publishing his annual compendium, *The World of Professional Golf*, and Seve Ballesteros was spicing things up. The modest doorstop covered the main tours' events and big money moments; it was a benchmark of how golfers across the globe measured up. For years this meant how well Americans had plundered tournament purses domestically and overseas. McCormack had already assessed Jack Nicklaus the game's leading money winner seven times, and from 1977 to 1980 Tom Watson had dominated financially. In the 1984 edition, looking back to the previous 1983 season, McCormack wrote, 'Domination of professional golf in the world was no longer the exclusive province of the United States. The latest and weightiest evidence of this came in 1983 when, from statistical yardsticks and subjective and objective viewpoints, Severiano Ballesteros reached the pinnacle of the game and became the world's No.1 player.'

Seve had become the first non-American to accumulate the most greenbacks in a year: $686,088. A lot of pesetas. McCormack didn't just tot up the cash, and although the official global rankings for golf did not begin until 1986 – with Greg Norman dominating for the first two seasons – he'd created a system weighted towards the majors, the other big events on the US tour, and, on the lowest rung, most of the counting European tournaments, then something of an outpost. Tallied on a three-year rolling basis, points for the commencement of 1984 arrived at the following as the game's leading quintet:

1. Severiano Ballesteros
2. Tom Watson
3. Raymond Floyd
4. Greg Norman
5. Tom Kite

Golf was changing: Jack Nicklaus was sixth, but Tommy Nakajima and Isao Aoki of Japan were seventh and ninth. Australia's David Graham was in 12th. It was testament to Nick Faldo's skills, determination and burgeoning reputation that he was in 14th. Many above and below him were playing in higher-ranking events week in, week out, but the young Englishman was building a solid résumé and led the European Tour Order of Merit in 1983. After Jack and Tom, Seve was only the third player to have topped the annual list. Yet typically he competed in events which, by McCormack's assessment, provided the points equivalent of chicken feed. Golf beyond the USA was virtually minor league baseball to the Americans. Now Seve was in their wheelhouse.

After recounting Ballesteros's 80-yard pitch-in at Wentworth to keep his match with Arnold Palmer at the 1983 World Match Play alive, McCormack observed, 'The Spaniard has traits and traces of Palmer about him, although he doesn't have that natural infectious warmth of Palmer with the galleries and others around golf. It's not part of his normal makeup and that is something that can't be learned or successfully acted out.' To be classed similarly to Palmer, the man who defined golf from the late 1950s, was praise indeed, but to limit some of

Seve's interactive skills seemed to miss he was from a different culture and language, and as yet only 26. Seve was a thoughtful, infectious communicator, and self-deprecating. At the 1976 Open prize-giving, aged 19, after receiving his cheque then being invited to take to the microphone, he bashfully stood, pondered for a second, then said, 'Señores y Señoras, muchas gracias.' The crowd clapped and shouted, laughed and cheered again. It wasn't a jingoistic moment of fun poked at Johnny Foreigner but collective delight at a young sportsman, who'd offered so much but lost a great battle, entering into the Corinthian spirit. Rather than fumble on and perhaps make a hash of a longer statement in a foreign tongue, Seve sensed less was more. Ballesteros gave a nice shrug of the shoulders, a wee wave of the arms, and sat down. It was as perfect as his most piercing long iron. The young player's personality played right into British hearts in those few seconds. After the battle against Arnie at Wentworth, the BBC's Alex Hay summed it up as a hero of yesteryear against the hero of today. The young Cantabrian had rattled in his pitch and looked mildly sheepish about sticking it to the man who practically invented modern golf.

For the Masters Tournament in 1983 McCormack outlined how he spotted Ballesteros on the 2nd hole at Augusta National during the first round. On the 555-yarder, which he would eagle as part of his final-day acceleration, Ballesteros's tee shot faded into the large bunker down the right, a trap conceived to catch the longest hitter of the day in the early 1970s, Mr Nicklaus. The recovery shot is – at its most ambitious – a medium iron, leaving around 150 yards in and a chance for birdie. Upon watching the Spaniard consider his options, McCormack was amazed the player selected a wood to extricate himself from the deep hazard. Predictably, Seve failed, leaving himself in the sand, facing a likely shot dropped. But this player was always looking to advance and McCormack's startlement was not over.

He'd been expecting Seve to hit a shot shy of the green and get up and down for a good par: 'Wrong again. With the same wood, Ballesteros hit a titanic shot that landed on the green and stopped no more than 20 feet from the pin. He was putting for a *birdie*. It would have been nice if he had made it, but I'll settle for what I saw, a par such as no one else would make.'

1978: The Open Championship, St Andrews

Jack Nicklaus Wins – Bobby Locke – Ballesteros at The Belfry

AS THE 21-year-old Spaniard practised – wide stance, wide takeaway and a high-speed descent into the shot – Alastair Lindsay watched, fixated. He was only two and a half but the vision in front of him would become his sporting hero. The golfer from Pedreña had that effect, on young and old. Alastair was sitting on a wall by the practice ground and, as the golfer finished his session, mind and body attuned for a day's play, he walked up to the lad, provided a few words of future encouragement and ruffled his hair. Another Seve fan was born. I hadn't quite started my own journey yet, but I recall almost to the day the first time I became conscious of the name, Severiano Ballesteros. Sunday, 16 July 1978 would be a good guess. It was the week before my ninth birthday and also the first time I heard the name Clint Eastwood. It was the Sunday after the then-traditional Saturday finish of the Open. Jack Nicklaus had lifted his third jug, his second at the Old and all seemed well. The greatest professional of all time had battled his way to a victory over New Zealand's Simon Owen, and it seemed right that not only had he triumphed, but he'd won again on the testing undulations of St Andrews. Nicklaus, with his diamond-patterned sweater, golden hair and beaming smile was a storybook ending to the 107th Open.

We were two families – the Reids and the Chalmers – who'd spent an entire week at the Open, with the children interested in the golf, roaming around the town, the course and the exhibition tent. I was never one for autograph books, but that week I was an official, voracious hunter. The Golden Bear did not feature on my pages, but Arnold Palmer and Bobby Locke did. Locke had won the Open at St Andrews in 1957, a few months after the birth of a young boy in Pedreña, Spain. I still recall Locke's kind face and smile, his moustache, shirt and tie, and that he appeared delighted to be signing autographs for beaming youngsters, most of whom almost certainly had no idea who he was. My dad would enlighten me. During our trip we had visited my uncle's family in nearby Falkland. One of the older cousins remarked how Clint Eastwood had been in the small town some days before, visiting Falkland Palace. This had been communicated excitedly, and I recognised the name as the actor from a film I had recently watched, *The Scalphunters*, and felt the mild glow of being able to contextualise what older people were talking about. It was months, maybe years later, that I realised it was Burt Lancaster who'd been in that film. Burt Lancaster, Clint Eastwood: exotic names to a child from provincial Ayrshire. I was an unquenchable consumer of films, but I didn't know my Clints from my Burts and even the likes of Charles Bronson, Lee Marvin and James Coburn all seemed to me to be the same person: rugged, deep-voiced, gunslinging Americans fighting corruption and evil. Or being corrupt and evil.

The other part of the conversation I understood, although I possessed no clear idea of who they meant. Some young, handsome golfer – my cousin Jayne was now telling this story – called 'Sevvy' had apparently whipped his ball over the

Old Course Hotel. Or had he hit his drive through a room window? The detail of it seemed pretty vague, but also exotic and fantastical. Here was a golfer in the game's oldest major and people were talking about his bad shots. Here was a golfer who, somehow, had managed to enthral a 12-year-old girl. It was confusing but I got the thrust, this was not ordinary.

* * *

A few months later, Seve stood on the 10th tee at The Belfry. The club he pulled was an aberration. With the water to be avoided, he faced a simple par four that roared mid-iron down the fairway, wedge on to the green. The Spaniard selected his driver. There was something of a stir in the crowd. The fairways and rough already a less vibrant shade of green, soon the falling leaves would lend a yellow, golden coat. It was late September, the first day of the Hennessy Cognac Cup, a match-play event featuring the Continent of Europe against Great Britain and Ireland. The terrain, trees and cooling conditions reminded Seve somewhat of his home back in northern Spain, as the days started to draw in and winter loomed. He was battling Nick Faldo, and despite being bunkered on each of the opening four holes, the Spaniard was one up come the turn. As well as pulling his big stick at the 10th, the young golfer – 21, but already a winner of eight European Tour events – took a slightly closed stance and addressed the ball.

> 'The point is it doesn't matter if you are like a beast before or after the hit, as long as you look like a beauty at the moment of impact.'
>
> **Seve**

The wide stance was the anchor, his bright-red sweater a counterpoint to the early autumnal conditions. He was taking on all 310 yards in traditional 1978 garb, slightly flared trousers, large and wide-collared golf shirt. He stood ready to unleash. His swing coiled and uncoiled, wound up before unwinding with ferocity.

'By Jove, he didn't hold back on that,' announced Peter Alliss.

The hole was shaped left to right, flanked on the latter by a stand of tall trees, and a massive cut or power fade seemed appropriate, but what wind there was came from the left and the player had hit a very high draw, going *over* the treetops. He spilled back on his feet and immediately walked straight left, tracking the ball in the air, seeking a view of the pin. His demeanour suggested only success for this crazed stratagem. The ball flew 300 yards, pitched 25 feet shy of the pin, jumped a bit left and ran out to about 18 feet. Alliss remarked that the shot alone was worth the BBC TV licence fee. In the *Glasgow Herald* Raymond Jacobs called it 'a stroke of prodigious power and precision, not to mention daring'. Severiano's rationale for taking on the shot? 'It was time to try something different.' That and trying to break Faldo's resolve.

* * *

I was minded of Seve's crushing tee shot on a flight back from a US golf trip when, in the Denver airport bookshop, the Tattered Cover, I noticed Geoff Dyer's latest, *White Sands*. I feel amused and educated when I read Dyer, who seamlessly blends the highbrow and the lowbrow, the popular and the serious. The book kept me happy for most of my 13-hour journey. Golf wasn't far from my mind, having played Riviera and Shadow Creek the week prior, mingling some faintly stellar shots with contusions of the mediocre and poor. I am always aware how lucky I am to play these courses, venues I could only never imagine visiting in my golfing adolescence – the people met, the course conditioning, the shared laughs and alcohol; the weather. But I *was* surprised to be thinking of Seve when going through the 'Space in Time' chapter about the author's trip to The Lightning Field, a piece of land art in the New Mexico desert, just west of the arse-end of nowhere. Martin Heidegger, German philosopher (handicap unknown), rarely pops up in golfing circles but Dyer invoked the Aryan egghead's 'Building Dwelling Thinking', outlining how the philosopher saw the relationship between man-made objects and nature. A bridge 'does not just connect banks that are already there. The banks emerge as banks only as the bridge crosses the stream. The bridge causes them to lie across from each other. From that it follows that the bridge effectively brings or leads the stream to flow under it and beneath these banks.'

In the deep of night somewhere above the north Atlantic I realised Seve Ballesteros connected the tee at The Belfry's 10th directly to the green when they had never been connected before. They were not meant to be connected, not by the designer and especially not by a player in 1978 on a dank autumn day. The tee was connected to the fairway. The fairway was connected to the green, usually by a soporific tee shot followed by a mundane approach. Until Seve's magisterial blow it was an average exam, a nice, modern idea that would get nary a mention in the media. With a single golfing moonshot, Ballesteros reconfigured that, made the hole psychologically pivotal as play entered the back nine, and the 10th went on to define a transatlantic clash with the Americans, and to define a change in mindsets. The Europeans were coming. When, seven years later, the Spaniard took on the green in the first morning foursomes of the 1985 Ryder Cup, and when Sam Torrance followed him, screaming a power cut round the trees right at the pin, the hole's symbolism and redefinition were complete. Come that Ryder Cup the drive had been shortened by 30 yards as Seve had shown how the challenge could beguile, how he could redefine not just the playing of a hole, but redefine the whole idea of it.

1964: Pedreña

A Young Spaniard – The Beach – A 3-Iron – The Power of Imagination

PICTURE THE boy: smiling, bright-eyed, his handsome face topped by a mop of black hair. He is smartly dressed, his parents take pride in his appearance, and in collared shirt and sweater he makes his way through the tight lanes and open tracks of the small fishing village across the water from Santander, the main port on the Cantabrian coast. Small, irregular walls guide the youngster towards the bay. The air is damp but the sun glimpses through a chilly Atlantic breeze that whispers through and around the houses. The boy carries his prized possession, a forged 3-iron, its shaft conjured by his own hand, a stick whittled to fit the hosel, left to soak in water, then dried to fit. He gazes seaward. It feels like a vast ocean, the city across the water seems like a metropolis, to its north the liquid horizon and a world he knows only from watching the first television in the village. Black and white, flickering and grainy images show *The Lone Ranger* and his sidekick, Tonto. Battling injustice, one man and his trusty second fight wrongdoing. It's only a generation since the end of World War II when seas nearby were stalked by the German wolfpack, U-boats hunting Allied naval vessels and merchant shipping. These ominous harbingers of death and chaos stealthily slipped in and out of Rochelle, France, and south-west of Santander, at Vigo, Spain. The coastline here is both beautiful and rugged. 'It seemed to rise from the sea like some rust-corroded wreck, as old and bleached as the rocks around it. There was no smoke or movement among the houses. Everything looked barnacled, rotting, and deathly quiet, as though awaiting the return of the Flood. I landed in a town submerged by wet green sunlight and smelling of the waste of the sea,' wrote Laurie Lee of arriving in Vigo. It was also 20 years hence from George Orwell scribbling the first words for his most famous novel, *1984*: a reaction to fascism.

Severiano inhales the invigorating air. The recent rain fuses the smell of the fields with the sea as the golfer makes for the greatest golf course, the links of an unbound imagination fired by his older brothers' love of golf and his uncle's talent. From the age of five Mozart would compose and play in front of royalty, but this nascent *golfista* plays majestic golfing symphonies in his own head, the beach his sheet music. The wind is gentle but often it howls off the Atlantic, scything through the Bay of Santander, the fishing boats in the village clattering in awkward percussion. Nearby hills and peaks take on a sheen of silvery green, sometimes shrouded in mist. The rain is an annoyance to the boy's playtime but it brings different qualities to his course and his play. To the outsider this feels more like Switzerland or Wales, not Spain with its vast blue skies, heat and humidity in the summer. In the winter it's more like Northern Europe with its darkness, foreboding clouds, wind and rain. Cantabria is the boy's patch, he knows nowhere else. His family has lived here for generations, tending the livestock, working the land. It is said the province has Spain's greatest concentration of cows, and his family is a proud farming one with, as is the way in these parts, patches of land dotted around and nearby. Just west of the mountains by the boy's home lies another range, the *Picos de Europa* and his country's first national park. There, his fellow countrymen and a few visitors from outside Spain trek, climb and canoe, take in the flora and fauna, avoid the occasional brown bear. His friends and other boys swim or sail or fish by the bay and out on the sea, along the pristine beaches sprinkled on the Atlantic's edge. Many play football and dream of becoming the next Alfredo Di Stéfano or Ferenc Puskás and running on to the pitch at the Bernabéu to the adoration of thousands. Seve imagines another *el clásico*; golf is his first love.

The boy's pulse quickens, the beating in his chest resounding as he anticipates the thrill of the elements, the feel of the sand, the club to ball, the flight of the well-hit shot. The tide has recently gone out, and the boy places his makeshift golf balls – pebbles – on the compacted, smooth, damp sand. The lies are tight and demand accuracy of strike, clipping each petrified orb cleanly and squarely.

> 'A shepherd tending his sheep would often chance upon a round pebble, and having his crook in his hand, he would strike it away; for it is inevitable that a man with a stick in his hand should aim a blow at any loose object lying in his path as that he should breathe.'
>
> **Sir Walter Simpson**, *The Art of Golf*

Sometimes a shot will veer from the intended line, and on the next hit he will cut across, keeping it straight; left to right for the pebble that tends left, and right and across the pebble that wants to go right. The physics of golf are a mystery but the chemistry of the game charges his blood and catalyses his mind. He does not yet understand the terms cut and fade and hook and draw but he knows what these shots look like. And how they feel. And how to play them. And how. Modulating his wrists, arms, upper and lower body, contorting them, at one turn making the ball fight against the path its shape demands and going straight, or moving quickly through the shot, exerting the touch and skill to move the ball more than gravity and the air appear to allow. He swings long and hard, a flying right elbow generating power, losing accuracy. These are some of the joys of the game. Like a young magician who always carries a deck of cards – never lets those cards leave his touch, caressing them, flicking them between his fingers, shuffling, sliding, flipping, new sleights of hand – the boy's tools are his single, ersatz club, never seeming to leave his hand, some round pebbles, the wind, the heat, and the earth; compact, dark sand; fluffy, white sand; scrub and brush; the water and its spray. He touches and feels these, his palms and fingers caress and touch the earth. Elemental sensations. The rhythm each shot plays on his hand and body, golfing lithographs for the future.

This bag of tricks is his constant companion, the shots and challenges his every thought. Nothing is more natural than, as the years progress, shaping the ball's flight into wonderful, gentle arcs, or whipping a fast and quick-turning shot into the wind or round some corner, real or imagined, towards the target. Some of his tricks are functions of memory and practice, golfing prestidigitation, while others are almost baffling, standard equipment used in ways that he invents and feels. None of his shots are trickery, no secret cabinets, mirrors or trapdoors, this is all natural, organic. The young Spaniard comes to understand more and more about his swing, the club, the reactions of the club and ball. In time, he would play the seemingly impossible shot, opening up a long iron, inherently understanding how loft and bounce operate, and almost waft the ball at degrees and speeds belying the face. The beaches, the wind, the rain, the sand, the turf, his passion, these are the young Severiano Ballesteros's instruction manual.

He dreams of playing against his brothers, all of whom work at the local golf club as caddies. He will build his strength on *his* course and by working on the family farm. One day he will play the big course on the hill, he will defeat his brothers and the other good players. He will caddy for the rich men who play there and live quite differently from his family. Many of them come to Santander and its surrounds for holidays. They dress well and have nice cars, life in Spain for them seems good. But the boy's country is a backward place, with no meaningful middle class yet to drive the accumulation of wealth, skills, and to improve the standard of living. Most of his countrymen are from *pueblos*, distant and isolated from Madrid, the hub of power. When people begin to flock to cities many *pueblos* wither, communities die, and the middle of society appears and commerce develops. The boy doesn't understand it yet, but these rich men who visit Cantabria and their families are of the Right, the men of power and possessions, of influence and persuasion. Spain is a divided country, the Right and the Left, the haves and the have-nots. The boy knows they are different, as his brothers will occasionally speak of them with some respect for their status in society and at the golf club, and they can often be the most generous payers for caddying. And often the worst golfers. Pedreña is rich with a sense of community, the fulcrum of daily lives and the nearby city meaning people do not have to stray far for work. They can work the sea, live on and work the land. The pull of urban migration need not attract the Ballesteros brothers.

The boy graduates from pebbles to real balls gifted by his siblings, or those he snaffles from the rough and bushes of the golf course. It's another rite of passage, boyhood mischief, to his advantage. On the beach, some days the young player will choose the sand away from the water, where it's powdery and undulates, mimicking rough or bunkers. His play is only constrained by the mind – its boundaries and variety limitless. He hits balls and marvels at their flight, how true and far they seem to fly, and how the wind affects them. He hits a shot into a stiff breeze and the ball soars, climbs like an aeroplane, before it stalls and falls. He finds ways to keep the ball low, cutting across the ball sharply right to left, hands low. The ball seems to go further but is harder to manage. He hits hard across the ball, turning the ball left to right into the wind. It flies up and into the elements, landing more softly, more like something he can master. The joys of discovery delight. He strikes a crisp iron into a strong wind blowing from the sea, he drives his hands hard and low through the ball and smiles as the ball rockets off the clubface, burrowing through the stiff breeze, straight and true. Severiano Ballesteros. Serious crossbowman. These *ballesters*, crossbow men, can be traced back to Spain's north-east in the 13th century. Perhaps this is in his blood.

Quick-running chipping areas, difficult bunkers, the mind's eye of a child, a putting green, a tricky lie, a buried ball; easy shots; unimaginable shots; slashing through scrub; lofting delicate chips; shots with the hands; thumping the ball with all the power his body will afford. Sometimes his mother – she adores him, treats him like the spoiled favourite – is not impressed when he returns with shoes caked in dense wet sand, good sweaters pulled here and there by bushes, sand in his face and hair unkempt in the Atlantic breeze. But she is happy her young, handsome son can amuse himself out in the clean sea air for days on end. Her brother, Ramon Sota, is Spain's greatest golfer, and a resident of Pedreña. The year before the young Seve was gifted his long-iron clubhead by his brothers, Ramon was seventh in the Open Championship at Lytham St Annes. In 1965 he would be sixth in the Masters, only one of four players from beyond the traditional golfing heartlands of North America and the Commonwealth of the former British Empire. The top three spots at that Masters would be filled by Nicklaus, Palmer and Player. Ramon had finished ahead of many a player of note. Carmen Ballesteros understands her son's love of the game and of the great outdoors. It is in her blood.

Day after day, hour after hour, the relentless, artistic timpani of shot after shot, the young man's brain, hands, muscles feel every strike, the bad ones delivering a shudder through his fingers. He is ahead of his time, days of practice laced with variety, different targets, different shots create a daguerreotype of all the shots a golfer might require. As well as the fields of his family and eventually playing on the course at Real Golf de Pedreña, he would practise on the beach until he was 13. The golf–course–beach is his playground and his classroom. His brothers play in the caddy competitions at the big course, and he sees what it means to win and lose, to succeed and fail. He watches his father compete in local regattas, big powerful men rowing boats as fast as they can across the bay, each team craving first place. He understands the power and the ecstasy of victory.

1970: The Open Championship, St Andrews

A First Open – Fred Daly – Pedreña's Caddy Competition – First Victory

THERE MIGHT have been a faint hint about me of umbilical nutrients when I attended my first Open, the 1970 affair at St Andrews. I was not yet one year old but the 99th playing brought my first brush with a beer tent and a major winner. As my dad left the on-course hostelry one day, me in a pram blissfully unaware of anything beyond masses of people, expanses of green and the click of club on ball, Fred Daly, the Northern Irish winner from 1947, stopped to chat. He took a liking to an infant being carted around the ancient Fife links. As a fellow Celt, perhaps admired my dad for realising that pushing a pram both justified the reward of a pint, as well as providing the ideal cover story for it. After all, Dad had been kind enough to take Kenneth off Mum's hands for a few hours. We were still three months shy of Germaine Greer's *The Female Eunuch*, at the vanguard of modern feminism, and while she would write the 'World has lost its soul, and I my sex', Bob Reid was not going to lose the chance of a beer.

'Ah, there's my wee friend, looking happy and smiley,' or words to that effect, said Fred. My dad would occasionally talk of this, taken by the Irishman's down-to-earth manner and friendliness, chuffed his son had this brief encounter with golfing lore. Daly assaulted five Opens in six years the way the Allies stormed Utah, Omaha, Gold, Juno and Sword beaches, finishing first, second, third, fourth and third again. Royal Liverpool in 1947 was his finest hour, becoming the eighth winner around the Hoylake course. He was in fine company, previous champions on Merseyside including amateur gods Harold Hilton and Bobby Jones, and early professional legends J.H. Taylor and Walter Hagen. Footage from the final day shows swathes of spectators across the links, but unfortunately the cameras did not capture American amateur Frank Stranahan – 'The Toledo Strongman', who'd twice win the Amateur, an LA Open, and earlier in 1947 had finished second at the Masters – almost holing out from the final fairway for a two, forcing extra holes. Daly was modest in victory and thankful for being able to take the Claret Jug to Ireland for the first time. 'And I hope the change of air will help it,' he told the watching masses at the prize-giving outside the Hoylake clubhouse. Not until 60 years later would the jug find its way back to the Emerald Isle, when Padraig Harrington triumphed at Carnoustie.

I recall absolutely nothing of the 1970 Open Championship. If Jack Nicklaus had baptised me with claret from the jug, it would be filed under the heading 'In search of lost time'. Knowing I had been at that famous championship, when Doug Sanders – seemingly a tortured man down the stretch, a condemned man at the end of it – looked up early for his winning putt only to see it break intently, sentencing him to a play-off with Nicklaus and a whole-life term of what-ifs, gave me a lifelong, direct connection to the Open. Up until his penultimate regulation shot Sanders had been one putt from destiny. Not until he hit that putt did he realise what that destiny meant. Nicklaus, already an Open winner at Muirfield in 1966, as well as six other majors, was remembered for taking off his sweater on the 90th tee and smashing his drive through the final green the way Panzer tanks smashed through Western Europe 30 years before. Then, upon holing his winning birdie putt in the play-off, in a moment of unNicklaus-like abandon, he hurled his putter high into the air and was quite lucky not to have injured Sanders, the caddies, and been arrested for wounding with intent. It was a stark representation of the difference between winning and losing at the highest level. Between those who became famous and adored, and those who came close to some kind of immortality. It seemed to me what championship golf was all about.

I was probably somewhere coughing up ice cream into my bib as Jack Nicklaus peeled off his bright-yellow sweater then pounded his final drive at St Andrews' 18th through the green. As I started bobbing along on my own golfing stream, pushed around the Old Course as my mum and dad took in the play, Severiano Ballesteros was 13 years old and continuing his own journey, hinting at an illustrious future. In 1970 he had his first encounter with national golf, as a caddy. He'd looped for his brother the year before in Santander, but this time he toted Manuel's bag in the Spanish Under-25s championship in Malaga – Seve's first trip away – and was furious that his sibling played so poorly. With no *fully* developed sense of winning and losing, and knowing what good shots might be hit, Seve's desire and high standards were founded on the possible, not the probable.

* * *

From the beach in 1964, the route to Malaga became more formal when, aged eight, the young Spaniard's golf schooling entered another phase – lugging 1960s golf bags around Real Golf de Pedreña. This part of his education was underscored by a realisation that, unlike his family, some who considered themselves golfers would be better off staying at home or going to the pub for a game of *tute*, a popular Spanish card game. The more he caddied, the more the desire to test himself on the course became unstoppable. As well as still playing and practising on the beach, he'd sneak on to the course at the day's close, playing golf in the growing gloom. Hitting full shots, chips and putts in the Cantabrian moonlight compelled the young Ballesteros to visualise and sense where these blows would go, imagining shots landing and rolling out to the hole, their lengths and lines mere perceptions. He'd feel the turf or sand under his feet telling him how the ground would react to a shot and how that shot must be executed. Would the sand or grass explode into a million fragments and would the club pass cleanly through impact? Should he compress the shot to drive it from its lie or was that too dangerous, uncontrollable, and did the shot require to be struck surely from the surface? By kinesthesis, he'd hear and feel chips, pitches, drives and irons as they left the clubface, the ball sending messages up the shaft into his hands and frame. As a very young Tiger Woods was constructed in a hothouse of Earl Woods's making, the boy Seve developed in a unique incubator, each shot a full-body experience, feet, legs and core fused with hands, arms and mind.

In the late 1960s – bios and his autobiography disagree on precise ages, the timeline muddled – Severiano entered his first Pedreña caddy championship. In his initial showing he took a ten on the 1st hole and finished fifth with 51 over nine holes. Two years later he was up a flight, his 79 over 18 leaving him the winner. Now, he would play against only the leading caddy players. He didn't win on his initial top-flight outing, but eventually he'd win the event more than once, courtesy of a 65 in one victory parade. This score could barely be imagined, and it gave Seve respect as others came to understand his talents. Already he had years of beach practice in his repertoire, plus the benefits of the dark sorties on the course and all his caddying. Despite his own play being confined to a small outpost in Spain, after turning 13 in 1970 the young Severiano reached a milestone: he beat brother Manuel. The eldest Ballesteros son was already a pro of a few years' standing who, in 1968, had won the Basque Coast Open, an event sufficiently notable that his win appeared in the Spanish national newspaper, *ABC Madrid*, and France's main broadsheet, *Le Monde*. The French daily spoke highly of the 19-year-old Manuel, calling him a revelation who beat – among others – Uncle Ramon, as 3,000 spectators followed play. As I first encountered major golf at St Andrews, Seve Ballesteros had begun to chart his course.

The 1984 Open Championship: Thursday

The Great White Shark – Tom Watson – Seve Sparkles

IT WAS a classic 1980s Scottish summer day – a real summer – sun ricocheting off the light waves in St Andrews Bay, the wind-beaten turf tattooed with gold, fawn, green and brown, and the temperature high enough for everyone in the country to flaunt bare arms and legs and pretend, briefly, they lived in Spain or the South of France. Scots loved those days, they felt so rare. The vast West Sands glowed while the flags around the Old Course protested in the breeze. Some families gambolled, played fetch with dogs on the beach; others made sandcastles, impregnable fortresses in the minds of the children who fashioned the walls and ramparts, their imaginations gleaming like Seve's had on distant Cantabrian shores, young plastic dreams shaped by the forces of curiosity.

It had been quite a journey from the sandy beaches of Pedreña to the hard-running, undulating, fiery links' turf of the Old Course, St Andrews, venue for the 113th instalment of golf's oldest major. It was the one they all wanted to win, but then they always said that. If Augusta National was conjured, the Old Course terrain formed over aeons, as if part of some 'Divine Golfing Plan', a sporting venue that stood the test of time and continued to outfox modernity. The Masters at

Augusta came every year, but Old Course Opens only came round every so often. Since the year of Seve's birth, 1957, when Bobby Locke won his fourth, the Auld Grey Toun had seen only a quartet of Claret Jugs handed out – Jack Nicklaus had two, 1970, 1978; Kel Nagle won the Centenary Open, 1960; and in between, the late 'Champagne' Tony Lema had won in 1964, defeating Nicklaus by five. Around the time of Lema's victory, a young Seve was given his first club and started venturing on to the sandy links of his febrile mind.

In 1978, 14 years later, Ballesteros played in the championship, and in the book *St Andrews and Golf* he would write, 'The first time I ever visited the golf courses at St Andrews, my mind drifted back to my childhood, when I was about 7 or 8 years old and just learning to play golf. It was a place close to our family home in Pedreña, Spain – at a small beach very near the local golf course. To tell the truth, the scene of that beach in Pedreña ... was so similar to what I saw in St Andrews that I felt myself carried back to my early boyhood days, as if through a time tunnel.'

In 1984 he was back for a second Open tilt at the Old. He was already the champion golfer of 1979, and twice a Masters victor, but Seve's form was sketchy. Following the 1983 Masters he won only four times, the last being the Trophée Lancôme in early October. His game had become, scoring-wise, ragged. He missed the cut defending at Augusta National, and although he managed a seventh place at the Madrid Open, his next best was 25th. A saving grace being he'd at least closed with a pair of 72s, and it was the weekend before the Open. If Seve believed in good omens, José Rivero's win, José María Cañizares's second place and Antonio Garrido's fifth must have given the Cantabrian a lift. Or, bad omens, Severiano was the fourth-best Spaniard. Newspapers were treating Seve like an outsider at St Andrews. He was struggling with his swing, and Greg Norman was captivating the USA. Most had the powerful Australian and Tom Watson as the men most likely to succeed.

In 1982 Greg Norman – the Great White Shark – was the leading player in Europe and the following year joined the PGA Tour. He'd already won almost 30 events globally, including two World Match Plays. In early summer 1984 the barnstorming Aussie went on a tear. In early June he won the Kemper Open at Congressional by five; two weeks later he lost at Winged Foot in a play-off for the US Open; he then shot a 67 on the first day of July to beat Jack Nicklaus by two shots at the Canadian Open; and two weeks before St Andrews the Great White lost out in another play-off, this time at the historic Western Open over Butler National. To Tom Watson. The USA loved a confident showman who could match words with actions and stateside scribes were bullish about Norman's chances at St Andrews.

In October 1983 at the Ryder Cup in Palm Beach Gardens, Florida, Tom Watson said to his captain, Nicklaus, 'Where do you think Ballesteros will be? I want to be there.' 'We wanted Ballesteros and Watson,' said Jack. All of golf would relish that clash, but Tony Jacklin put the Spaniard out in his first game, depending on him to get a point. In the end Watson clinched the Ryder win, but from Bernard Gallacher. Prior to 1984 Tom Watson had not won much in the previous two seasons, but he had picked up three majors. Including his win at Muirfield in 1980, five majors contributed to his tally of 13 wins since the summer of 1980. Although considered as being in a PGA Tour slump, Watson began to show compelling form and in outlasting Norman in the Western Open play-off he won at the third extra hole, draining a 25-footer then saying, 'I had a great feeling with my putter. I made everything I looked at.'

* * *

With early season form tending to some disarray and others exhibiting form, the omens did not seem great for Seve, but his Open started much like any other and Ballesteros appeared in front of the Royal and Ancient (R&A) Golf Club clubhouse just before his 2.50pm tee time. Some spectators spotted their golfing hero: the young conquistador, dashing matador, leader of the Spanish Armada, whatever Hispano-based cliché dripped from the pages of newspapers and magazines. The terrain of the Pedreña beach had been supplanted with the Old World's most famous course, but a sense of being at home underscored the challenge. Seve's jet-black hair flapped in the breeze, his bronzed features caressed by the Scottish elements of the season, wind and sun. Light-grey slacks, black sweater, dark golf shirt, he was not one for bold or dizzying stripes and checks. Little distorted the message of his beauty and grace. On the Thursday morning Mitchell Platts of *The Times*, in an article entitled 'Readers of the bumps predict Watson win', had written, 'The enigma of the championship is Severiano Ballesteros. The Spaniard has been struggling: his confidence is as low as it has been throughout his professional career, and there would appear to be less power in his swing than a year ago. If he can recapture an aggressive outlook, then the inspiration he requires might enable him to repeat his victory of 1979. More likely, however, Greg Norman will emerge as the player capable of thwarting the Americans. He has done so twice on their circuit this season.'

But already that week, Seve had found *something*, courtesy of practice-round partners Jamie Gonzalez of Brazil and Argentina's Vicente Fernández: 'They noticed a flaw in my swing which I corrected, causing my confidence to soar.' Gonzalez told the papers he thought Seve was joking when he asked for advice, but he spotted a reverse pivot and the Spaniard was able to make a change in his action.

Ballesteros started steadily, without taking the chances afforded by most of the front nine being downwind. Out by the loop – where the 7th led to the 8th and around and back to the 11th – fans channelled back and forth to catch a glimpse of the finest players on the planet. There was chatter and the hustle of spectator traffic, laughing and joking as they bumped into pals, mused about the day's golf or other topics of the hour. Seve appeared in good spirits approaching the result of his drive at the 12th. Crowds to the right lined the fairway, others snaked homewards as the afternoon grew long. Expectancy danced in the wind for those taking in this next shot. The figures at the ropes were dotted with brightly coloured T-shirts, sweaters and windcheaters, plus innumerable dark blues, blacks and browns, traditional shades for a summer in Scotland.

Ballesteros had covered the opening stretch drama-free, birdying the 3rd and capitalising around the loop, birdying twice with four threes in a row, the ones at nine and ten being gains against the card. On any day when the wind at the Old Course is blowing from the town, the 12th hole, called Heathery (In), is where the exam begins. With the first seven holes directly from the town to the Eden Estuary, and the final seven coming back, 'In' and 'Out' were literal, representing a tricky journey in to the clubhouse. On paper 12 is innocuous, but bunkers in the fairway and gorse left were designed to catch the ambitious or wayward tee shot, and the ultimate target, the green, was fiendishly shallow, only 12 yards deep where the hole would typically be set. The Spaniard's drive had come to rest on a slight upslope, adding to the test of punching a short iron through the firm breeze. He eyed it up, considered his options and played. His swing had a seamless fluidity and sweep, his weight slightly on his left side to ensure he didn't come off it. His practice swings had been tempered, flowing, his lower body in sync with the terrain. As he played, it seemed like classic Ballesteros, but his shot did not sound clipped, as the club dug into a fraction of the upslope, instinct being to stay down just a tad too long, overcompensating for the headwind. He turned away in disgust as the ball just made the top of the false front of the green, and with some spin went into reverse. On the BBC, Bruce Critchley remarked on the player's anguish, and the two testing putts he'd left himself. Anguish in the face of Ballesteros's brand of perfection. When you are a magician, surely you can pull off the simplest of tricks? Seve was three under but always pushing, especially when he knew there were birdie chances and players lurking. Greg Norman, Nick Faldo, Tom Watson, Ballesteros all had their own brands of steel, the inner force that drove their desire to perform and to win. Critchley was not wrong in his assessment of the birdie putt: about 40 feet up a four-foot-high 'little' slope, wind blowing left to right across the line. One saving grace was that there was not much to be considered; it was all about pace and how the wind affected the ball, as the nasty upslope was fairly uniform on the line. Seve would not expect too much lateral movement.

In his 1982 biography with Dudley Doust, Ballesteros put great stock in correctly aiming putts, something he recognised many amateurs overlooked. After some studying, Seve rapped his ball directly at the cup. Caddy Nick DePaul lifted the pin out of the hole and stepped back, watching intently. The ball ran strong and true up the slope, heading straight for the middle. 'Get in,' came a shout from the sidelines. Seve lifted his putter aloft and milliseconds later the ball galloped into the hole. Cheers, shouts, roars, and the player recognised the crowd's delight as he walked in the direction of the 13th tee, with his free hand acknowledging the fans. He was beaming, smiling, nodding his thanks. Bruce Critchley, 'Oh, how about that!' In the space of 15 minutes there were anguish, joy, mediocrity and magic. Seve was Rage Against the Machine and Beethoven on the same playlist. Four under par, one behind the leaders. He knew the birdie was a double boon as he'd saved a possible three-putt and gained a shot to par before the gruelling final six holes. He parred the 13th and 14th, hit a super drive down 15, then prepared for his approach.

'A lovely rhythmical swing from Ballesteros,' came the TV announcement as Seve flowed through the ball. It landed right next to the hole and rolled out about 12 feet. The entire Ballesteros orchestra was in concerted melody. The conductor himself looked at ease, unhindered by expectation. He hit a nice putt for his birdie, but it was too far right of the hole to take enough break. He strolled up to his fourth shot, the ball lying a foot behind the hole. He marked it, turned the ball to the hole, aligning the name to the target, placed the marker in his pocket and characteristically gently brushed his hand over the right edge of that pocket and hip, subconsciously checking the marker was there while priming his mind. With the confirmation of his pre-shot routine, he knocked in the putt, remaining one shot off the lead. Peter Alliss commented the player sensed a good finish would seal a well-played opening round. The safe tap-in was accompanied by the screeching of seagulls and chatter of the spectators dissipating in the wind. The Spaniard strolled to the 16th tee looking contented.

Seve seemed to have regained some equilibrium. However, before the relatively mundane 18th he still had the Principal's Nose and Deacon Sime bunkers of 16 to face, and the 17th to contend with. The Old Course's benchmark, 'The Great Reducer', the Road Hole. Grace married with strength resulted in the powerful, flowing Ballesteros action and he seemed to be enjoying his golf, strolling after his shots as if he was on Real Golf de Pedreña without a care. Bruce Critchley commented that the depression of previous weeks seemed to be slipping away. Perhaps the tension of those months had depleted his power, any swing fault shaving yards and control from even the strongest of actions. At the next, Ballesteros slashed his tee shot straight down the left side, the ideal spot to both miss the dangerous bunkers and approach the pin middle right. He'd swung just past the parallel and whipped the ball away, his customary recoil from such a hit seeing him step back on to his left foot as he came out of the shot, rocked back and righted himself. There was a little applause, the ball was safe, too safe to provoke a massive reaction from the gallery. Ballesteros regarded his driver and putter as the two most important clubs in his bag. *It is good for my confidence to start a hole well and finish it well.* He talked of rhythm and clubhead speed in his biography with Dudley Doust: 'When you have good rhythm, and you want to hit a really long drive, you don't swing fast. It is not the answer. Instead, you make a longer swing, take the hands a bit further back. You slow down the swing, backswing and downswing, but you speed up the hands through impact. That is all.'

His second to 16 seemed similar to the one at the 12th, a slight miscue on firm-but-powdery turf was not rewarded on Scottish links, a millimetre here or there translating into yards not gained, especially into a breeze. Maybe he was too relaxed, swinging too easy. Seve knew the purer the strike through the wind the less the ball would be affected. Perhaps he was fighting to control the clubhead. It was as if he very slightly decelerated through the shot. He finished at the front of the green, 35 feet from the hole. No anguish this time, perhaps because of sterner tests to come. He hit a lovely approach putt to 18 inches and tapped in. Now it was his turn to face the 17th. He'd struggled here in the 1978 Open, five, six, six, five, six over par at the Road Hole alone. He finished seven shots behind the winner, Nicklaus. Surely there was some of that mental residue sticking to his ego, especially when one poor hole could be a real setback, having played oneself into contention. In the recesses of Seve's golfing brain, he knew his previous woes, surely. It was human nature to know; managing the memories was the key. The Road Hole is unique in championship golf. The player must hit over the boundary to find the short stuff, the other option being a drive so safe as to be 'unsafe', in the rough with a testing angle to the pin and green. Physically, there is one way to play the hole, a straight drive on the correct line followed by a perfect iron shot for length and line. But the mind games are so strong they often dominate even the best. A birdie at the hole will not win the Open today, but a traumatic double or treble not only scars the scorecard, it plays with the mind for the coming rounds. Donald Steel in the Open Programme: 'Perhaps the most famous single hole in the world, as respected and feared as ever although modern wizardry with the wedge has limited the toll it exacts somewhat. Even if the skyline has changed over the years despite the recent reproduction of the old coal sheds, the drive is a classic example of the calculated gamble necessary if the best position is to be gained for the second shot. Many still obey the principle of playing the second to the foot of the green on the right and treating the hole as a par four and a half, thereby avoiding the road and the Road bunker but that is always easier said than done. Still only on rare occasions does anyone attack the flag.'

Earlier, Tom Watson had found the bunker; Nick Faldo, the road. Bill Longmuir hit the wall and came back on to the green, and Greg Norman had flirted with the sand. The 17th was a conundrum many struggled to resolve. And the Old Course Hotel had turned back time, putting in sheds to mimic the old railway ones that both threatened the tee shot and hid the line for the confident, bold or insane. Seve took a few easy, almost deliberately slow, practice swings, calming mind and body. He'd had a long wait, and the game behind had joined his on the tee, play backing up as the field in front had repeatedly failed to unpick the secret to making par. Fellow Spaniard Antonio Garrido, and son and 12-year-old caddy Ignacio, looked on as Ballesteros was about to pull the trigger. The crowd was at such close quarters by the tee, tucked in the corner, that it looked as if some could almost reach out and touch Seve. All would feel him. Like many legendary sportsmen and women, actors and actresses, Seve had that ability to command an audience, to draw them in with his presence, will and focus. Richard Burton's first mentor, Philip Burton, spoke of the actor's 'astonishing audience control – he could do anything he wanted with the audience'. Seve possessed that magnetism. 'Finally, Ballesteros. And after a long wait like that, let's see what he can deliver,' noted Mark McCormack for the BBC. The swing was a controlled belt: shaft to parallel, the ball started left of the sheds and tried to cut back a bit. Giving his driver back to caddy DePaul, Seve did not seem unhappy as he looked onward while removing his pristine white glove. Europe's most attacking, aggressive and gifted player appeared to have played safe, and perhaps the leftovers from 1978 had played a part. Safety would soon look like calamity. 'The lie won't be too bad, the angle not too good,' postulated McCormack. The commentator reflected what Seve knew. The second shot was the hard one, not the drive. For his 4-iron approach, underestimating the grass – the rough here was a shade tougher, more tangled and did not disintegrate on contact, unlike other parts of the gilded links – Seve hit what can be described best as a snipe. From 240 yards out, it travelled maybe 150 yards, left.

McCormack's Midwestern twang – a lat, a lat, a lat of trouble was his assessment of the ball's resting place – captured the tone. Ballesteros was no doubt looking to chase the ball up. Right choice, rotten result, and perhaps less club would have delivered more loft, height and a better outcome. Seve fans' anxiety would now be peaking at the prospect of the kind of mishap his drive had been designed to avoid. He was 50 yards shy of the gaping Road bunker and chose to hit a pitching wedge left of it, towards the pin. It was both ballsy and his only meaningful way to rescue something from the hole. All other left or right options, if hit poorly or too much, could leave him in dire straits, but his shot compounded matters. It came up short, albeit not in the trap. For par he faced a putt round the left rim of the bunker; this wall of death offered both the ideal and most dangerous line, flirting with a disastrous drop to the sand.

This was loved/hated by Ballesteros fans, there was an animalistic thrill watching him at work. How could a player with such gifts get into such a mess? Is this what happens when a player's course management is 100 per cent about moving the ball towards the hole? Safe shots sideways tended to never feature. Sitting on his haunches, right hand resting on the putter like a knight would rest on his sword, left arm on hip, Severiano surveyed the puzzle. A wrong decision or poorly executed shot now would undo a lot of the previous three hours' work. It would rekindle thoughts of 1978, and this parallel would be drawn on TV and in newspapers. Despite these and an obvious temptation to get greedy or play too safe, Ballesteros simply played an excellent putt firmly over and slightly around the bunker lip so his ball passed to the right of the hole, the bold side, given where he was coming from. It was mastery of touch and nerve, as it would have been easy to flinch, over-hit it madly or look up early in hope. His fourth finished five feet beyond the hole. He eyed his bogey putt with stealth and purpose, every movement and nuance dedicated to its holing. As if it was meaningless and he didn't even have a card in his hand, it was knocked straight in the centre, rolling nicely.

As if it were never really in doubt, Seve strode to the hole, picked out the ball and waved to the crowd. All business now, no smile, joy or relief, just pure belief and an air of mild, knowing assurance. It was a bogey that took the emotional energy of a double bogey but delivered the boost of a great par. One of golf's paradoxes, a boost, the kind of escape that totally deflates opponents. He dropped a shot further behind the leaders, but it was no disgrace. Thursday's stroke average at the Road would come to 4.87. The Spaniard had lost a couple of dimples to the field. Up the last, Tom Morris, a hole of 354 yards, a tee shot and a wedge later Ballesteros had 12 feet remaining, his ball just beyond pin high, on the low side. He could expect the ball to move from his left and would fancy his chances. The crowd all along the road, on the stands to his left between the 1st tee and Grannie Clark's Wynd, and behind the green, clapped and cheered their appreciation. Seve would miss the putt, just kissing the right lip, and walk off with par. A 69. He'd stamped his mark on the first round and dished out dazzling putting, solid iron play and some nerve-jangling recoveries. He was smiling.

1984: Some Cast Members

Going Supersonic – The 1980s – The BBC – The World's Best

THE MAJESTIC white bird banked smoothly, glinting, floating in the blue skies above the mottled fields of Fife. The Eden Estuary's platinum waters scintillated below. As golfers battled it out on nearby courses Ladybank, Lundin Links, Scotscraig and Leven in Final Qualifying, Captain J.W. Monty swooped across the kingdom, preparing Concorde for landing at Leuchars, a Royal Air Force station on the banks opposite the double green of the 7th and 11th at the Old Course. The British Airways captain steadied the pride of Anglo-French engineering.

The sleek, supersonic machine was the plane spotter's dream date traditionally attracting crowds of onlookers hypnotised by the form of the delta-winged icon. Flocks of people and streams of cars had descended upon the countryside, hoping to catch a glimpse of the sky's fastest passenger plane. She always created a stir, her shape marking her out. Travelling by Concorde at twice the speed of sound was one of the perks of being an elite sportsman, businessman or global celebrity. In a few hours G-BOAF had flown across the Atlantic, her precious cargo the golfing might of the US tour. Upon disembarking, Ben Crenshaw, Johnny Miller, Arnold Palmer, Bill Rogers and

Fuzzy Zoeller posed for a photograph on the tarmac: 20,000 people came to see them land.

Fans of sport, golf lovers and the dedicated couch sloths who couldn't or didn't normally attend the Open Championship could witness it all unfold on terrestrial television. The 1984 event at St Andrews saw the BBC emerging into a form of modern broadcasting. On the weekend, all 18 holes would have coverage, helped by the Old's squeezing into the ideal broadcasting template, a classic links strip betwixt arable land and sea, only four holes – 1st, 9th, 17th and 18th – with standalone greens. Twelve long hours of broadcasting started around morning tea and didn't finish until 11pm, when the highlight show appeared, wedged between a ropey film and the current affairs programme *Newsnight*.

Like those frequently in Open attendance, the many at home had a form of ritual to follow as the stalwart commentators dished out golfing wisdom, humour and a variety of non-sequiturs. The BBC presented great weeks of summer sport, one constant being that not often did anyone from Great Britain or Ireland win anything of importance in the 1980s. Wimbledon, the Olympics and the football World Cup offered great television where British viewers sooner or later attached themselves to a favourite from somewhere else on the planet. The annual parade of the Open was ideal for this type of hero adoption. Jack Nicklaus's powerful consistency aside, and the Californian glamour that the likes of Johnny Miller brought to the game, golfing exotics were few and far between in the late 1970s, and most of the domestic players appeared drab. Lee Trevino was a bundle of fun allied with outstanding ball striking and touch. And Greg Norman was starting to appear. The BBC commentators, on-course analysts and presenters were revered. In the days before 24-hour news, endless TV coverage and social media, they provided glimpses of great sporting inner sancta. Golf was a fine example of this tradition. The Corporation was almost an integral part of the event, hard to imagine an Open Championship without it. Since the passing of the eloquent Henry Longhurst, Peter Alliss had taken on the mantle of TV's golf doyen, but Longhurst had set the standard. Privately schooled, followed by Cambridge, fond of a gin and tonic, Longhurst was a good golfer in his own right, having won the 1936 German Amateur. He'd nailed the nature of links golf on the Old Course in a 1957 article in *Esquire* magazine 'Even the experts would not claim to appreciate the full quality of a masterpiece of painting or music at the first time of seeing or hearing ... What is the secret? Partly, I think, that before playing any shot you have to stop and say to yourself, not, "What club is it?" but "What exactly is it that I am trying to do?"'

In 1955, Peter Thomson of Australia had answered the question, winning the second of five jugs. Peter Alliss missed the cut, but had registered top tens in the two years immediately prior. Longhurst died in 1978, and Alliss was now firmly in the lead commentating seat and had already written or jointly written a dozen books focusing on the sport. In early July 1984 *The Open: The British Open Championship Since the War* had been published and he shared his views on the top players of the day, as well as the championships won and lost. The golfing purists would baulk at the use of 'British' in the title, while the history purist would ask, 'Which war?' Alliss was a highly accomplished player with 31 tournament victories and eight Ryder Cup appearances, including the famous 1957 Lindrick win, an extreme rarity. Other golfing notables joined Alliss. Clive Clark was a Walker and Ryder Cupper who scored the first televised ace, a 2-iron at Augusta National's 16th hole during the 1968 Masters. Clive tended to be out and about, looking at players' lies, and interviewing them after their rounds. Bruce Critchley, never a pro but played in the 1969 Walker Cup, lent the gentleman golfer's view. Alex Hay was one of the most recognised voices, and laughs, in British television sport. With a slight Anglo tinge to his Scottish accent he and Alliss were a fine two-ball for commentating badinage and it was common to hear Hay chuckling in the background at some of Alliss's chatter. Another distinct tone came from Cleveland, Ohio, lawyer Mark McCormack, the founder of the International Management Group and redefiner of sport, and sportsmen and women, into lifestyles and brands. With this group, the BBC brought a range of perspectives, expectations and styles, and it fitted the zeitgeist as Britain retained the vestiges of deference, respect and the Class System. Rounding out the coverage was the presenter Harry Carpenter, whose calm, assured demeanour was a perfect fit for the game. If Harry said it, the public believed it.

* * *

In the 1930s, Paul Gallico understood in *Farewell to Sport* how major golf can go. Writing of the US Open: 'But in the field ... that tee off on the first day of the Open, there are a great many guys named Joe of no particular reputation or record. And there is no telling when some hitherto unknown will suddenly go crazy, get hot, hook up four low rounds, and win the tournament. Almost invariably one of these unknowns is leading the field at the end of the first or second day. Someone playing with little or no gallery shoots a 69 for the first round, or hooks up a 69-73 for the first two days and is leading the nearest big name by two or three strokes.' He'd unpicked the formula before major sport truly, properly existed with all its pomp and pressure. Pretenders would come and go in a single event, a single moment, the cream would rise as others soured. It was the incubator for bringing on new stars as well as the report card for those who dwindled or underachieved. Majors saw honest battles where the best challenged and often prevailed, others learned and fought another day or disappeared, badged as a great tournament player, journeyman or Warholian one-hit wonder. In 1984, golf was a popular sport, but tournament play was not yet globalised. Curtis Strange (ranked #21 by McCormack at the end of 1984 and the future winner of the 1988 and 1989 US Opens) could choose to not even play in the Open in 1984. Today the internet would shame him into entering. Then shame him back to Virginia if he didn't play well.

The print media also had a formula. On their July front covers the UK's *Golf World* featured Tom Watson, *Golf Monthly* had Watson alongside Nicklaus, while in the USA *Golf Digest* featured Jack Nicklaus in a non-Open headline; along the top of its cover a strapline suggested that both Americans were marching towards history. The British newspapers were full of home hopes, Faldo prominent, and the Scottish rags delighted in a list of 'Tartan terrors' who might take home the jug. Their list ran to 11, Sandy Lyle, Sam Torrance and Ken Brown being the most likely to succeed. There was such a slew of coverage, and of others to consider, that just about every journalist in every paper across the land could perhaps claim some foresight come Sunday.

Before the main event, all the golf-focused newspapers carried a range of snippets on outliers, those who squeezed in via the 36-hole Final Qualifying gauntlet: Wayne Grady, Larry Mize, Bill Longmuir, Wayne Riley, Mike Clayton, Morris Hatalsky and Magnus Persson. Three would make news. Longmuir for his first and second rounds, American Hatalsky for getting the Open under way on Thursday, and Persson – a Swede who in 1982 aged 16 played in the Open at Royal Troon – for his caddy, George McLeod, who sported a dress white shirt with sleeves rolled up, kilt, belt, leather sporran and woollen socks with red flashes. He cut quite a dash, his red kilt a contrast to the golden links. Those who knew about wearing a kilt on a warm day, never mind while carrying a hefty golf bag, would hope the looper's nether regions were as well lubricated as Ben Crenshaw's putting stroke. Despite one man's traditional Scottish dress, the Open Championship was ahead of its time. The 1984 edition had entrants for qualifying from 33 countries beyond British and Irish shores. The BBC and other media had rich pickings for their words, images and sounds.

* * *

Fred Couples was low amateur at the 1979 US Open but this was his first Open foray. Turning pro in 1983, he made his mark winning the Kemper Open in a five-man play-off, and he won the Tournament Players Championship (now The Players) at TPC Sawgrass in early April 1984, edging it by a stroke. From Lee Trevino. He'd played in the final round with Ballesteros and Watson, and although the Spaniard pushed him for a few early holes, the 23-year-old from Seattle prevailed. Couples was so good-looking, his action so smooth, he made golf sweaters appear chic, and he wore them effortlessly. His opening 70 involved no strained muscles.

Jack Nicklaus. Major championships: 17 victories, five Masters and five PGA Championships and four US Opens. Three Opens, his first at Muirfield. Prior to 1984 Jack had finished in the major top tens 71 times. But, yet again in his career, he was deemed to be in a slump. Only this slump seemed to be concurring with the top of a hill; he'd won his own Memorial the month before. Still the Golden Bear hunted the big ones, and his last had been the 1980 PGA Championship at Oak Hill where he'd routed the field. That year he'd also won his fourth US Open, at Baltusrol, edging Isao Aoki by two shots in a thrilling denouement. At the Old in 1984 Nicklaus had dumped his second shot of the event into the Swilcan Burn, falling prey to the hole's flatness, TV viewers greeted with a clop as ball hit water and stone bed in quick succession. 'I thought that was perfect,' he explained to caddy Jimmy Dickinson as the ball splashed down. From that point Nicklaus knew his feel was off, the messages twixt brain, sinew and muscle not quite what he had hoped, perhaps because he'd felt unwell and pulled out of a past champions' reception. The legend from Ohio did manage to get up and down after his drop and penalty shot, but he worked his way round in a frustrating 74. 'I just couldn't find my touch.'

Greg Norman was the number-one player without a major, although no one was talking about the lack of one. Everyone was focused on when he'd win. The Great White Shark was a late-to-the-party golfing prodigy, winning his first event on the Australian Tour in 1976, a mere six years after turning professional. Club professional, that is. In 1977 he joined the European Tour and won the Martini International at Blairgowrie, Scotland. Norman was loved for his attacking style, taking on golf courses like an enraged fighter. It wasn't enough to beat the field, he wanted to beat each and every hole into existential submission. He was thrilling to watch, even in times of strife. The US Open at Winged Foot would ultimately be remembered for the calm demeanour of the winner, Zoeller, but Greg holed from about 60 feet at the 72nd, after a blocked approach, forcing the play-off. It was ultimate TV golf. He was renowned as the straightest long driver of the ball, attacking those 1.68 inches with malice. His name was also a gift to British journalists with a penchant for the mediaeval – articles abounded on Norman conquests. The UK bookmakers had him at 9-1 and, in typical fashion, he'd rewarded his journalist fans with a 67 in the first round.

Bernhard Langer was the first elite threat to emerge from northern Continental Europe. The Bavarian was steely, determined and various other words that one might use to describe a typical German – all compliments. He'd won eight times in Europe, including in Scotland (the Glasgow Open in 1981), but was famed for two other headlines. He'd successfully defeated the curse of many golfers, the yips, the nastiest of putting palsies. Then, at the Benson & Hedges International Open in 1981, his second into the 17th rested up a tree. Langer scaled the trunk and played out, all caught on national British television. I recall it all unfolding. Cue many jokes in the media about a tree-iron. Despite a virus that he felt would limit his chances, Langer opened with a steady 71, sitting just outside the top ten.

Nick Faldo was the great British hope, but a man whose determination was inversely proportionate to his charisma. He seemed to be on the march to achieving something great. At Birkdale the year before he'd been in the top four in the first three rounds but faded with a 73. Despite this malaise, he'd 11 titles on the European Tour, making him the winningest player after Seve, as Langer and Sandy Lyle clipped at his heels. Faldo was inspired to pursue golf after watching the 1971 Masters on a colour television and being captivated by the power and attraction of Jack Nicklaus, even though the Golden Bear only managed second place that year. In 1984 at St Andrews Faldo matched Seve's opening round, 69.

Sandy Lyle was an Anglo-Scottish long-hitting prodigy who could keep a 1-iron shot on a frozen rope. Ballesteros said himself that if God was arranging a tournament based on raw golfing talent, Big Sandy would win, Seve second. Lyle had won nine titles in Europe, but his major record was sketchy. However, he had tasted some of the bigger time, having played in the 1974 Open at Lytham aged 16, and being twice runner-up (to Greg Norman, then Seve) in the World Match Play.

Lee Trevino's form suggested he was past winning majors, but he'd been a multiple champion, taking home five of the banner events from 1968 to 1974, two being Opens at classic Claret Jug quick-running arenas, Royal Birkdale and Muirfield. When Lee was around, anything could happen, such were his shot-making gifts. Super Mex fired a firework-free two under par 70 in 1984's opener. He'd go on to win the 1984 PGA Championship at Shoal Creek, Alabama.

Ben Crenshaw had been the next big thing, the next Jack Nicklaus. In recent Opens – at the Old Course, Lytham, and Muirfield – he'd finished second, second and third. Despite winning the first tournament of his pro career, it took Gentle Ben's win at the 1984 Masters to see his first major. He opened in 72 blows.

Lanny Wadkins strutted around a golf course like it was a challenge and as if he owned that challenge. He golfed his ball with a no-nonsense, quick-fire approach and he recorded a 70 in the Open's first round. The Virginian had recorded nine top tens in majors since 1973. He'd torched Southern Hills in the final three rounds of the 1982 PGA Championship with 68, 69, 67 but was second to Raymond Floyd, who'd opened with a 63 and led thereafter. But Lanny had won that major in 1977 at Pebble Beach. It appeared Wadkins liked surf and turf.

Frank Urban 'Fuzzy' Zoeller looked so relaxed and easy-going it was amazing he could be bothered. He'd won six times in America and made major news twice. He became the first modern player to win the Masters on his debut, in 1979, and he presented Seve with his green jacket in 1980. He'd won the 1984 US Open with mild insouciance at Winged Foot, eventually running out the winner against Greg Norman in the play-off. He carded a 71 at St Andrews.

Tsuneyuki 'Tommy' Nakajima was, according to Mark McCormack, the seventh-ranked player in the world. This probably felt like being the fifth Beatle. By the end of 1984 he'd have notched up 20 professional wins. He was also known for two golfing disasters. Nakajima had taken a 13 at Augusta National's 13th in 1978, and a few months later had an altercation with the Road Hole. He found the green in regulation, then putted into Road bunker. He recorded a nine. This was a predictable gift to the UK newspapers: the Sands of Nakajima. Disasters aside, Tommy was a most consistent player, and his 70 at St Andrews had him handily placed.

Isao Aoki, beyond the actual playing of golf, was everything Nakajima appeared not to be: cool, easy-going and with an elegance that meant he was – and still is – the only golfer to make a black glove look truly hip. When it came to playing, Aoki looked relaxed with his hunched stance and toe-in-the-air putting style. Zoeller and Couples look stressed in comparison. Come 1984, Aoki had won over 40 times but, like his compatriot, made noises around with two memorable golfing moments. In the second round of the 1979 World Match Play an ace at the 2nd saw him win an apartment at Gleneagles, and in 1983 he holed out on the final hole in Honolulu with a wedge to win the Hawaiian Open (McCormack judged it shot of the year). He had four major top tens to his name, including a seventh at St Andrews in 1978. The laid-back son of the Chiba Prefecture started 1984 with a steady 70.

Tom Watson was the greatest links exponent, five wins already at the Open. As defender of the Claret Jug he adorned the front cover of the official programme, his hands held aloft as he emerged from the throng on the last fairway in 1983, making his way to the 18th green at Royal Birkdale. Perhaps because his reputation spoke for itself, he needed no small bio within the £2.00 programme, but the 1982 edition from Troon gave the flavour of what the public could expect: 'Whenever the Open is held in Scotland, Tom Watson is the man to watch. Following his victories at Carnoustie, Turnberry and Muirfield, Troon would complete golf's equivalent of a royal flush.' Troon gave

Watson that royal flush, and St Andrews was the opportunity to add an ace to that winning hand. Watson's 71 saw him under the radar in round one of 1984.

Prestwick

Starting Out, Starting Golf – Scotland in the 1970s

IT SEEMS that the primordial soup meant for me to be a golfer. Somewhere in that prebiotic chowder over three million years ago, phosphates, proteins and carbohydrates got together and agreed that aeons down the line I would pop out, ready for action, suffused with just a few of the qualities and attributes a golfer should possess. Thoracic flexibility, good hands, and place were on my side. I was born to one golfer and into another golfing family and emerged from that placenta-based hazard without penalty into a decent lie. My coming to golf was familial and geographical, enough to send me on my way to the links. When I emerged from the warm darkness in 1969 the maternity hospital practically abutted a golf course, one of the local munis. And I was three miles from Prestwick Golf Club, 'Home of The Open'. Days later I was in the parental home, half a mile from where Willie Park Sr won that first major, 109 years earlier. If location wasn't enough, my parents had met through golf, Dad having beaten my mum's brother in the then-big regional event, the Tam O'Shanter. Another match was struck. In the way of modern marriages, I guess both might have felt four down on a few occasions, but life generally was one up and both my parents found the fairway or penalty areas were negotiated with some ease.

Two weeks prior to my free drop into reality the 98th Open began at Royal Lytham & St Annes and on paper a poor third round cost the venue's 1963 champ Bob Charles a win, as Tony Jacklin's 280 gave him a two-shot victory. Curry Kilpatrick (a journalist, not a Scots-Indian restaurant) made much of Jacklin's win in *Sports Illustrated* by drawing parallels to Charles Windsor's recent investiture as the Prince of Wales. Prince Charles had been granted the title Prince of Wales back in 1958. With his formal ascent coming 11 years later, it was the kind of slow play that would see J.B. Holmes banished to a supermax. Jacklin was already a man of rare achievements, winning the 1968 Jacksonville Open Invitational by two strokes from the likes of Doug Sanders.

Quite an achievement on two counts. For any foreigner to win in the USA was rare, and for anyone to win an 'open' that was an 'invitational' rarer still. The next year Jacklin would win the US Open by seven shots at Hazeltine, Minnesota. Like a golfing wormhole of yesterday, today and tomorrow, the future Ryder Cup captain, who revolutionised the matches along with Ballesteros, won the Trophée Lancôme four months after his American major, beating Arnold Palmer and Ramon Sota by a single shot. Before bursting through Jacklin won quite a few times in the 1960s, beating the likes of Adrian Sadler, Sean Hunt, Tony Grubb and David Snell to the top of the leaderboard. Sadler, Hunt, Grubb and Snell sounded more like a third-rate law firm in Clacton-on-Sea than the future powerhouse of Eurogolf. Jacklin's major promise didn't advance after Hazeltine and he became what Dan Jenkins would call others, 'a dogged victim of inexorable fate', notably at the hands of Lee Trevino. In 1972's third round at Muirfield the Texan squirted a bunker shot at the 16th that on its second violent hop landed straight in the cup; minutes later, at the 18th, a chip in for birdie; and on the final day, on the penultimate hole, Trevino holed from off the green again, this time for the scrambliest of pars. It unnerved Jacklin, who then three-putted from 18 feet and in majors was never the same again.

We moved twice around when I was starting primary school, for a few months living in a house that my parents soon realised needed too much work, one third of a mile from what was the first tee of the original Prestwick layout. It's in this house's garden on Prestwick's Marina Road that I hit the first shot I recollect. Perhaps in a bid to impress the adults, I teed up a ball and swiped it with a putter, the old-style blade that was closer to a nasty 1930s long iron than today's tech. It was a fair blow for a five-year-old, smashing through the window in the garage at the bottom of the garden, almost hitting the throng on its way. There was hell to pay, the shock and anger on my dad's face not so much the result of the shot but more that I had actually been stupid enough to hit it. Aside from this exuberance-based glazing incident, I was a good child who'd picked up some of the golfing bug.

By now, my brother had arrived, almost a full five years after me, and he would go on to be a proper golfer. I'd just play the game, whereas he could *play*. Like many young, 'mobile' families in Scotland in the 1970s we moved into one of the new, burgeoning estates, practically up the road from what had been the second family home, the one before I'd taken up putter-based anarchy. Into this fourth home we settled, a single road from a park with its own pitch and putt. Surely only in Scotland could one live in a series of houses that were sometimes only an iron or a few well-hit shots from the nearest green. This was the start of a kind of upward mobility available to the young couples and families of the 1970s. Seve came along when the United Kingdom was starting to change. He appeared at just the right moment for golfers to get behind a Continental player who had some swagger.

My dad's job involved something that a few generations before would not have existed as a career: he sold oil to commercial customers, first for Shell-BP, and then for BP. This meant a car. And suits. And corporate days away and training courses in exotic places like Hemel Hempstead, itself a sign of a new Britain or, more technically, where old met new. Hemel was originally a mediaeval settlement, and following World War II it became a focal point for exo-London growth and eventually the site of a New Town. The New Towns Act of 1946 eventually saw 27 such sprawls built. Seve Ballesteros emerged on to a changing social landscape, as the UK peered from the gloom of a generation of post-war thinking, rooted in the past and the great halcyon days of Empire, to something a bit more vibrant and, hopefully, more modern. Whatever modern meant, change was not going to be easy. The UK was almost bankrupt, taxes were high and opportunities not plentiful. On BBC Radio 4's *Desert Island Discs* in 2020, the actor Mark Strong captured the times: 'You have to remember, the 70s, that time, it was the three-day week, there was rubbish piling up in the streets, there were power cuts. Frequently the lights would go out, you all had to scrabble about for candles.' It should be no surprise that this fomented music by the Sex Pistols and Black Sabbath, and their nihilism, anarchy and fascinations with death, war and the occult. All pure escapism of a particularly strident type. It's always been fashionable to choose music as a sign of the times, so it's worth noting that the week after Seve hit the mainstream golfing scene in 1976, the UK's No.1 was a Demis Roussos EP containing 'Forever and Ever'. This was escapism, albeit via a tune that should be seen as the attempted suicide of pop music sung by a man who looked like he'd be more at home wrestling on ITV's *World of Sport*. Owning a record by a Greek crooner was some kind of social mobility-by-proxy, allied with a Europhilic outlook. The UK was on the turn.

While society was changing, golf in Scotland in the 1970s and early 1980s remained a simple affair. Primarily it was played by men and boys, the equipment used now looking medievally crude, with heavy, clunky irons. Putters tended to be either old-school blades or a range of modern disasters mimicking dysfunctional Bauhaus. A lot of kit was simply a bit too expensive for the common man. Even in my early teens a PING Anser at £35 was a lot of money to spend on a single club. It was no accident that when they came along, the smooth, forged muscle back of my first set of Mizuno Pro Original irons felt like finely engineered pieces of modern art. Just to run my hands gently over those blades brought a sensory satisfaction. Golf bags tended to be nasty, too, either leather and very expensive and a nightmare in Scottish rain, or plastic copies of those leather ones, with the design quality of reinforced bubble wrap. Lugging a wet Scottish golf bag around a golf course in the 1970s was probably what it feels like to dispose of a dead body, 18 times.

Those Ballesteros Hands

Artistic Touch – Ben Hogan – Power – Control – Feel

THE PAINTER, the sculptor, the musician. So much of their art is about the hands, how the brain and body connect and shape their creations. Seve's hands came with long, strong, supple fingers. On the golf club they seemed to envelop the grip wholly but delicately, the club in its rightful place. The fingers had *touch*. And Ballesteros's right arm was slightly longer than his left, allowing the player to naturally fall into place when addressing the ball, right hand below the left, with the traditional overlap, the Vardon grip. Ballesteros seemed genetically engineered to play the game. Frank Deford, the American sportswriter, described hands as 'exquisite, divinely human instruments that God gave us to separate us from the beasts of the field'.

Gary Player said of Seve's hands, in Ballesteros's autobiography, they 'are actually hard and muscular, so it does not matter how your hands are formed, either you have got that feel or you do not, and he is a true wizard around the greens'. Seve's hands were primed and aged and educated on the beaches and land of Cantabria. In his resting state the Spaniard appeared always ready to strike, even if it was a putt. He was intent, intent to hole a putt or chip; intent to continually strive towards the hole, especially in times of strife, when a drive or approach had gone astray. But the intent was underscored by a kind of beauty. Not since Ben Hogan had a golfer seemed so elegant.

I look at a picture of Seve and his caddy brother, Vicente, in the mid-1980s. Vicente appears to be looking at the bag, wondering, talking to Seve about the club to hit. In contrast to Vicente, dressed head to toe in petrol blue, a bright-white shirt underneath, the golf bag and headcovers are bright red, the Slazenger name and logo accompanied by that of the La Manga Club. Seve is poised, looking at the target in the distance. His right hand rests lightly on a mid-iron, cradling its sole, and its soul. It must be a practice round, an exhibition, or some form of unofficial event, because Vicente has no caddy bib or traditional overalls on. I know it's in Europe, because Seve wears a Slazenger shirt. I survey what I can see of the clubs. It appears all the irons have lead tape applied towards the toe of the muscle-backed blade, the effect being to fractionally slow down that toe, discouraging a pull or hook, one of Ballesteros's weaknesses. He knew how to control the clubhead and clubface like no other, but he also knew he could lose that control. Seve looks straight ahead, fixed on his target, but we can sense he is also listening to his brother, processing all the information available to him. His begloved left hand rests at his side as the other strokes the forged steel, the gentleness of that caress belying the power of the forearm and hands, and the clear message of intent that will follow when the shot is executed. Or might it be less power and more finesse, a hold-up cut into a gentle breeze, or a controlled draw into a tight pin position back left. Seve seeks to resolve this conundrum.

I am captivated by his intensity. Eventually the internet tells me the photo is from the 1985 World Match Play at Wentworth, and that Seve was playing the reigning US Open champion, Andy North. Ballesteros would win that year, demolishing

Bernhard Langer 6 and 5 in the final as he successfully defended his title.

> 'Hands have a history of their own, they have, indeed …
> their special beauty.'
> **Rainer Maria Rilke**

Seve's hands seemed to have that special beauty, assured of their place in time and space. Laid upon a club they were resolved yet relaxed. Hung at his sides they framed the golfer; confident, at ease, but ready. One day I found myself listening to a BBC podcast featuring Clive James discussing his admiration for the iconic American actor Steve McQueen. Stumbling on the show was a small nugget in this book's ceaseless stream. As I listened, I was conscious that across from me, on a bookshelf in my house, was *Steve McQueen: A Tribute to the King of Cool* and upstairs was a framed photo of McQueen in a T-shirt, atop a German motorcycle, wondering how he was going to evade the Wehrmacht and the Gestapo, and continue *The Great Escape*. I loved Steve McQueen, that icon of the fantasy life of many boys and men. My dad had told me how, in 1963 aged 24, he went to the cinema to see the classic war film. As Hilts, the Cooler King, played by McQueen vaulted the menacing border fence on the motorcycle the entire auditorium rose to its feet and roared in a frenzy of ecstatic approval. Every time I watch the film I think of that moment and the power of the shared experience. I wonder what it must have been like to have been brought up during the war and to see that film just 18 years after the fighting stopped.

It seemed that Hilts was the apotheosis of the hopes of a generation. In the podcast, Clive James read a passage from his novel, *The Remake*, in which a chauffeur, Eric, was a McQueen aficionado: 'What about the way he checks his grease-gun in

Hell Is For Heroes, remember that bit? … The way he shakes the shotgun cartridge beside his ear in *The Magnificent Seven* to see if it's properly packed. Spins the chamber of the long-barrelled Colt, same picture. Checks the back-sight on his Lee-Enfield in *The Sand Pebbles*.' James recounts his own joy at McQueen on film. 'He would put his gun in his holster with an elegance you'd never seen before in your life. Throughout the movies this wonderful sense of movement … How is he getting that much attention, what's he doing? Well, largely, it was a matter of what he wasn't doing. And then chose very carefully what he did do; very selective … He would think himself into the script … no one could get out of a car like McQueen … He moved beautifully. All the great male actors do. All the great male actors move as beautifully as women. All of them.'

Seve's draw was about movement. When he pondered club selection, he would clasp the clubhead in his hand, gently, like a piece of fine china. It was a cradling of a tool of his craft, the thing that rendered his art. With one tool Ballesteros could do many things. He fingered clubheads and shafts and grips like the finest artisans from a Spanish village specialising in leather or ceramics. He handled his sticks like precious objects. He'd spent his childhood with a club in his hands, and they were an extension of the self, his self, himself, like the magician who'd spent years handling and fingering his cards, who'd shuffled and played tricks until the deck became part of him, his mind, like another limb or organ. It seemed like Seve's every movement was a flow and extension of his golfing self. Before golf psychology caught on, the Spaniard carried himself like a champion. Like a golfer capable of *anything*, he moved and rested like a champion. This set Ballesteros against the good players and challengers of his day; he was capable of things they could not imagine. He knew it, they knew it. We loved him for it.

Steve McQueen was a renowned scene-stealer, an improvised movement or line drawing attention his way. Ballesteros and his demeanour didn't steal scenes. He simply *was*. Those charismatic people have what we call *presence*. We focus on certain elements, looking at what makes them great or special. But it's not about a single quality, or a few, it's their everything. *They have it*. Seve's presence and skill and power and touch meant those scenes were just his, like some hidden line of kingship. Seve's hands were essential to his art, his game. Throughout his career his swing could sometimes seem on the verge of breaking, it was rarely a thing of metronomic consistency. In his heyday, shots could be things of beauty delivered by a set of movements with gleaming angles, shattering power and blissful elegance or raging might: and his hands were at the core.

ROUND TWO

'Don't try to rush things: for the cup to run over, it must first be filled.'

Antonio Machado

1983: The US Open, Oakmont

Another Battle with Watson – A Winning Strategy – American Depth

STAKES WERE high come mid-June, 1983, not far from the Allegheny River, north-east of Pittsburgh. The Oakmont Country Club was hosting the US Open for the sixth time. The course, opened in 1904, was envisaged as one of the game's toughest: its quick, canted greens, and bunkers – notably the famous Church Pews – designed to throttle the prospects of the wayward, designed to challenge the best. It was not the kind of United States Golf Association (USGA) endurance test in which Seve Ballesteros was meant to excel, but entering the final round he was atop the leaderboard with Tom Watson. In his *World of Professional Golf*, Mark McCormack observed of the 15th hole in the third round, 'Ballesteros played his 1-iron from the tee, and then followed with one of those shots that remind you of the young Byron Nelson and Ben Hogan. It was a 3-iron that covered the flag all the way and stopped four feet left of the cup, which was sited on the back of the green. It was among the more glorious long-iron shots we are likely to see in championship golf, both for direction and distance, and it demonstrated once again what a wonderful long-iron player he is.'

On the opening day the *Pittsburgh Post-Gazette* cited Las Vegas odds with Watson and Craig Stadler favourites, then

Raymond Floyd – then not yet an US Open winner – followed by Seve, Lanny Wadkins, Tom Kite and Ben Crenshaw at 8-1. The European led on Thursday with an impressive 69. More typical US Open service was resumed with a 74 on Friday, but another 69 in the third round left him in first place with Watson, and the only player to have two scores in the 60s. Two others on 69 after Thursday, John Mahaffey and Bob Murphy, had succumbed on the Friday to 79 and 81.

The final-day ABC telecast spoke of a Grand Slam for Seve, invoking the name of Bobby Jones. Could the 1983 Masters champion prevail? For Watson, the 1982 US Open champion, Ben Hogan was noted as the last to win the national open back-to-back, in 1951 and 1952, the former being his famed win at Merion upon return from a near-fatal car crash. Both protagonists were being talked about in the same breath as the greats: and past US Open winners at Oakmont included Tommy Armour, Hogan and Nicklaus. The Masters had seen Ballesteros and Watson paired together, Seve triumphantly wiping out the field with his dramatic opening surge, closing with a simple chip in that oozed class and a certain knowingness about his arsenal of talentful shots. Or maybe he was just lucky. The two were paired again, the golfing world was excited. Even *The Age* newspaper in Melbourne, Australia led its sport pages with the story, over the state of Victoria's traditional mainstay, Aussie Rules. The paper may have taken Thomas Boswell's column from *The Washington Post*, but it didn't have to lead. Or maybe it did, given the Capitol Hill journalist's assessment:

> **Watson, Seve duel for glory: Top two tied in US Open**
> Anyone who's ever had a glimmer of affection for golf owes it to his soul to watch the final 18 holes of the 83rd US Open from Oakmont today. Tied for the lead in golf's premier tournament are the two greatest players of the

> day, Tom Watson and Seve Ballesteros at one-under-par 212 after three rounds. They hold the wishbone of contemporary golf between them and both are pulling with one thought.

The 'wishbone of contemporary golf'. Watson and Ballesteros had the game by the giblets. The story accompanied a photograph of a frustrated Ballesteros, body dipping, face contorting as he missed a birdie putt. Seve was intent on winning the US Open to defy the naysayers who cautioned he was too wayward, too aggressive, his prestidigitatious short game undermined by USGA rough. Boswell pointed out the leading duo were one shot ahead of Calvin Peete, who could become the first black man to win a major, and two ahead of 40-year-old Ray Floyd vying for a first US Open title already having a green jacket in his wardrobe and two Wanamaker PGA Championship trophies on his mantelpiece. Floyd had game, and Peete was beyond consistent with his driving, though surely the main battle would be Tom versus Severiano?

Boswell continued: 'These two are at the peak of their mighty games. Ballesteros is golf's most titanic hitter, its most spectacular escape artist and one of its hottest streak putters. Watson is almost as long, almost as daring, a better tactician and manager of his own temper and, probably, the best putter, long range or short, on earth.

Both say they're hot and expect to win.

> '"I played very consistent today," said Ballesteros, prospering with a new conservative game plan that has him hitting 1-irons off 11 tees. "I was in the rough just once. A good record for a little Spaniard, no? … Perhaps I will continue to be lucky."

> "'My putting was exceptional today," said Watson, who has hit more greens and had fewer holes over par (six) than any other here. "Because I won last year, I think I'll be more relaxed this time … You know me, I love competition. Sometimes I need a rude slap in the face to get things done.'"

The article set the scene, and sold it. The players fancied their chances, with Seve having a pop at being perceived as lucky. Watson acknowledged the solidity of his game, relishing the opportunity to win back-to-back. Golf wanted an epic shoot-out between the best player of his generation, an American, and, for the first time, a European lauded by many as the best in the world. With another Masters under his belt, Seve was now in with a chance to take the most coveted American golf championship of all. He had even prepped well.

The power of imagination and ambition fused to create the USA's greatest output, the mythology of winning. Culture, lifestyle, thinking, entertainment and sport all craved the greatest, the ultimate. Jammed between Mexico and Canada the 48 contiguous states and their cousins in Alaska and Hawaii demanded clear winners. It was the Wild West transplanted into society – the good and the bad, the winners and the losers. The entire competitive nature of America was underpinned by statistics and who was better than whom. America is full of winners, grown men focused on their pasts as player of the year at high school or winner of such and such in college. The lies, damned lies and statistics of a million games and a thousand seasons allowed so many to lay claim to being the best, even for a fleeting throw of a football or the miraculous, one-off, three-point basket. Uncle Ramon told Seve not to go to America, it was difficult to win there. But Seve went, and Seve won.

> 'Americans love to fight. All real Americans love the sting and clash of battle. When you were kids, you all admired the champion marble shooter, the fastest runner, the big-league ball players and the toughest boxers. Americans love a winner and will not tolerate a loser.'
> **General George Patton**

Aged 18, Ballesteros had a tilt at the PGA Tour School in 1975. The mentally fittest scorers would prevail, and for any young man raised in the close-knit, homely environment of Pedreña, the USA was *the other*. Seve was homesick and, realising he'd miss life in northern Spain, practically threw his chance of a Tour card on the back nine of the final round, missing out by four shots. Living a family-oriented existence in Pedreña and on the European Tour was a real contrast to plying one's golfing trade across the Atlantic back then. And in Europe Seve was not alone, as other Spaniards started to make an impact. In contrast, the PGA Tour was a tribe of the individual: winners or prospective winners need only apply. The Tour School was the start of a love–hate affair with the United States, but a great career move. Winning his card would surely have changed the course of Seve's career, and his and Europe's immediate golfing destiny.

The hate part of Seve's stateside affair became the US Open, the PGA Tour Commissioner Deane Beman's needs around minimal playing commitments, and a range of US players Ballesteros saw as foes unequal to his talents, some of whom he disliked because of their standoffishness. Although, in a United States on the slide from the 1950s middle-class boom, the assassination of John F. Kennedy and the Vietnam War, the American approach to a Spaniard arriving on their shores was, perhaps, understandable. Despite Seve's own occasional pettiness, he detested that Americans felt he was coming to steal their money. Surely golf was meritocracy based on the numbers on the scorecard? Seve knew he painted some beautiful and interesting numbers.

The love of Seve's transatlantic life was the Masters Tournament. His first meaningful introduction to American golf came on the rolling grounds of the former flower nursery in Georgia. When the April 1977 edition of *Golf Digest* appeared, the cover – 'Can This Teen-ager Win The Masters?' – was accompanied by a photo of Ballesteros exploding through a shot. It accentuated the question. The USA had invented the teenager, the cocky kid with his quiff or flattop, sneakers and leather jacket, and now one from Spain was on the prowl. The accompanying article covered Seve's family, how to pronounce his name, something of his early golf history. Billy Casper, a great putter and thrice a major champion, remarked, 'The kid has one of the finest short games I have ever seen … and he's an animal off the tee.' Ballesteros would win the 1978 Greater Greensboro Open, and then the Masters in 1980 and 1983. If Augusta National was his great American romance, the courses of the US Open were forbidding mistresses. But encouragement in 1983 came immediately prior to Oakmont, as the maestro had won north of Manhattan, 400 miles east. Seve prepped for the Manufacturers Hanover Classic at Westchester Country Club (WCC) in an air of uncertainty as the sore of the Spaniard's relationship with the PGA Tour continued to pustulate. Having won three majors and secured a regular PGA Tour victory, Seve felt his place in the game should allow him to play in America more often, at his discretion. Despite being the leading player in Europe, he was dependent on playing in the States by way of sponsor invitation (these making him exempt from the regular tour playing rules). PGA Tour Commissioner Deane Beman was not overtly receptive to these requests for wider play; rules were rules. For every five tournaments played in the USA, one could play a single event in the competitor's home country. For Seve this meant Spain, but they had not enough professional tournaments to match a trade-off with the US, and this would constrain the rest of the Spaniard's play in Europe. Did this spur Seve to victory at Westchester?

Focusing on the US Open warm-up, at WCC Seve opted for a 1-iron off the tee when prudent, finding fairway after fairway. He opened with a 69, followed with 67, then endured a lacklustre 70, leaving him one shot ahead of Fuzzy Zoeller going into the last round. This was the Spaniard's first US appearance since winning the 1983 Masters and it became an early head-to-head battle with the man from Indiana. The crowds were openly rooting for the American, a recent winner at Harbour Town. Playing uncharacteristically safe golf, Seve found his game a bit out of sorts, and when he three-putted the 11th and 12th some fans jeered. For a New York state crowd this was not unusual, and Seve was up against one of their guys, albeit Fuzzy was from Midwest. The 11th hole preached caution, a creek around 255 yards out enforcing safe play from the tee that would then lead to the accurate approach demanded by a three-tiered green. Seve's three-putt just added to the pain of a hole played in near regulation. By the 13th tee he'd failed to record a birdie all day, had the crowd on his back, and he and four other players had at some point been in the lead.

Ballesteros had struggled on the long par-three 16th all week but on Sunday found the green with a long iron into a sizeable 30 feet. He *slammed* the putt in for a two, startling the crowd into a supporting rethink, caught by his tenacity. He came to the 72nd tied with Andy Bean and Craig Stadler and his regulation 1-iron tee shot and two approaches could set up a tournament-winning birdie. Severiano pulled driver. He melted it 300 yards, a colossal tee shot with a bit of oil-hardened wood and some rubber. But the 1-iron strategy meant a gap in his bag, offering the choice of a 4-wood, too much, or a 3-iron that needed jumped on, hit perfectly, much like his drive. Seve opted for the iron. Wide stance, ready for a wind-up and detonation, every centimetre of the ball needing to find and run up the centre of the clubface at the speed of a nuclear reaction, he crushed it. Killed it. Perfectly struck, it sailed directly at the pin, the player imploring, '*Vuela, vuela*' ('Fly, fly'), and it finally came to rest two yards from the hole. Seve knocked in the six-footer for eagle, a two-shot win, and around 11.5 million pesetas. The $81,000 winner's pot was the third highest so far in the 1983 US season; only the Masters and the Tournament Players Championship put more in a player's bank account. It was a stunning end, the stamp of Seve all over it. Later Ballesteros told reporters that after the long birdie putt at the 16th he heard someone in the crowd shout, 'We love you, Seve.' 'I knew that I would win,' he said. Seve loved to draw power and confidence from crowds, be they for or agin him. He also felt that the WCC was ideal preparation for the US Open and a course he'd never seen. Stalwarts of the American game disagreed. Raymond Floyd and Fred Couples both saw little comparison between the PGA Tour test at Westchester and the brutal Oakmont, noting the greens at the US Open would be much faster than those in Rye, New York. It was like comparing kindergarten with a maximum-security prison. A national US broadsheet reported that one wag on the Tour suggested that if you wanted to catch Seve Ballesteros at Oakmont, you'd better be there Thursday and Friday, as he'd be gone come the weekend. But on the eve of the major, in *The New York Times*, Johnny Miller declared to journalist Gordon S. White Jr, 'Seve is the best player in the world right now.'

* * *

In Pennsylvania, ABC's televisual juices were flowing, Jim McKay setting the scene: 'Will it be Seve Ballesteros from

Spain marching towards a possible Grand Slam, of Masters, US and British Open, and the PGA. It brings memories of that other Grand Slam when Bobby Jones won the US and British Amateur and Open titles in 1930. Or will it be Tom Watson, Kansas City's Tom Sawyer grown to manhood, trying to repeat as US Open champion.

'Watson and Ballesteros, the two greatest players in the game today, are tied for the lead with 18 holes to play. The last Open champion to successfully defend was Ben Hogan, that was 32 years ago, when he won at Oakland Hills … will it be the kid from Spain, becoming the first from his country to hold the title, or the defending champion, middle America's hero, Tom Watson.'

They nailed it, despite having a history of intros that pitched the US Open final round like a clash of civilisations upon which rested the entire future of Western culture. David Fay did the first tee announcing using a loudhailer, the kind of instrument probably more reserved for local cheerleading practice. Major golf, 1980s style. 'This is the last pairing for the final round. The players are defending national open champion, Tom Watson, Kansas City, Missouri.' Claps and cheers from the small crowd on the minimalist bleacher behind the tee, and those standing around it. On TV, McKay added, 'Trying for those back-to-back opens, the greatest player in the world for the past four or five years.'

'And Severiano Ballesteros, Santander, Spain.' Fay announced the final player on the tee, a US quirk, the leader doesn't get the honour, he ceremonially hits the final drive. The ABC telecast had Watson astride the rest of the field, sitting on one under par, but this was no anti-Seve bent, as the American broadcasters often had the habit of placing the best names in their minds at the zenith. Ballesteros's 69 in round three made him the leader.

McKay talked of Europe pitched against the USA. Of high drama, and a confrontation of the two best players in the world against each other. Who was the best, who would win? McKay (pronounced *mah-kay*, but only in America) dropped the must-ask question of the day, his distinctive voice familiar beyond sport as fate had left him to explain the events unfolding at the 1972 Munich Olympics when Palestinian terrorist group Black September took Israeli athletes in the Olympic Village hostage. Dave Marr responded to McKay's 'greatest player' comment, 'I would sure think so over the past number of years. And, of course Seve, is … is underrated, I feel, in this country. He feels like we call him lucky, but when you keep doin' it, Jim, you're not lucky, you're just good. Maybe some of the people just don't wanna admit it. But anyhow, here's the defender.' Watson took the tee, waggled and slashed a wood just left of centre, a solid start under great pressure.

What followed for a few holes was a ding-dong battle between the world's best, accompanied by ABC commentating gusto. Ballesteros stuck with a 1-iron, knocked just into the first cut of rough, then to a blind pin tucked right of centre, missing the green from 215 yards. He struck a nice shot, but his body language silently urged the ball to find the putting surface. On the course for ABC, Bob Rosburg, 1959 PGA champion, meditated, unsure if, head-to-head with Watson, the iron-of-the-tee strategy would reap dividends. McKay asked Rosburg to assess the mood of the players: 'Very, very tense, I thought, as well as I know them. There's one other point out here, too, they had to wait already on the 1st hole: now, the pace of play, both of these players play very, very quickly, that might have something to do with it.'

Watson had 175 yards and tweaked his approach left. The two players were immediately struggling but Watson found a favourable lie and hit a lovely long running pitch to about five feet. Seve was in a classic US Open spot and, to emphasise his dislike for the thick rough around greens, his chip came up 12 feet shy. But with that familiar crouched putting position, putter toe in the air, he stroked the putt in and raised the club in his left hand, signalling both the crowd's and his own appreciation. Par. Seventeen to go. Watson matched him. They both led on one under. Dan Jenkins of *Sports Illustrated* had his own view of the events unfolding: 'Both Watson and Ballesteros started nervously, rescuing pars at the 1st green with gutty putts, but it quickly became evident that Watson was aching to get even for the knockout blow that Ballesteros had laid on him in the Masters in April, the last time they were paired.'

On the 2nd from 125 yards out Watson almost hit the pin, his approach nestling behind the cup, his putt not dissimilar to the 1st. Seve had already approached with a decent shot to about 25 feet, but settled for par. Watson, knees bent, crouched at the waist, rattled his putt in for birdie. The commentary team watched with rapture as the American took the lead on minus two. ABC's enthusiasm was infectious. Seve was one adrift and then another shot behind was Larry Nelson, the 1981 PGA champion. Holes three and four brought into play the famous Church Pews, a 100-yard-long bunker complex with 12 grass-covered ridges, likened to those austere seating arrangements in places of worship. Prayers were optional on Oakmont. But recommended. Watson drove down the middle and appeared to be into his stride. He found the short rough but had hit a long one. Ballesteros continued with the iron. Rosburg and Jim McKay were renowned for their double act, Rossie typically calling a shot impossible, only for the player to pull off something wonderful, and he was changing his tune already and starting to endorse the Seve iron play, the value of putting Watson under pressure by playing first. Seve needed to find the short stuff.

Each fighter was finding his range, eyeing the other for an opening. Both made pars at the 3rd, but the 4th was an arduous 591 yards. Watson ended up in the rough from the tee but pulled a decent lie and was able to persuade a wood not far from the green. Seve had just missed the fairway and ended in a poor spot. He had to lay up well back, 100 yards or so. On Seve's long walk to his ball he surveyed the green down the hill, his focus punctuated by aircraft streaking across the sky, Sunday commuter planes taking travellers home after a weekend, or onward to work for the Monday morning. He then clipped a beautiful wedge beyond the flag. The American had a long greenside bunker to negotiate, the pin not too far beyond. He swung his sand wedge surely, delivering the ball on to the green and allowing it to roll out to three feet. A wonderful shot any day, any time. There was a noticeable spring in Watson's step as he rounded the bunker towards the front of the putting surface. For ABC, Peter Alliss commented on Tom's angelic smile, not his killer instinct.

Seve's play looked stretched, the lack of length telling, quality a bit of a struggle, but he did have a birdie putt from 20 feet. He appeared to just tap the ball. It rolled towards the cup as if on ice, imperceptibly snaking towards its destiny. It dived in the right side, the crowd roared, understanding its importance. So did Ballesteros. In acknowledgement the visor came off and he saluted the gallery, his pursed lips signalling renewed determination. Alliss reacted, having acknowledged the Spaniard needed to make a few putts, 'Isn't he quite remarkable, it almost wriggled away. Look at that look in the eye … I'll show you. He really has, eh, enormous talent. Let's look at that again. He hardly seemed to hit it hard enough, looked to be going quite slowly, then it looks as if it's drifting away to the right, and I thought it was going to catch the edge and not go in. But it did. This is classic, almost match-play stuff between Ballesteros and Tom Watson.'

Watson now had a four-footer to ensure he remained two in front, but he was a great champion, imbued with practical and earthly powers. He stroked his ball straight into the heart, four under par. He still had both hands on the trophy. Three birdies in four holes were stellar stuff. Watson was sizzling, Ballesteros starting to cook. The 5th was a short par four and both players hit iron. Watson found the fairway but Seve hit a poor one, leaking it well right, almost in a creek. Seve really seemed to be taking his time; he and caddy Nick DePaul surveyed the second shot, pin tucked left, and an overhanging tree branch above them. Once decided, Seve went right at it from 165 yards, those powerful hands slicing through the rough and under the ball. Rosburg witnessed a beautiful-looking shot, but the ball ran beyond the putting surface. Watson struck a solid iron to the back centre, 20 feet from the cup, and in a safe part of the target, given all the danger lurking. Peter Alliss once more admired Watson's momentum, especially after his mediocre opening hole.

The sparring between Watson and Seve was in danger of breaking out into full-blown golfing pugilism, but when Seve got to his ball it appeared his next punch would be with one hand tied behind his back. He was a yard off the apron. Jack Whitaker was describing the travails of Ballesteros in the deep rough. Bob Rosburg took over, describing it as terrible, bemoaning the USGA set-up around the greens. As Seve eyed the shot, the lie, the distance from ball to hole, and the pace of the green, he appeared to fancy it. He gave the ball an educated dunt, hands and arms fixed through the ball. It landed on the green and hit the left side of the hole, lipping out. Seve spun round in surprise, frustration and disappointment. From travails to deep rough to near chip in, this was what Seve did for a living. 'Oh my!' came Dave Marr's response. 'My Lord, wouldn't that have been something,' mused Whitaker. 'It's probably too early to say, but it almost looks, Dave Marr, that Watson's trying to do to Seve what Seve did to him at the Masters.'

Forty-five minutes later ABC showed the players walking across a bridge above the Pennsylvania turnpike, heading to the tee that would take them to the turn, as the telecast went to an interlude about the man, Severiano Ballesteros.

The picture cut to a graphic of the Iberian Peninsula, Portugal signalled by a burned orange, Spain a sickly oozing yellow, emphasising the distance from the lush green Allegheny River and its surroundings. Spain seemed like a faraway land of heat and dust. McKay explained, in a poetic bent with some ropey Spanish-sounding guitar music to accompany him, that great golfers came from Texas, West Pennsylvania, or great cities of the US Midwest, like Columbus, Ohio or Kansas City, Missouri (or, in other words, great champion golfers were Ben Hogan and Byron Nelson; or Arnold Palmer; or Jack Nicklaus and Tom Watson). They did not come from anywhere else, not Europe and especially not Spain. Not from some place called Santander. Panning across the Santander Bay in this interlude – that had the 1980s production qualities of a high-school media project – ABC explained Seve came from an even smaller place. The screen showed a leafy, sunny country single-track road, a horse and cart chugging along, a bucolic throwback to simpler times. The segment charted Seve's humble beginnings, the century-old farmhouse in which he still lived, and that his great-grandfather had sold some farmland in 1929 to allow the creation of the Real Golf de Pedreña. McKay acknowledged that had that not happened, a young Seve may have been a farmer, not a golfer on the grandest stages. ABC outlined his major golfing résumé, and remarked of the win at Lytham in 1979, 'He was a slashing, swashbuckling Latin hero at just 22 years old.' Of his 1980 win at Augusta National, 'He pelted the long ball, and putted the greens to perfection.' And it all started in a caddy shack in Pedreña, where Seve and his brothers talked about and learned the game.

Surely, to be a true great, ABC said, Seve needed to win the US Open. What followed was impossible to imagine today. Seve interviewed, detailing why his record at the US Open was so bad, practically a sworn affidavit on why he would never win it. He had also been quoted thus in the US newspapers. Perhaps it was a function of Seve's analysis when it came to his own golf, Spanish directness and honesty. Ballesteros explained how the US Open demanded mechanical play, that finding fairways and greens was key, and that par upon par upon par was required, and that did not suit him. Few would argue, and the final round at Oakmont was proving the point, as the irons off the tee continued to leave long approach after long approach. 'The rough at the US Open is very difficult, that is my problem,' he felt. Maybe the real issue was that for someone as natural and imaginative as Seve, the US Open felt like work. Like a job. Like a grind. It didn't allow a golfer like him to play, to enter the spirit of play. His interlude words were to prove prophetic as he failed to birdie the 9th and his struggles continued. The big clash between Watson and Ballesteros played out for a few more holes around the turn, but the rough, the longer shots and the demands of USGA golf nibbled at the Spaniard's ability to score. As Seve started to recede, and Watson maintained his position, Larry Nelson pecked at Tom's dominance.

A weather delay bumped the final few holes into Monday and when the siren to halt Sunday sounded, Watson was on the 14th green. Nelson was on the tee at the par-three 16th, a hole of 228 yards that would ask a wood of the player. Larry had fewer holes to make mistakes on, but starting at a long-short one is no one's idea of fun, especially to a pin hiding back right, protected by a trap. On the resumption of play, major sport took one of those turns that emphasises why we can spend hours watching and waiting for a signature moment. Watson had a birdie try and hit a decent putt but settled for a par. Nelson had found the green with his wood and minutes later hit a beautifully paced, snaking left-to-right 60-footer that dropped right into the heart of the hole. A hoop and a holler came from some of the gallery and the player allowed himself to break into a canter, a mixture of surprise and understated delight. Nelson was now five under to Watson's four, the latter three head of the rest of the field. Seve had faded to two over. As Tom approached his ball in the middle of the 15th fairway he asked Bob Rosburg what the cheering was. Rossie suggested later it must have been an 'awful jolt' to hear the news of Larry Nelson's gain. That's how it goes, was Watson's ultimate assessment. For the first time in many hours, he was not ahead or sharing the lead in the defence of his title. Larry Nelson would become the US Open champion. The Watson-Ballesteros clash, ultimately, did not match the hype, but the front nine had seen all the drama of great shots and great recoveries. Another day would come. Seve was still Masters champ, and Watson had his Open Championship defence to look forward to at Birkdale.

Santander

Isolated Spain – Ballesteros Backstory – Hogan, Palmer, Player, Nicklaus

FIRST SETTLED in Roman times, Santander, the Cantabrian city overlooking Seve's home, was founded for its natural port defended by the sea and the mountains. Grassy hill farms and sometime snowy peaks snaked along much of Spain's northern coast, geographical, psychological and meteorological separation from the *meseta* to the south. Pedreña lay across the water and, given its latitude, sometimes the only hot and glowing thing about it was the ABC graphic that appeared on the US Open telecast. Ted Walker, English poet and author, arrived in the late 1970s: 'The warmish Maytime air of Santander, away from the waterfront, carried and mingled scents no visitor to Spain disremembers: fresh bread and over-ripe melons, shellfish, chopped onion, red meats being cooked in sauces containing bitter dark chocolate … the beginning of slow-to-simmer soups and stews, newly-crushed garlic heads releasing juices into hot olive oil; and the fragrances of late breakfasts: pungent coffee, newly-fried churros, the smoke of black tobacco.'

Severiano Ballesteros appeared in Pedreña, Cantabria, northern Spain in April 1957, a son of the soil and a cousin of the sea, his early life rich with the fruits of both. Born in

1919, his father became a man as Spain passed into a period of turmoil, war, hate and recrimination. In 1936 the Spanish Civil War broke out, and Pedreña was in a Republican – the side of change and equality – region that stretched from the east of Santander, San Sebastián in the Spanish Basque Country, to west of Gijon. This sliver of revolt was a salient, hemmed in by General Franco's soldiers, the Right, the Spanish Establishment, vested interests who benefitted from the power of wealth, land ownership, the Catholic church or public office. Around the time of Baldomero Ballesteros's age of majority, the Civil War was going from bad to worse, and it wasn't the conflict of the modern popular Northern European imagination, skirmishes here and there with one side led by a guy in a funny hat versus some idealists from Spain and the rest of the world in red neckerchiefs. Spain was the litmus test for a global conflict, as Germany and Italy supported the Right, Russia the Brigade on the Left, and Britain and France remained shamefully neutral. Over 50 nationalities fought on the side of the Brigade and the Republicans, but seen from afar the Spanish war still has an air of the artistic ideal, intertwined with many of the good and great of early 20th-century art and literature.

Seve would remark that his father was for General Franco, believed he was best for the country, and shot his hand to avoid fighting for the Republicans. This appears as if it was a straightforward course of action but the war was a tragedy that set Spain apart from the rest of Europe for decades. There was the very real chance that someone like Baldomero Ballesteros would be killed, regardless of politics. The war was brutal and descended into the opaqueness of all civil conflict, but from the opaque came the notorious and the iconic. Guernica appeared to be an innocuous market town in the heart of the Basque Country, some 60 miles east of Pedreña. Fatefully, it was a bustlingly parochial centre of commerce and a psychological and physical gateway to the north for Franco's troops. It was the heart of the Basque Country and home of their famous oak, a symbol of the people and culture, the first planted in the 14th century when Robert the Bruce of Scotland was fighting the English and when the native Mississippi culture was at its zenith in what would become land of the United States of America. The Basque town was strategic, and the army wanted to push up from outside Madrid and into the Republican-held north of Spain, a hotbed of resistance. In late April 1937 the planes of the Nazi Germany-led Condor Legion carpet-bombed Guernica, the first time in any conflict civilians had been deliberately and almost solely targeted in this way. It was the start of cynical airborne assaults, home of the euphemism 'collateral damage'. Guernica became the war's most infamous event, made real by Picasso's mural shown at the International Exposition of Art and Technology in Modern Life in Paris in 1937. On the streets of Guernica that day, on the canvas, and in the exhibition halls of Paris, art and modern life fused. The technology of mass warfare had arrived.

In June 1937, as Baldomero Ballesteros elected to wound himself and side with Franco, the Falange and the Fascists, Pablo Picasso completed his most famous work. The artist did not like to append meaning to his paintings, but the uninitiated can see the faces of contorted human and equine suffering, the agony reaching from the canvas: 'tangled horror', as Jan Morris called it. Like many civil conflicts the struggle ignited petty, historic wrangling, which became just as lethal as ideologies. Wicked opportunists took the chance to profit from confusion, fear and suffering. Local squabbles, family feuds, minor criminality turned into bloodthirsty, barbarous disagreements where one side was as capable of a savage act as the other. Conservative estimates have 200,000 dead in combat, and the same number killed in cold blood, driven by revenge and murderous intent, or slain at the hands of right-wing sympathisers and itinerant thugs. Such is the world that informed Seve's father's early adult life and the privations that followed.

Whether Baldomero Ballesteros's support of Franco was the result of tempestuous youth, commitment to beliefs or driven by purely local sympathies – he was from people who owned and worked the land, perhaps fearful it would be taken – he is marked as Seve's father, his DNA part of what made Seve tick. Seve explained how his father had shot himself to escape 'conscription' to the Republican side. A very dim view of such activity was taken, and often remedial medical treatment – administered without anaesthetic – became a form of mediaeval punishment for trying to avoid the fight. The future for any young man of fighting age and ability was grim. Be enlisted by the Republicans whose side was on the wane and would lose 60,000 men in the Battle of Santander, or join the Fascists and find yourself in immediate trouble in a Republican area, risk being executed on the spot. Few of us face such decisions. History tells us that, in general, siding with the *Franquismos* was the winning thing to do, but morally corrupt. Paul Preston's book title, *The Spanish Holocaust: Inquisition and Extermination in Twentieth Century Spain*, says it all. The war was a battle of beliefs, interests, convictions. It's not difficult to see how Baldomero passed this on to his own flesh and blood. Combined with the tempestuous and mercurially individualistic-but-family-loving Spanish way, you have a combustible mixture of passions. The rents in Spanish society remained long after the war; many remain today. Spain became virtually bankrupt, ignored by the international community. Dogs and cats disappeared from city streets as hunger gripped the nation. As Seve grew up, some Spaniards were living in caves, eking out near-prehistoric existences. This erstwhile colonial powerhouse's once-gleaming jackboot was reduced to a tattered espadrille.

As the young golfer took to the beach with his artisanal golf club, the Spain of 1964 was a conundrum. Land by the shore was not typically of value, it was rocky and had no use for arable or livestock farming but, in the north, in Cantabria, the oceanic, more northern European climate brought rain and a fertile landscape. It was not the Spanish heartland of package holidays and sun-kissed beaches. The political and social landscapes were imbued with the 'Twenty-Five Years of Peace', a nationwide 'celebration' of a quarter of a century since the end of the Spanish Civil War. Francisco Franco and his fascists were still in charge, still paranoid. They warned of plots and turmoil emanating from Europe, 'secret machinations, subversive action and the power of occult forces'. Economically, politically, geographically and psychologically, Spain was haunted. This was the background to Seve's upbringing. How might this all have informed his sense of (in)justice, opinions and actions regarding the powers of the PGA Tour and its European cousin. In his autobiography, Ballesteros talks of Pedreña's telephone exchange operator being a confidante of the local priest. This fact is presented in a mildly amusing, gossipy way about how the woman would know everybody's business in such a small town. So would the priest. So would the local police, most probably. Power can work in mysterious ways. As Tom Watson was growing up and starting to win local and state competitions in the furnace of Midwestern progress, Spain was hurtling back to the past.

There were three cars in Pedreña – one uncle Ramon's, while corrupt politicians and the rich in Madrid drove plush Mercedes imported at vast costs. Spain was a backwater. The country was neutral in World War II but, spared the carnage and suffering, it received no benefits as a war economy, became isolated as a fascist regime, saw no boom from post-war rebuilding of towns, of infrastructure. In 1946 the United Nations had passed a resolution for a boycott of Spanish trade, but the Civil War had already cut income to 19th-century levels. Spain was alone and weary. To be spared the menace of the World War was a godsend, but there were real macroeconomic benefits for most of Northern Europe once fighting had ceased and the continent and its peoples began to get back on their feet. The Allies' defeat of Hitler's and Mussolini's fascists left Spain looking like a morbid, moribund curiosity, an annoying right-wing canker on the rear of a new, democratic Europe full of ambition. As Severiano Ballesteros walked through his boyhood golfing dream, British travel writer Jan Morris wrote in 1964 in *The Presence of Spain* that the country was quaint in its lack of industrialisation and progressiveness, much of this attributed to the country's diverse cultures and geographies, and the shadow of the caudillo, Franco. Morris spoke of a great fighting tradition and historical turmoil: 'The Spaniards were withdrawn from the world so long that in many ways there they have a Victorian look. The Spanish forces may seem archaic, but nobody has recently doubted their ability to fight, and in Spain the profession of arms commands a special kind of esteem.'

The British travel writer also seized upon that special brand of Spanish fury, the psychology and tumult of the bullfight. Half a decade before Morris, Frederic Raphael had travelled and seen that 'in Franco's kingdom time seemed to have stopped; in 1939. Spain was in bondage', while the rest of Europe was free. The Civil Guard were everywhere, watching the daily machinations of a stunted life. The priest was watching, the telephone exchange listening. Raphael observed that Spain saw 'cruelties of peace were better than the disasters of war'.

* * *

Severiano Ballesteros Sota – the Spanish convention being father's surname, mother's surname – was born two years before Raphael travelled to Spain, the country effectively bankrupt.

Two days before Seve's coming, on the other side of *el mundo*, Doug Ford won his second major, the Masters, coming from three behind Sam Snead to triumph by three, sealing an unexpected victory by holing a plugged bunker shot at the last for a best-of-the-week 66. It was also the year of the first 36-hole cut at Augusta National, and Ford had tied the lowest final round in a major and the lowest four-round total at the event. Golf was entering a new era as the next edition at Augusta saw Arnold Palmer win his first major and Grand Slam golf's first five-figure cheque, $12,500. Also in 1958, Herbert Warren Wind coined the term Amen Corner for Augusta's treacherous 11th, 12th and 13th holes. In his article ('The Fateful Corner', *Sports Illustrated*) Wind recounts, 'down in the Amen Corner where Rae's Creek intersects the thirteenth fairway near the tee, then parallels the front edge of the green on the short twelfth and finally swirls along the eleventh green' Bobby Jones dedicated the bridge at the famous par three to the legendary Ben Hogan, and the bridge from 13th tee to its fairway was named for Byron Nelson. A generation hence a young Spaniard would be attacking those holes with vigour. In 1959 Gary Player won his first Open at Muirfield, pocketing £1,000. In 1960, en route to Dublin for the Canada Cup (as the World Cup was then known), Palmer and scribbling sidekick Bob Drum would conjure up the modern Grand Slam, a reconfiguration of Jones's Impregnable Quadrilateral of 1930, for the professional game. Jones squared a perfect circle by winning the Amateur Championship (Old Course), the Open (Royal Liverpool), the US Open (Interlachen, Minnesota) and the US Amateur at Merion, but Palmer and Drum ensured that forever the modern Ark of the Covenant contained the Masters trophy, the US Open silverware, the Claret Jug, and the PGA of America's Wanamaker. Already in 1960, as he and Drum soared across the pond, Palmer had won the first two, defeating Ben Hogan and a young amateur, Jack Nicklaus, in the US Open at Cherry Hills. Modern golf could have been quite different – Arnie was a replacement in the Canada Cup for Ben Hogan. After his final round and Palmer's charge at Cherry, the Ice Man was in no mood to travel. Modern golf's formula for immortality turned on a single shot on a singular day.

* * *

Hogan was playing with 20-year-old Jack Nicklaus who, at one point, led the 1960 US Open on five under par. At the par-five 17th, its green practically surrounded by water, Hogan turned to ask who was leading.

'Palmer.'

Ben shook his head, 'How could that be?'

Palmer blistered round in 65, using the mile-high air as a trump card when driving the 1st green at 346 yards and holing the putt for eagle, setting his scorecard alight. That fire would rage for years, change modern golf and reinvent the Open Championship as Palmer then Nicklaus understood the importance of winning where the game had become formalised and the early working-class greats rose to become champions backed by the few, adored by the many.

Hogan hit a perfect approach – too perfect, strike-wise – to the penultimate hole at Cherry Hills, and it spun back into the water. Palmer went on to win, take Hogan's spot in the Canada Cup, and conjure up the modern Grand Slam on his way to Portmarnock where he and Sam Snead would win. In Pedreña, a carefree three-year-old was perhaps already dreaming, as golf's guard was changing and solidifying. Palmer and Snead won in the year that witnessed the founding of Mark McCormack's International Management Group (IMG), while parts of Spain appeared stuck in the Middle Ages. The contrast between Seve's early and later lives was stark, but for many Spaniards home remained home, an acute sense of place was life's cornerstone.

* * *

Those pastoral parts of Spain that survive – many small towns on the *meseta* or in remote mountain communities have dissolved into the ether – retain that sense of their long history and uncomplicated role in the world, a salute to the simple pleasures of work, play, family, culture and custom. Pedreña provided all the nurture and lessons for which a growing boy in 1960s Spain could ask. Severiano was the fifth son of Baldomero Ballesteros Presmanes and Carmen Sota Ocejo. One son died a tragic death, the result of an attack by a swarm of wasps, and the Ballesteros's next child would also be called Manuel. The older Ballesteros brothers, Manuel, Vicente and Baldomero Jr, worked the family fields in the hills around Pedreña, and the young Seve would help, usually assigned the most basic and earthy of tasks. While Manuel was a stocky, shorter boy – the classic Spanish male template of his mother's side – Seve was already a more modern-looking Spaniard: rangier physique, handsome shining face, lithe. Vicente was the same. Growing up, the family benefitted from the mixed diet of a burgeoning new Spain before the country began to blossom. Meat, fish, vegetables courtesy of Pedreña, farmland by the sea. These simple luxuries were not available to most of his country folk, and nor were the sporting genes of his paternal and maternal bloodlines. Baldomero Ballesteros was a strong, vital man who had been in winning teams in local boat races, the annual events where Cantabrians take on their nearby foes, including the Basques. Communities would turn out in their thousands to cheer on and support the rowers, each winning crew welcomed as heroes, spectators enjoying the taste of victory. These competitions of strength, determination, rhythm and teamwork have their origins in the famous fishermen and seafarers of the north of Spain, men who pioneered both transatlantic travel, and long-range, transatlantic fishing. Iberian fishermen were likely harvesting the cod fields of North America before North America even existed. Fishing close to the shore was also important, and after a hard day's work boats would charge back to the land, rushing to be the first to sell their catch. The template of Severiano Ballesteros was forged not just on the beaches and the fields. Meanwhile, in the USA, another golfer was blooming.

Missouri

Young Tom – Stanford – Missouri State Champion – Turning Pro

TOM WATSON and Seve Ballesteros hailed from similar places in the UK psyche, parts of the world the British felt they knew. But Kansas City, MO is no Disney World, no *Cheers*, no Yankees or LA Lakers heartland, it's a place all of its own, but quintessentially American, with a rich, unique history. *Mizz-oh-rah*, as they call it in the west, on the cusp of the Great Plains, that vast region constituting much of the western breadbasket, is where Old Macdonald met Ronald McDonald.

> 'A Missourian gets used to Southerners thinking him a Yankee, a Northerner considering him a cracker, a Westerner sneering at his effete Easternness, and the Easterner taking him for a cowhand.'
>
> **William Least Heat-Moon**, *Blue Highways*

The British 'knew' Tom Watson, he even looked like them. He'd won our Open, America was our friend, and Tom shared essential British traits: modest, thoughtful, sporting and gentlemanly in his ardent competitiveness. Adversity was met in a calm, stiff-upper-lip way. In the same way that Seve Ballesteros was clearly not British, but something of the exotic, and that we 'knew' Spain, Tom Watson could quite easily have been Scottish. But he was a Missourian, an American through and through, but he was no cracker.

Thomas Sturges Watson was born in Kansas City, Missouri, in 1949, part of the explosion of the USA's middle class with a new America emerging post-World War II. Hot off the back of victory, America was the world's grain store, manufacturing hub, the world's policeman against the Red Menace of the Soviet Union; the world's philosopher with new ideas of society, economics and consumption. New models of everyday life took root in the USA in the 1950s and 1960s. The country exploded into modernity with home ownership, white goods, and a car for one or more in the family, all of which saw the USA's economy surge, as if World War II had been some perverse, elaborate plan of obscene infrastructure spend to kick-start an entire swathe of the planet. The USA could have guns and butter. And America was the world's bank. The Marshall Plan – $13 billion ($100 billion in today's money) of aid to war-torn Western Europe – appeared in 1948, and with the USA's GI Bill of Rights you had thousands of young American men going to college or university, learning trades. This Petri dish was the backdrop to Tom Watson's early life of growth, vision and seemingly untold opportunity.

Ray, Tom's father, was an insurance broker in flourishing Kansas City and the family were part of the upper strata of Missouri society and business. Sallie Bet was a stay-at-home mom who looked after two sons before Tom, as the 1950s represented the single-most lucrative period of economic growth for the average American, fostering unassailable confidence. World War II was the Big Win. Come 1963, the British prime minister was talking about the white heat of technology, but the US had been bathing in that warmth for a decade. The middle class had time for leisure, and money to spend on those pursuits. For some, that meant golf. In his classic instructional book *Getting Up and Down: How to Save Strokes from Forty Yards and In*, Watson recounts his earliest golf memory, and gives us an insight into one of the qualities that made him. He recalls the summer of 1956, six years old, arriving at Kansas City Country Club (KCCC) with the family, and being given the chance to putt on the practice green for the first time. Watson would 'never forget the excitement of that evening, since it was … my first real golfing experience, hooked me on the game forever … it was fun and a new challenge'. He enthuses about his early years and, instead of hitting full shots, the challenge of putting, reading the breaks and speed of the green. He acknowledged the first lesson his father taught him – *get the ball into the hole*. In the same way Ballesteros cultivated a game unbound by convention, golf holes and their layouts, the Watson boy ingrained an iron-clad short game and putting stroke at KCCC.

As Watson grew up, America changed. A form of waking nightmare began with the assassination of John F. Kennedy. The events of Dealey Plaza, Dallas, on 22 November 1963, shook the US's sense of what it was and stood for. American progress also had the shadow of annihilation by the Soviet Union as a backdrop to the Cold War, and it almost became a Hot War with the Cuban Missile Crisis of 1962. While Spain and Seve's family conjured with a move to the modern world, the United States of America, Russia and the rest were struggling to understand what modernity meant with its complexities and contradictions. With the Arms Race the superpowers toyed with the idea of destroying economies and belief systems at which Spain could only glance.

The USA was already in Vietnam. Troop sizes tripled in both 1961 and 1962, and JFK's successor, Lyndon Johnson, escalated the country's commitment. Before the US really had a hold on or an understanding of what this war would mean, they were deeply involved. This moral maze had profound implications. Events in Dallas seemed to draw the country into prolonged trauma. In 1965 the once-firebrand-but-mellowing Malcolm X was gunned down. In 1968 Martin Luther King Jr and Bobby Kennedy were assassinated by lone gunmen. America was in crisis, and the continued escalation, protests and disagreements about Vietnam were tearing the country apart. Adding the insecure, unstable and paranoid President Richard Nixon to the mix did nothing for the USA's sense of destiny and meaning. If Seve Ballesteros was born into a relatively backward and isolated society in northern Spain, Watson grew up and matured in a time of great prosperity, then angst. A doubt-ridden USA was the place Seve saw when he first came to play stateside. The game of golf is meaningless in terms of global socio-economics and the US military-industrial complex but the 1970s was not the ideal time to be launching long-driving and blistering short-game raids on American tournament purses. US golfers were usually Republicans; uncertainty, military defeat and financial pain were not typically on their menu. They benefitted and suffered from a 'Victory Complex'.

Victory was their right, and when they saw Seve appear, some saw a direct threat to their destiny. And their pockets. Early in his career Seve heard comments in locker rooms about him coming over the Atlantic to plunder the purses of the players on the PGA Tour. He took these slights personally. In many ways this reaction from US players was natural, protective, although the strongest players saw Seve and his game as an opportunity to prove themselves. Others, like Ed Fiori complaining to commentator Ben Wright about him referencing Seve's great shot-making, felt aggrieved. Maybe if we'd played in 11 majors between 1978 and 1984 and missed six cuts we'd feel aggrieved, too. Ballesteros took umbrage at being called 'Steve' in the same way baseball legend Roberto Clemente detested the press and others referring to him as 'Robert'. Ballesteros had a tendency to take things personally. This also drove him to greatness.

Ballesteros and Watson were outwardly differing people in almost every way but their competitive streaks were fostered in familial challenges on similar land. Tom was often against his brother, Ridge, and his father, Ray, and these informal lessons and games led to informal graduations. Tom's game would advance rapidly and he had an older quality player to look up to. While Seve had his maternal uncle, Ramon Sota, and his brothers, Watson's father was his primary golfing bloodline. Ray held the amateur course record of 64 at KCCC, he schooled his three sons on the game, Tom the keenest. KCCC had been formed in 1898 after some friends who'd been playing on a cow pasture wanted to organise their play.

Albert Tillinghast laid out the original course, one of many in a career that charted some of the US's greatest tracks like those at Baltusrol, Bethpage, Winged Foot and Quaker Ridge. KCCC became Watson's playground. He'd play hole after hole, beat ball after ball, tuning his brain and swing to an ever-improving game. In a 1983 article in the Stanford University alumni periodical, the imaginatively titled the *Stanford Magazine*, the Kansas City pro, Stan Thirsk, spoke of playing his single ball in a better-ball game against Ray and Tom when the former suggested the number of shots in the match to ensure that if Tom performed, the father-son team could win. But Tom had to perform, there were no free passes and the patriarch was a great negotiator in combining his knowledge of golf with that of actuarial probabilities.

This allowed Watson to take his skills from the hours spent on the course alone to meaningful levels. All amateurs love to match themselves with the local pros, but the games with and guidance of Thirsk meant a lot to Tom. Watson knew the value of those formative years, both technically and on how to compete, how to scrap, how to scrape a win. He'd play in 'the gangsomes' on the local professionals' day off, and Watson would join Thirsk and others as they toured the metropolitan area playing competitive games against each other.

Golf for the Spaniard seemed more informal, but also more intuitive and experimental: trying, copying, failing, succeeding. While the US was pumping out excellent players by the tankerload, most of Spain's talent was being panhandled on local tours – although a handful of very good working-class golfers had, by dint of their talents, found their way through the sporting labyrinth dominated by Spain's elite. Meanwhile, Watson was at the heart of his country's upwardly mobile golfing stratum. Tom would focus on the great players and try to mimic them – Jack Nicklaus for his sound grip and tempo, Ray Floyd for his fearless putting. Watson tried to learn from others all the time. Come graduation from high school he'd already played exhibition matches against Arnold Palmer and Jack Nicklaus.

In his autobiography, Nicklaus recalls playing, in 1967, in an exhibition match in Topeka, Kansas, with a 'fine seventeen-year-old amateur by the name of Tom Watson'. More detail Big Jack does not provide, beyond a brief account of his own terrible putting display that day. For any young, aspiring sportsman these competitive battles can be catalysed into intense ambition. They allow calibration against the barometer of good play, course management and personal control at the highest level. These matches functioned the way Seve's formative golf did. Without the pressure of a card, money, TV cameras or vast crowds, success or near-success comes relatively cheaply, without any scar tissue if play is bad or a heavy defeat dished out. While a win and other good things can be drawn upon, unsullied. It's one of golf's fundamental allures that on a given day, on most courses, any player can score as well as the next, be it on a hole, a front or back nine, or complete round. This offers false hope, any success an imitation of the real thing, but Tom Watson was starting to look like just that: the real thing.

While in boyhood Seve dreamt of sweeping all aside, formal opportunities were scarce in Cantabria. Tom was living that dream. He won the Kansas City Amateur at 14, triumphed in the state high-school championship twice, and in 1969 came fourth in the then-stroke play US Amateur at Oakmont. The *Sports Illustrated* article on the final round of the event made no mention of Watson, it was keener on dissecting the not-too-healthy diet of winner Steve Melnyk. Fourth was stellar, given the depth and reach of the championship, but the USA liked winners. Melnyk would go on to win the (British) Amateur, and the runner-up at Oakmont, Vinny Giles III, who'd been second previously, would win in 1972 then take out the British version in 1975. The field at Oakmont included Lanny Wadkins, Andy North and Tom Kite, but Watson's ascent was low-key. He didn't come from the historic East Coast where US golf began; he didn't hail from the sunny West Coast and its wide and deep pool; he wasn't from the monied history of golf in the Deep South or the hard school and pan of Texas. Missouri was off the beaten track, but Tom's comprehensive talents had brought him wins at city and state level, where the might of many sports matched that of whole countries. The USA was a country of vast raw golfing material and the golf industrial complex produced armies of excellent, structured players and stiff competitors. Missouri and Kansas City were places of honest work and endeavour, where everything was possible but nothing was free.

After high school Tom went to north California and one of America's most prestigious universities, Stanford, a place to excel in games and academics. Ray had also been a student there. Watson wasn't on a scholarship and set on a career in business. He explained to the author of the *Stanford Magazine* article, 'I had come from Kansas City, a community where discipline is ingrained, to Stanford, where an individual had total freedom. During college I was searching always for ways to improve myself, but finding the right direction wasn't easy.' Going from Missouri to just south of San Francisco in the 1960s must have been eye-watering, from mom's apple pie to tie-dye. Watson originally enrolled for economics, then turned to psychology, but his KCCC work ethic remained, both in class and at the golf facility. He was renowned for his commitment. Friend and foe would remark on his long hours of practice and play, honing, seeking, tweaking, ironing out creases in his game. Perfecting. Back then, given the equipment and understanding of the game, Watson was deemed to be around the perfect height for a golfer, and in his introduction to Watson's *Back to Basics*, Lee Trevino noted how Tom's action involved 'no wasted motion'. Watson's game and process involved no dilly-dallying, no long ruminations, but instead a walk straight to the ball; yardage and shot assessment, set-up, waggle, strike. Shots could be executed in the time taken to type the last two sentences.

This approach fed into Watson's distance from the tee, a strong ally to a strong short game. In 1969 he won the NCAA Long-Drive Contest. Not because he drove his car to Missouri, but because he had three tee shots averaging 294 yards. He began to realise golf was his main talent, part of the cream just below the rich meniscus of the USA's best. As well as Kite and Wadkins, contemporaries included Ben Crenshaw and those following – Jerry Pate, Bill Rogers, Jay Haas, Curtis Strange and Craig Stadler. And after a US Army Tour in Vietnam, a young Larry Nelson was learning golf courtesy of Ben Hogan's all-time-best-selling instructional, *The Five Fundamentals of Modern Golf*. Between Stanford and turning pro in 1971, Tom Watson won the Missouri State Championship four times and from '69 to '71 he was the lead player on the Stanford golf team. Watson's prodigious talent and propensity for practice marked him out. The Stanford coach, Charles 'Bud' Finger, fingered Tom for possible greatness in the team's press guide. Large part sincerity, it also sent a message to opponents. 'Tommy has awesome distance off the tee, but is also a sharp iron player, accurate with the wedge and deadly with the putter. He could rise out of the college ranks to become one of the world's great players, just like Arnold Palmer, Jack Nicklaus, etc. … he loves to play the game.' Watson was the hottest thing out of Missouri since Chuck Berry.

Although Watson won only two collegiate events, and was 'only' a second-string All-American, and despite being in the shadow of Kite and Crenshaw, Finger saw Watson's inner steel. Others did, too, and some of his father's friends clubbed together to pay the young Watson's expenses in return for a percentage of winnings. Auspiciously he would get his Tour card at the first time of asking, in 1971, and collect $1,065 (about $6,500 in today's money, or even more today if adjusted for the 'Tiger Woods effect'). A nice, quick haul in his first tourney. But in five other starts he would barely add to this. In '72 he played in 33 events, made 22 cuts with one top ten, collecting $30,413. The near-$74,000 won in 1973, eight top tens and two third places saw the young, now-married Watson gain exemption to all PGA Tour events the following year. For Tom and Seve 1974 would be pivotal. It also set them on course to battle each other, despite the years that separated them, despite the thousands of miles that separated their upbringings, and despite the two very different places in which they were raised and how they fostered two remarkable talents.

1984: La Manga, Costa Blanca

A Death in the Family – The Walker Cup – Jack Nicklaus – An Encounter

COURTESY OF a *Golf Illustrated* diary, 1984 became the only year I attempted to keep something of an ongoing record of my movements. I was no James Boswell or Ronald Reagan and entries were triumphs of brevity: 'French Vocabulary'; 'Played in the medal today. NR. Total rubbish'; 'Bulging eardrum', more suited to the back of an illiterate's fag packet or range of unsellable bumper stickers. My life appeared to be a series of homework exercises, falling off my bike, going to pals' houses, and playing pretty ropey golf, sometimes all on the same day.

The summer of 1984 did not start well. My charismatic, maternal grandfather died. The shock was seismic. He'd been suffering the then-typical vagaries of age but was not expected to go to the big golf course in the sky. I had spent a lot of my childhood with him, listened to what he said, laughed at his jokes and anecdotes. He was a successful bookmaker and cut a dash. Not the bookie beloved of American gangster films – trilbies, nice duds, cars, prohibition and submachine guns – although he had the threads. And the hat. And some of the cars. I recall one day not fully understanding why we were in a dusty office in Glasgow, grandpa draped in cloth as a man circled him, taking measurements and chalking up the material. He enjoyed the finer things and sought to educate me in some of them. Our relationship was a function of the time. Each Saturday my dad's routine was to head to golf, play mid-morning and then spend the afternoon in the club bar chatting and sharing jokes and stories. The great dividend was Mum, me and, eventually, brother Alan would often drive the 40 miles to my grandparents to spend the day. Their place was old and solid and mature apple trees grew in the back garden. The upstairs had been converted into a double bedroom with canted ceilings and this room held the 'Treasure Trove', my grandpa's name for the long attic that housed all kinds of esoterica and bookmaking paraphernalia. By the main door hung a large print of *The Dance Class*, in which a group of young ballerinas are instructed by an older gent. My grandpa came to Degas through the artist's renderings of horses and jockeys. Graham Emmerson loved racehorses, wanted to be a jockey, but literally outgrew that dream and instead made his living amongst those things he loved. This also meant he did not have to make a living, like millions, in factories, pits, fields, or the heavy industries fired by the pits' coal.

His other love was golf. Eventually weekend adventures would take us to his club. Ralston had white sandy bunkers and many holes played up, down or across hills. I found this challenging, and the rolling ball I was used to on the flatter, firmer Ayrshire courses was not forthcoming. One day Grandpa told me he'd been given a putter by Jimmy Walker, I now presume to settle a bet, a club that Jack Nicklaus had given him during the 1961 Walker Cup at Seattle Golf Club. Jimmy and his partner, Brian Chapman, had been trounced by Nicklaus and the deadly accurate Deane Beman. Travelling from Scotland to Seattle today is a trek. Back then, to lose heavily, it must've felt like an odyssey. To make the team, Walker had won the Scottish Amateur at Western Gailes. The next year would be a milestone on the Scottish amateur scene. Ronnie Shade lost in the final at the Muirfield, then he reeled off five championships in a row, dominating at Troon, Nairn, the Old Course, Western Gailes and Carnoustie. Like a Faustian quintilateral, his worst margin in the final was 4 and 2. Then, in 1968, he won at Prestwick, the second playing of the Scottish Men's Open Amateur Stroke Play. The wins and venues lend colour to Shade's nickname, 'Right Down the Bloody Middle'. RDBM Shade also played in Seattle, but even he went home empty-handed as the US prevailed 11-1.

Sports Illustrated magazine might only have been six years old but Alfred Wright's article, 'A Talent for Adversity', suggested the GB&I team seemed to thrive on losing, the long trip from British and Irish shores a penance for acceptance of US dominance. This was brought into relief by the GB&I captain, Charles Lawrie: 'Your chaps just strike the ball better. It's that simple. You hit the ball with more authority.' The inferiority was as physically hardwired as it was mental, as Wright outlined the US's pivot swing technique. Aside from Michael Bonallack and Martin Christmas, GB&I's more traditional swings depended on timing and co-ordination, qualities that had to be underpinned by confidence, concentration and a desire to perform. Combined with pressure, wiry rough, different playing conditions, travel weariness and the US opposition, losing makes sense, but the mentality suggests they'd lost before weighing anchor. I am sure each player did not feel this, but the strategic mindset was defeatist. For years, other great British players, pro and amateur, lost all sense of perspective at the faintest whiff of apple pie, two bars of the 'Star-Spangled Banner' and the arresting taste of a gherkin. The USA could churn out quality golfers like McDonald's pumped out Big Macs. Emphasising this, the week after the Walker Cup Deane Beman was on the cover of *Sports Illustrated*, not Nicklaus, even though the Germanic Ohioan had already notched a second and a fourth in the national open and was just nine months shy of winning at Oakmont. In beating Palmer by three in an 18-hole play-off for the 1962 US Open, Jack won his first major. A generation later, a young Spaniard called into question notions of global golfing dominance.

Beyond the USA and around a handful of players – Player, Bob Charles, Jacklin, to name some of the few – golf in the 1960s and 1970s was defined by an inferiority complex founded on outdated outlook, outdated technique and an ongoing mental capitulation to anyone playing under Old Glory. Beside Uncle Ramon warning America was a difficult place to win, Seve knew nothing of this complex. He was programming himself for greater things, knocking down targets like the shibboleths which distorted the thinking of many players from outside the States. For those who saw the great US players it was clear, then, they did play the game differently, hit that ball more majestically. Nowadays, with modern swings and clubs, many can hit the ball far and high although, *still*, the greats seem to hit it yet further, higher. When Seve, Faldo, Langer, Lyle and Greg Norman were learning, the USA were Goliath. I sensed this even in 1987, 26 years after captain Lawrie's comments, when the US Walker Cup team arrived for the Amateur Championship at Prestwick. It was mesmeric. Drives inspired by NASA, their iron play seemed like the work of General Dynamics, a brand of golf that seemed futuristic. I watched a US player hit his tee shot at Prestwick's 14th. In my mind it was Billy Andrade, but it may have been Bill Loeffler or Len Mattiace. The drive soared into the piercing blue sky well above the level of the clubhouse and it seemed to be up there *for ever.* For a few seconds you could imagine it soaring over the entire town. Intoxicating. The wide stance and the big takeaway creating plenty of room generated shots unlike our native game, where swings could be inhibited (or wrecked!) with the cold and the wind. I caddied in that Amateur, in a group featuring a GB&I Walker Cupper. His game was beyond steady and it was great to spend three hours watching him, but you wouldn't have paid for it. Simply, it was a pleasing, highly efficient version of the UK game. The USA team in 1987 gave me a glimpse of Seattle. The Americans were assured, exquisitely turned out, professional and focused. Business-like. These were amateurs, mainly students, who didn't yet play for money, but already the game of golf was not a game, it was a job, and one they did very well.

The young Seve saw another way. Constant attack married with the ability to overpower trouble or craft astounding recoveries. Greg Norman was similar, his great strength – literally – being his long, straight tee shots, going at them full tilt. Here lies a paradox. Seve's early game was wholly dependent on feel, timing, spirit and *duende*, not the structured swings of his US foes. These qualities were inherent in his double helix via the maternal bloodline to golf, the paternal one to rowing. These genetic attributes were enhanced on the sands of Cantabria. The US game was focused on one milieu, the conveyor belt of college golf. Coaches at Wake Forest, Houston, Texas and Arizona did not construct a template to win the Open, or to hit raking draws and devilish slices, they had built games to win NCAA tournaments, translating nicely to the PGA Tour. The very things – power, quality of ball strike, holing untold putts in a row from four feet and in – that became the strength of the depth of the US game, ripped out its heart. The robotic skills of the PGA Tour, as mightily impressive as they were, and the money offered, paved the way for Greg Norman and Severiano Ballesteros. They liked the money, too, but they prized the win, especially on US soil.

* * *

Grandpa's sudden death drew us all closer, and it became an opportunity for me – after a first holiday in Spain – to visit

St Andrews for the Open. It was coincidence, given Seve's sponsorship connection, that we were going to an apartment in La Manga. One customer of my dad's was a potato merchant in Glasgow who, seeing Bob was a decent sort with a young family, offered him the use of the family holiday home. We were invited to meet Mr and Mrs Mathie at their house to learn about that part of Spain. Mr Mathie told us how he sometimes didn't fly to Alicante but instead drove down in his Porsche 928. I had noted it as we arrived, the colour of rich cocoa: nice way to travel. He told a story of how he and his wife had, during a recent trip, been buying gifts. As he paid with his gold American Express – then an exotic charge card reserved for the well-heeled – another customer also settled with Amex. This gave them an unwritten bond and they shared a few pleasantries, exchanged business cards. Back in the La Manga apartment, Mr Mathie was caught by a niggling feeling that he somehow knew the other customer. Unable to shake it off he went to his wallet and dug out the card. Severiano Ballesteros.

1974: The US Open, Winged Foot

Watson and Ballesteros Start to Converge – Early Struggles, Early Hopes

CASTING OFF on that ceaseless stream, flowing into others that might be in spate, slow to a trickle or intermingle in the waters of memory, sometimes there is a lack of clarity, detail becomes blurry. Take Ballesteros's most famous shot in a Ryder Cup, his gravity-defying 3-wood from the fairway bunker on his final hole at PGA National in 1983. Legend would suggest all was going swimmingly, but Seve was in that bunker in two. He'd hacked out of the rough a 4-iron after a tee shot hooked, to quote caddy Nick DePaul, into 'the left trash'. Having been four up after 11 holes, Seve had been pegged back by Fuzzy Zoeller and was now looking like losing. The American saw what Ballesteros had done with his first two shots, and laid up on the long par five, deciding against going for the green. The smart play against 99.99 per cent of players. Then the Spaniard dug so deep to hit one of the game's greatest shots, because to have led his team out in the singles there was no way he could give up a point to the USA. It was all or nothing; nothing was staring Seve in the face.

Similarly, the precise timing of Ballesteros's turning pro is unclear, but come the start of the 1974 European season he'd signed a few forms and passed an exam or two, that was all it took. He was primed to expose himself to more courses, players, and the pressures that come with playing for money. But as well as a lack of true tournament scar tissue, his continued living in the familial home meant every penny was not yet a prisoner. On his first trip out of Spain he shot 89 in the Portuguese Open at Estoril on his 17th birthday. Hard to imagine a worse present, a grinding shock of some magnitude, but easy to imagine, golf-wise. A shot leaked here and there, an unfamiliar course, new people, new surroundings, a different language. Add the difficulties of focusing in the face of great expectations, and 89 starts to feel completely right for a player emerging from a golfing chrysalis into the harsh light of the competitive day. But that light was refracted somewhat by the assistance and encouragement of others. There was also a bit of luck. Estoril was the start of a series in Iberia, plus the French Open, and Seve and brother Manuel bumped into radiologist Dr Cesar Campuzano, a man already known to the older golfer. When they saw him again at the Madrid Open, and after Manuel explained enthusiastically how good he expected Seve to become, the good doctor promised 500,000 pesetas and more encouragement over the coming years. Now Severiano Ballesteros was a golfer to trade with some backing. What he'd hoped for as a boy, now looked a possibility.

When he first appeared in a pukka European Tour draw, the Spanish Open at La Manga, it was a mere four years since he'd still been using the beach for practice, latterly for chipping and putting, the fast-running compact sand the ideal test for the slick, pure greens that awaited some of his future. Dripping with untrammelled belief and the determination of someone who hadn't competed in many formal events away from home, Seve's golfing education – an imaginative free-for-all – was initially his greatest hindrance. His play was not benchmarked against any course, player or tournament of note. Leaving Cantabria to compete meant Seve was a literal innocent abroad. Because of his lack of scarring, he could not be sure quite what he would find and how he would cope, although his 15th club, unstinting self-belief, would be a lynchpin. Unsurprisingly, he was incandescent with disbelief after an opening 83 at La Manga. Fifth from last. Followed by a 76, the new pro had a one-way Portillo bus ticket back to Pedreña. In hazy symmetry with Tom Watson's early career struggles, one of the $100,000-a-year men on the PGA Tour, Jerry Heard, would win the event in Spain.

Seve's next outing, the French Open, saw the bad taste softened with a hint of onion and garlic. He made the 36-hole mark but succumbed to a 54-hole cut. His play was steadier (76, 75, 74) but his three-round tally was the same as his two in Spain, 15 over par, although his scoring progression was promising (and on the European Tour then, a 75 was not disastrous). Nowadays it's almost certainly pay-cheque limiting. Vicente Fernández would finish third in France after closing 74, 75. And in Spain Peter Townsend had matched those scores in two of his rounds and finished third. Seve had much work to do, but he didn't quite have a mountain to climb. After picking up golf aged seven with an ersatz club and a bag full of desire, he was now plying his trade.

In the latter part of 1974, having been perhaps the greenest pro ever to step on a tee, after no success and missed cuts in his only two events of the year, Ballesteros picked up his first cheque, in Italy's national open. He finished five shots behind winner Peter Oosterhuis, three behind second, featuring Dale Hayes and Johnny Miller. Fourth was Simon Owen, who'd nearly win the 1978 Open. The young Spaniard was in, for the European Tour, exalted company, and he finished ahead of luminaries like Jacklin and Brian Barnes. He beat Manuel by six. Could another changing of the guard in the Ballesteros household be a harbinger? He also made a small cheque in his fourth and final event of the year, the El Paraiso Open in Malaga. Oosterhuis won again and Manuel was runner-up. The season was not the conquering campaign the young man envisioned, but Seve was still only 17. It seemed a solid start for one so untested.

* * *

Six weeks after Seve played in his second Euro event, Watson found himself leading the US Open at Winged Foot. The course in Mamaroneck, north of Manhattan, was the toughest test since Olympic Club in 1955, when Jack Fleck stunned Hogan in a play-off. Of the 1974 edition, Dick Schaap wrote *The Massacre at Winged Foot*, and the events of the golfing bloodbath speak for themselves. Jack Nicklaus set the scene, hitting the 1st green in regulation, then putting off it. Greens were compared to like being on the hood of a VW Beetle. In the first four holes the Golden Bear took 11 putts. He shot 75. Johnny Miller had 76, and Lee Trevino would shoot a pair of 78s to comfortably miss the cut. Apart from the severity of the examination, in the guts of the Associated Press's (AP) reportage was the mention of 'a pair of youngsters' seeking a maiden win, the Toms Kite and Watson, and the latter was in the lead after three rounds.

Watson already had tried to close out two wins but instead garnered a reputation as a choker, strangling his own chances with some shaky play or poor decisions. An AP syndicated article in the US Sunday papers highlighted the mental challenge. Watson talked of 'hanging on'. When Watson reputedly asked Sandy Tatum of the USGA if he thought he could do it, Tatum posed, 'Do *you* think you can do it?' The AP wrote of the World Open at Pinehurst, and failure in Hawaii. Watson mentioned recent near-successes at Riviera, and at the Danny Thomas Memphis Classic. He had made great progress in his short career. The European Tour players of the early and mid-to-late

1970s couldn't hold a 5-iron to their American counterparts. Tom Watson was in the most intense golfing environment and it seemed his own mention of two recent losses signalled doubt married with intense desire. As a psychology major, Watson understood getting over the line was a journey, and he would be forgiven for not being the first person schooled in a discipline who struggled to integrate it into his own routine. The young Ballesteros expected to win straight out the traps. Tom would know he couldn't expect to when first presented with the opportunity. But that doesn't make for good copy. And for many sporting greats, it was failure that ultimately made them.

In February 1973, Watson had surged to a 54-hole four-shot lead in the Hawaiian Open, holing putts of 20, 25 and 30 feet in the last four holes. In reports after the final round Watson was only mentioned for his 75 and seven at one hole. John Schlee was the winner, a renegade with a heart of gold who followed astrology and was reputed to have slept sometimes with his hands taped together to form the perfect grip. Towards the end of that season, Watson would command in spectacular fashion. The World Open at Pinehurst was the game's most lucrative event, but it could've been sponsored by the Marquis de Sade, a 144-hole hellacious golfing equivalent of water torture. Played over 72 holes one week, then same again the next, only the top 70 players progressed.

In the fifth round Watson whipped round Pinehurst No.2 in 62. Fourth-round leader Gibby Gilbert saw a five-shot lead change to a six-shot disadvantage. Watson was rampant. The next day Tom slipped to a 76, but still led by six. It had been a windy day and remarkably Gilbert, who'd opened with a 62 the previous week, slumped to an 82, surely a record reversal. Watson would follow with another 76 – including a ball out of bounds; shades of his college-golf wildness – and despite telling the press he was focused on winning the $100,000 first prize, he slipped to a 77 in round eight. Was this choking or, after a 62, had Watson lost some of his game while fatigue set in?

A year on from Hawaii, Lee Trevino drove into Inverrary Country Club for a pro-am. He saw in a practice bunker Watson, a player he deemed too wild to last, a notion supported by balls out of bounds and too many double bogeys or worse. When Trevino left, five hours hence, the young Missourian was still in the bunker. Watson was sowing the seeds of something, surely. For all sportsmen, defeat is not the thing. How the player reacts is the touchstone. Come the US Open at Winged Foot few were looking to Tom Watson as victor. *Massacre at Winged Foot* outlined in fine and sometimes amusing detail events of that week. Tatum was asked if the USGA was trying to embarrass the best players, and Schaap recounted the response, 'We have certain feelings about what a champion should be required to do. Those feelings begin on the tee. We feel the golfer should be able to drive the ball within an area of forty-five yards wide. If he does not, he should be penalized half a stroke. His next shot should be placed properly on the green.'

Watson assessed himself as impatient but stressed his absolute belief he would prevail. A winless Tom had the chance to take home his prize but Schaap's account of the fourth round was the unfurling of that dream. On the 4th, 460 yards, Watson had a six-foot putt for a two-stroke lead after Hale Irwin had missed from just outside him. He missed. At the next, Watson three-putted, albeit from 60 feet. Both parred seven where Irwin holed a brave six-footer. They bogeyed the 8th to bring the field a bit closer, and then Irwin made a break. He holed a twisting 35-foot putt over a ridge at the 9th for that hole's second birdie of the day. The usually stoic Hale did a little kooky dance, showing his delight and a change in the air. Both players bogeyed the 10th, Watson's with a three-putt. Then Hale rolled in a 25-footer at the 11th. It felt like the chess of some struggling grandmasters, not a sport of long balls and deft touches. But like the chequered board, it was a war of mental attrition. A wrong move would bring the endgame into view. When Watson – trying to force something to happen, perhaps; or impatience, again – hooked his drive into the trees at 12 it seemed like old spectres had re-emerged. After bogey, Watson was three behind and, ultimately, the final holes were between Forrest Fezler and Irwin. The other Missourian, Hale Irwin, held on to win by two.

Watson looked like he'd collapsed, his back nine of 41 total anathema. He'd leaked a shot here and there on the world's hardest golf course for that week, and the many weeks before and after. Irwin won the US Open, but Winged Foot won the week. The winning score was an unflattering seven over par, a 72-hole tally usually resulting in a pro having a myocardial event. Watson was badged again as a choker, and after his round admitted to having 'played terribly … I just had no feel for the game today'. Those who knew golf knew this happened sometimes at the worst moments, just when one needs to be up and not feeling flat. Watson set himself very high standards. On reaching peak performance, sometimes all the required psychic energy is used on the journey. In golf, getting into that perfect position of optimal thinking, playing and decision-making, over a single event across a number of days is not a given and usually a player's wins involve some form of toughing it out, playing through those tricky interludes when the usual feel and confidence are not present. It's also why luck is a strange companion, it has to be managed positively, and any negative breaks have to be accepted. For Watson, Winged Foot was not the place to achieve the needed resilience. The following Tuesday, the AP posed, 'Was 1974 Open Game of Chance or Skill?' The reporter likened the championship to the Anzio beach head, or a journey into the heart of darkness. They dubbed the course the Winged Monster. It ate up most of the field before regurgitating them in the locker room. But the monster in Mamaroneck would become a blessing for Tom Watson.

1975: The Open Championship, Carnoustie

Spain Emerging – Ballesteros's Open Beginning – Major Tom

FOR THE peoples of Spain, home and a sense of place underpin existence and community, interleaved with food, play, and the Spanish and regional cultures peppered across the Iberian Peninsula.

While the Basques feel they are the original people with the original language, and while some in Galicia believe in witchcraft, the people of the southern coasts lived a more free and easy existence, a combination of heat, sea and the influences of the Moors. The Cantabrians were different again as the more northern, oceanic climate meant the rhythms and seasons of life differed from the costas Blanca, Brava, del Sol and de Almeria, although foreign tourists did eventually come to the north, discovering arresting coastlines of rugged outcrops, sandy stretches and azure-coloured inlets. The Basques have a rather unfortunate saying when it comes to the beaches of their neighbours along the coast surrounding Santander – *cagar y volver* – the rough translation of which would be perform a bodily function, then return, although it was really just an edgy euphemistic reflection of reality. Basques would visit Cantabrian beaches in the summer, then head homeward after a day of fun. And scatological humour.

Severiano Ballesteros was at home in three places: Pedreña, Augusta National, and on the links courses of Old World golf where greens and fairways were protected by hungry bunkers and ingenious humps and hollows designed by cosmological forces. Seve's love of links wasn't always there and building a game on the beach was never the schooling for a trip to Carnoustie and his first Open Championship, in 1975. The beastly track in Angus, around 30 miles due north from St Andrews, didn't just feel long and demanding, it was long and demanding. It just didn't feel as if you had to hit the ball long and straight, you did have to hit the ball long and straight. Seve had all the length, little of the accuracy. After shooting 79 and 80, he didn't recall his visit with fondness, but he developed an understanding. 'Overcoming the problems links courses posed for me was going to be a real challenge. But I came to realise this style of golf required a player to use his imagination, that it demanded that I create shots, and this fitted well with my style of play.' Carnoustie was also Tom Watson's first Open Championship and he learned a thing or two.

* * *

Cap sheltering his face from the elements, Tom stared down the fairway through the murk, over the Barry Burn to the 18th green for the fifth competitive time, the 90th hole of the 104th Open. Twenty-two years earlier, in 1953, another becapped American had walked these fairways. The Ice Mon, as the locals came to call him, Ben Hogan, that season already had a green jacket to keep pressed and a US Open trophy to polish when he made his only Open start. Ben added to his legend, taming Carnoustie with 73, 71, 70, 68, and the fanciful among us would like to imagine he could've continued lowering his scores over at least another couple of rounds, even though it had been just over four years since almost losing his life in the most severe of car wrecks. His return to golf was as much a miracle as his survival. Tom Watson had a sense of history, as well as the opportunity to engrave his name on the Claret Jug alongside Hogan and Jones, Nicklaus and Palmer, Taylor, Braid and Harry Vardon.

The day before, after consecutive bogeys by both Australia's Jack Newton and South Africa's Bobby Cole, Tom had the chance of his young lifetime, a shot at tying the 72-hole total. In contrast to playing partner Johnny Miller, who'd knocked his tee shot into the right-hand fairway trap then tried to blast an over-ambitious 6-iron on to the green, leaving it in the sand, the young golfer appeared a model of calm. Watson had been hard on himself after Winged Foot the previous year, but it had been a new beginning. Two weeks later he was up to his usual tricks. After 36 holes at the Western Open, the oldest event on the formal tours outside the Open and the US Open, he was in contention then struggled to a nasty 75, including two balls in the water and an eight at Butler National's 14th. Facing the final circuit, he trailed then-reigning Open Champion Tom Weiskopf by a comprehensive six shots. Then a headline Watson felt was inevitable. *The New York Times* reported, 'Watson Rallies to Take Western Golf for His First Pro Victory', alongside a photo of the player with a trophy the size of a satellite. Tom beamed at the manifestation of his hard work, greeting the silverware like a much-awaited friend. Watson would go from being a non-winning, relative newcomer to dominant force. In May 1975 he picked up the Byron Nelson Classic at Preston Trail Golf Club, before his move into overdrive. He'd win five of the first nine Open Championships in which he competed, staring down and defeating all in his way.

Carnoustie, demanding supreme patience and supreme accuracy, did not seem to fit Tom's purview, but 71, 67 and 69 saw him placed fourth and in the final lap of regulation play, in a stiff wind, he grinded, finding himself one shot behind. He clocked a beautiful drive at Home, the 448-yard final hole, and as he stared down that arrow-straight test he appeared to have about a 7-iron left. With that simple, swift action he knocked it 18 feet shy and slightly right of the cup, and when he rolled the putt in, shortly after Miller had missed a chip to tie the lead, Tom's right hand punched the air and he beamed with delight. Only a rare birdie from the final pair could change things. Jack Newton could win, and Bobby Cole could tie, although, through a mixture of bad decisions and ropey play fostered by the Scotch broth of pressure and expectation, both had bogeyed 15, 16 and 17. In near symmetry with Watson, Newton stuck a 9-iron approach into just over 20 feet but on the same line, and Cole knocked it into the same distance as Tom, closer to pin high. Watson's putt had been a solid, confidence-laden slot directly into the hole. Newton's putt was weak and, in the circumstances, woeful; and Cole's was always left. Watson finished with real intent, while others had left their nerves strewn across the Angus fairways. Where many failed, Watson had outscored most players in the top ten. He had a chance to win on the highest stage.

The play-off between the Australian and the man from middle America was taut, marred by occasional, nasty Scottish summer weather. In an important few minutes Jack Newton pitched in for a surprise birdie at the long 14th to get ahead, only for Tom to pitch in for eagle and take back the lead. Such events today would engender a form of mayhem and supporter madness, but on the dreich links the reaction was more subdued. It was remarkable stuff but the more solid moments were the difference, and in contrast to 9-irons being hit in to the 72nd hole, the Sunday play-off's final exam was a drive and a long iron. Newton was up first, finding the bunker, short left of the green. As part of the template that would become familiar – anchored on the fairway, over the ball with his solid stance and straight back – Tom Watson had a 2-iron in hand. The crowd could hear the solid smack, the ball on the middle of the clubhead for as long as possible before exploding through the air with a hint of fade, dependably on to the green, resting 30 feet away. Watson of the solid putting was on display and he almost holed to win outright. Minutes later Newton missed his par putt and Tom joined Tommy Armour, Henry Cotton, Ben Hogan and Gary Player as winners of the jug on one of the hardest courses the game could offer. From the fairways of Kansas City, he'd elevated his play to become Champion Golfer of the Year.

1976: The Open Championship, Royal Birkdale

The Kid from Spain – Johnny v Seve – Short Game Gusto

THE YOUNG man looked up at Johnny Miller with a simple, knowing smile. He seemed to enjoy the shot as much as everyone else. Spectators applauded and greeted the audacity with stentorian approval. And despite the very British tone, one outlier shouted, 'Yes!' as the ball was halfway through its journey, as if he knew what the final result might, in years to come, mean. A chip-and-run from baked, wispy rough with a 9-iron covered 30 bumpy, dry, slightly uphill yards, rolled between two bunkers and came to rest four feet from the hole. It was a shot of daring. It was the shot of a thousand shots hit on a distant beach. In that moment it was perfect.

Hours earlier, things had been different. Seve Ballesteros, playing in his second Open, and having made his first cut, allowed the world to contemplate the unimagined. He was in the final group, with the 1973 US Open champion, Johnny Miller. Seve played for fun, he told us, enjoyed every shot. The British golfing public enjoyed them, too. This was the drab 1970s, when brown was the new black and when Britain enjoyed its most equitable decade. It seemed equally bleak for most. The country was on a precipice, and a pall of financial uncertainty hung across the isles. But here was a Spanish antidote to the lingering sense of the daily grind and political turmoil. The youngest Ballesteros had emerged from the British heatwave of 1976 to stamp a mark on the oldest major. With uncomplicated Western-style gunslinging simplicity Raymond Floyd had dubbed Seve 'The Kid from Spain'. The Kid played a game all golfers could relate to, they had played some of those shots in their youth. Or wished they had. Wished they could. For legions of juniors, Ballesteros's attributes of strength, deftness and adventure were to be aspired to, a golfing matrix no one had ever considered.

This is what would catch the attention of my cousin in 1978. Sometimes being a hardcore fan of a sportsman, sportswoman or a team was about secrets: the sauce, secret talent or secret mindset that allowed some to step from the everyday into the realm of the fantastic. What spiced up their play, injected their talent with a greatness that seemed beyond all of us? Could we, upon finding the secrets, ascend to such giddy heights? Our heroes were our fantasies. 'A slashing player with a glorious, uninhibited swing, a talent for playing spectacular recoveries that his inevitably wayward driving makes necessary, and a wonderfully smooth putting stroke. He … wastes no time even in moments of crisis,' wrote Mark McCormack in *The World of Professional Golf* looking back at 1976.

That glorious summer heralded the arrival of a unique talent. Ballesteros led the championship from the off, jointly on 69 after round one, then over the field by two after adding 69 and 73. Slashing and thrashing, powering and ripping, chipping, pitching and putting his way into the hearts of British golfers and minds of world-class players who knew a thing when they saw it. It was fitting in the final round he would go head-to-head with a similar player. Except Johnny Miller had already won the US Open in 1973, dismantling a soggy Oakmont course in 63 blows. He'd flirted with the Open and the Masters by way of three second places, including the Troon Open of 1973, as well as Carnoustie. John Miller felt he'd paid his dues and the links was ready for his brand of attacking golf. Like Seve, the 29-year-old Californian assaulted the ball with malice, clearing his left side like it was an extreme inconvenience. For three years his iron play had been, simply, stellar. 'I had a stretch there for a few years where I played some golf that bordered on the Twilight Zone … I can remember that I was literally getting upset that I had to putt,' Miller told *Golf Magazine* in 1982. He did not mess about. He and Seve had played together in the third round, and by his own admission the American had let the younger man's scrambling and imaginative saves get inside his head.

Ballesteros's style would be his undoing, what brought him to attention became the downfall. He lost the lead at the 6th as Miller notched up a four at that most exacting of holes, and by the 11th a triple-bogey seven saw the young Spaniard skewered by the horns of his own play. It's no coincidence that perhaps the most famous picture of Seve at this Open, atop a hillock, flanked by spectators, swiping an iron towards his target, had come earlier that day, during another altercation with the rough, at the 8th.

As the prospect of victory dissolved, Ballesteros would emerge from the gloom as the two players went on a scoring spree. Miller recorded a two at the 12th. Seve birdied the par-five 13th after a lovely 20-yard chip stiff. He'd shake the hands of Miller, congratulating him on an eagle, as the American chipped in on a different angle. Handshakes were returned at the next as Seve made birdie to claw back his second consecutive shot. One player relaxed and fell into a winner's rhythm, and the other rediscovered his purpose as the burden of expectation drifted away on the gentle summer breeze. Ballesteros was a couple of shots adrift of Floyd and Nicklaus, who were two holes ahead and soon entering the stretch of the 17th and 18th, back-to-back par fives. Miller ran away with it, finishing birdie, eagle, par, par, par, birdie, birdie. But Seve matched that tally: birdie, birdie, par, par, par saw him arrive at the 17th only two shots behind third, and three behind Nicklaus. Ballesteros was scrambling – normal service had been resumed – for pars, and Spanish *gusto* lit up the 17th with a long drive and a crisp iron into 25 feet. When he holed for eagle, Miller and Ballesteros once again shook hands. The 1973 US Open champion tip-toed around the rim of the Claret Jug as Seve climbed back to the realms of respectability and beyond. The Californian, now virtually on parade, with some words of Spanish encouraged his young playing partner as Seve sought to ascend the leaderboard one last time, something to reward three days of dazzling play and excitement yet for the taking. After a drive and a somewhat mediocre iron – perhaps a reaction to being long the night before – there was that chip at the 18th, 30 yards of bouncing, trundling immortality and a place in the golfing imagination of fans everywhere. Sometimes second place is a winner.

In *Sports Illustrated*, Dan Jenkins, the golf scribe who hid much of his wisdom behind a veil of lacerating humour, wrote, 'The world may not hear more from Severiano Ballesteros, he of the strong left grip, the wristy swing, the whiplash of a full swing and the nose for always finding the golf ball in the bushes.' For once, Jenkins was wrong. He was right to focus on the swing and the flaws, but he couldn't quite see the incandescent desire. Despite the boyish good looks and clear joy, the undercurrents of Seve's hours and hours on the beach and on Real Golf de Pedreña – and in battles with his brothers and other caddies – ran deep and elemental. Understanding what Ballesteros brought to Birkdale that week, Mark McCormack hinted at the future. 'One of these days some young British golfer will take a lesson from Ballesteros, who showed that youth is no impediment to success if you can keep your head and your heart in good condition as well as your swing and your putting stroke. He also showed that golf is not necessarily a game of torment and misery but has something, too, of gaiety and gallantry if you elect to play that way.'

Of all the fires ignited on the Birkdale links that week after a roasting start to summer, there was a sense that perhaps Seve had lit the touchpaper of future dramas, possible triumphs. McCormack chose his words well, as Ballesteros was gallant in both courage and respect. He'd unlocked his potential. In the following weeks he finished third, and in the Dutch Open he shrugged off a second-round 73 and won by eight. Seve had climbed on to the *meseta* of European golf.

* * *

Like a powerful drive that bounds down the fairway and finds just the right line and series of hops to retain momentum for as long as possible, that chip on the Lancashire coast catapulted the young Spaniard towards his greatest aspirations, competing against the best on the best courses in the greatest events. For the player this would seem logical, natural. His progression would be a series of psychic shocks for many others. Aged 13 he was still practising on the beach. Aged 17 he was on the European Tour. Two and a half years later he was centre stage. It seems uncanny and natural all at the same time. Perhaps he'd visualised, on that boyhood beach with fast-running sand, something like his ball slipping between two bunkers, running up to the pin. His timing was perfect to connect with a British public lurching forward in post-imperial, early post-industrial and financial doldrums. That timing was also perfect for global golf. As the mantle of contemporary greatness was just about to pass from Nicklaus to Watson, this young European appeared. Two hundred years after American Independence, US domination of the fairways was about to be threatened. Seve would see this as an unalienable right. He also tapped into something more than the British zeitgeist of moribundity, doom and gloom. Illuminating the sport, the Spaniard channelled a fundamental human need: play. The need for play, the freedom to play and, what those ultimately lead to, organised competition and the personal satisfaction and validation of victory. Seve Ballesteros gave us, his fans and the millions watching through distant TV screens, play by proxy.

In obvious ways, Severiano Ballesteros's continued popularity seems to do with more than absence and loss, more than nostalgia. Handsome, dashing, daring, iconoclastic yet embedded firmly in the European professional golfing tradition, what made Seve truly enduring? I had been conjuring with this idea for years, then, during the pandemic lockdown, I read a book about driving – cars not tee shots – and it hit home, part of that sinuous, fluid timeline of luck and chance, recognising Ballesteros had changed the domestic golfing landscape in a particular way. Having come so close at Birkdale, and having been so likeable and open, he already felt like a hero of our own making. Why? How?

After attending two practice days at the 2010 PGA Championship, then on my way back from Mt Rushmore and the Devil's Tower I pulled off Interstate 90 – a modest turnpike stretching from Boston to Seattle – into Murdo, South Dakota, the town named for Murdo McKenzie, a native of Tain, Scotland, born in 1850. Four years after Murdo crossed the Atlantic to join the Prairie Land and Cattle Company in Colorado, Old Tom Morris was laying out the golf course in his hometown. I checked into a motel and settled down to watch the final afternoon of the PGA and Martin Kaymer win his first major. After crossing US time zones one way then almost doubling back, the next day I rose early and drove 500 miles. Heading west, the Mississippi had taken my breath away, its scale staggering to someone from a small country on a small island. In Britain our big river is the Thames, a streak of muddy waste in comparison to the legendary artery that cuts through America from Lake Itasca in northern Minnesota to the Gulf of Mexico over 2,000 miles south. After a day at the wheel, I stopped in La Crosse, Wisconsin. On an unwinding early evening stroll I encountered Pearl Street Books, a gem, with thoughtfully curated selections catching my eye. I went for Matthew B. Crawford's *Shop Class As Soulcraft*, a lyrical, personal and occasionally intense treatise on the deep, simple rewards of working with your hands. Surely it was the kind of philosophy Seve Ballesteros would understand? And as the Spaniard might appreciate the joy of a forged wedge's design and shape, I handled Crawford's book, admiring its US design cues, and the touch of its matt cover. Quoting philosopher Alexandre Kojeve, *Soulcraft* outlines, 'The man who works recognises his own product in the World that has actually been transformed by his work: he recognises himself in it, he sees in it his own human reality, in it he discovers and reveals to others the objective reality of his humanity.'

Seve's product (golf) recognised his own meaning, while providing the same to his fans and admirers. Surely, there was something transcendent here. Eleven years later I was reading Crawford's third book, *Why We Drive*. An entire decade after a 2,000-mile drive brought me to page 15: 'To dare, to take risks, to bear uncertainty, to endure tension – these are the essence of the play spirit.' Surely this was the source of Ballesteros's attraction, somewhere in the damp, lush mountains and hilly pastures of Cantabria. Like storytelling, like appending meaning to our own existences and death, human beings have an inherent need for play, or as the author of the above quote, Johan Huizinga, put it, the *play spirit.* Seve tapped right into this.

I'd been given the *Drive* book as a birthday gift, and my late July reading came directly after the virtual Open that the R&A had put in place of the cancelled 2020 event. Seve placed third, behind Jack Nicklaus and Tiger Woods. A few months prior, the Twittersphere voted 1984 as the Official Open Film they most wanted to see. From the outset of Seve's fame, via the 1976 battles with Miller and tying with Nicklaus at Birkdale, he shone a beaming light on links golf, his game seemingly totally free, embodying a primal sense of the desire to play, and in turn he created stories with tension, drama, no clear ending. Part of Seve's art was imperfection; winning gets boring. Perfection is aspirational but truly unattainable, nature tends towards entropy. When Ballesteros came along, he represented a kind of impossibility, the flawed nature of sport executed in some kind of perfect way. That is to say, not perfect. His golf seemed unencumbered by detail, the detail of how to get round the course conventionally, and the notion that one had to be on the fairways and on the greens in regulation to score well. Seve Ballesteros represented golf laced with uncertainty, tension and drama. For me, Tiger Woods was the total opposite. Of course, there were the amazing dramatic shots and amazing recoveries, but they appeared part of the perfection Woods sought when playing. Seve was a perfectionist in his own flawed way – we are all flawed – but *playing* came first. Arnold Palmer was the same. He had to play in his own game. As did Greg Norman. So did Jack and Tiger, but their playing was very structured and calculated. It was all great golf, but it was the uncertainty of others that created Nicklaus's and Woods's greatest tensions. Wanting to understand more on our primal need for play led me to Huizinga's book *Homo Ludens* (1938). It seemed to explain a lot about modern politics, sport and the formation of clubs, those being logical progressions to organised play, where like minds get together and bring structure to what they are playing. Another part of this evolution is rules, regulations and conventions. Golf had been doing this since some guys got together at Leith Links in Edinburgh and came up with the first codification in 1744, 240 years before Seve was trying to win the Open at St Andrews. Seve and the play spirit – and almost every other sporting hero – gave us something to hope for, something to emulate. And through emulation we make a connection to those we seek to mimic or match.

Play is at the heart of the competitive instinct. For Homo sapiens it's not competition that drives play, it's the other way around. Ballesteros had the play instinct in spades, the spades worth of sand he trampled over and played on for years. Every single shot from the fast-running putt to the smashed drive was steeped in Seve's desire to play the game. When entering the public consciousness in 1976, he was a young man playing golf. He appeared multitalented yet struggled to control his instincts. He was everyman elevated to the elite, undermined by the same impulses and desires weekend golfers struggled to manage and contain. He was the golfer we all wanted to be. His game seemed less cynical, and the young Seve Ballesteros had taught himself that if he just played, having spent years decoding the mysteries of club to ball, he expected to win.

1977: The Open Championship, Turnberry

Spanish Ascendence – Ballesteros Goes Mainstream – Watson v Nicklaus

DESPITE HIS arrival and subsequent Euro-tear, Seve didn't feature prominently in the Open for a couple of years. In January 1977, he started national service in the Spanish air force and, although he would be released early, just before the German Open in August – golf in the Spanish military being as useful as flower arranging in ISIS – it didn't stop him winning the French Open in May, and the Uniroyal International Championship in a June play-off with Nick Faldo. Birkdale hadn't just ignited Seve's career, it lit a fire under the entre Spanish golfing scene. Before Ballesteros's second victory in 1977, other Spanish winners that year were Manuel Ramos, Antonio Garrido, Ángel Gallardo and Manuel Piñero. By the end of the season three of the four would be in the continent's top ten, joined by Francisco Abreu from Tenerife. Seve would be the fifth Spaniard, sitting atop the Order of Merit.

Another Spanish star, Salvador Balbuena, had won the Portuguese Open a few months before Seve arrived at Birkdale, and in November of 1976 he picked up a win in Morocco, defeating Curtis Strange by three shots. Tragically Balbuena would die suddenly, while preparing for the French Open in 1979.

Seve was news beyond golf. The chip-and-run at Birkdale had won him a place in the British golfing heart, a small pot bunker of love on our favourite hole, and he appeared on the front of a British institution, the *Radio Times*, the BBC rag outlining the television and radio schedules. It was the media aggregator of the day and circulation was near four million, 14 per cent of the population. His cover appearance was every bit as remarkable as his 1977 *Golf Digest* one in the USA. The *Radio Times*' lead story was territory reserved for the British entertainment staples of gloomily realistic kitchen-sink dramas or comedians whose material lay somewhere between the music hall and a 21st-century public order offence. Iberian sportsmen were not its typical preserve. In the magazine, journalist Bryon Rogers provided insight into a modern phenomenon, driven by a love of golf, covering Seve's early life and golf on the beaches and the course at Real Golf de Pedreña. Looking towards Turnberry's inaugural Open, Dudley Doust penned 'This year's homegrown hopes', tagged on at the end of the main article. It read like a pile-up – at a demolition derby, Brian Barnes, Peter Oosterhuis, Neil Coles and a fading Tony Jacklin – of the UK's hopes for a winner. Doust did target Nick Faldo, in his first full year as a pro – as a wild card – but had listed Eamonn Darcy as a possible winner.

Although Darcy had won the Greater Manchester Open a few weeks prior, it was the stretch of a dysfunctional shaman to suggest the Irishman could win the Open at Turnberry. These were great players, of course, but Seve was already box office, while the vast majority of UK sticks were usherettes at his matinee, and they were all the short film to the US players' main feature. As sidebars in the TV listings, Coles and Barnes appeared, but the main spiel on the programmes for the Open seemed to capture the flavour of the moment as well as the golfing future:

> The testing 'Ailsa' course at Turnberry Hotel on the Ayrshire coast is a new venue for this, the most historic of golf championships.
>
> With winds blowing off the sea, this course demands strength and accuracy. JACK NICKLAUS, therefore, although not having won the championship since 1970, must remain the man to beat. JOHNNY MILLER, last year's winner, does not seem to have found his form this year but the Spanish challenge, headed up by last year's joint runner-up SEVERIANO BALLESTEROS seems to be well in form.
>
> A host of young players have successes on the American circuit this year and the one to watch will be the current Masters champion TOM WATSON, who won the Open 1975.

The 1977 Open was scheduled to be an all-American show. Watson and Nicklaus took *that* to new heights, but the *Radio Times* introduced a young Spaniard to the mainstream UK public, and put him on the front page.

The end of the 1977 'Duel in the Sun' at Turnberry is so well documented and famous it seems fatuous to outline it again, but if we could encapsulate all of sport and what it means to those who love it, the final hole and previous 30 minutes of play are, in microcosm, what play and competition at their highest levels mean, where one man and then another transcend the moment. Twice. Having gone toe-to-toe for the final 36, the 18th saw Tom Watson fizz an iron straight down the middle of the fairway, while Big Jack peeled off another sweater and blootered his drive. Down the right, almost into a bush. With all his might he hefts a wedge on to the front of the green, and Tom clips an iron into about a yard. Game over, surely. Nicklaus digs so deep on his 40-foot putt that he holes it, a remarkable turnaround after a drive that seemed to have guaranteed second place. An older pal of mine, then aged 17, recalls leaping from his seat in front of the TV at home, punching the air while shouting, 'Did you see that! Did you see that!?' Upon turning round, he found he was alone. Watson followed his swift routine and stroked in his putt for a second Claret Jug.

The 1984 Open: Driving

Arriving in the Auld Grey Toun – Lord Golf – A Lucky Bounce

I DON'T recall my own journey to St Andrews in 1984 but we were certainly in a car, not Concorde. For golfing mortals, the drive is one of anticipation. The roads wind through rolling livestock and arable farmland of the Kingdom of Fife, the hedgerows and two-lane blacktop interrupted by small towns, villages, a small steading here and there. Bus stops punctuate the route, staging posts for those who travel to work in the Auld Grey Toun at the university, in golf, or another trade or workplace that services the town's two big attractions. The A91 descends into the small village of Guardbridge then climbs up a short, sharp hill before the land flattens, more coastal suddenly, hedges more uniform. Despite making this journey for over 50 years, each time it's the same. As I near the Home of Golf, the warmer the glow of what lies ahead. Dotting left and right, zigzagging, the town appears bit by tantalising bit. Initially it's like a faraway green one may hope to reach, but as the seconds pass, spires begin to loom, harking back to ancient times of a god-fearing folk and the English-speaking world's third-oldest university. A light tingling of anticipatory pleasure develops. As you whip round the series of bends on St Andrews' outskirts the road becomes a sweeping right-to-left curve and the town appears with solid old buildings, clean, winding streets with their relaxed, pleasant feel, people strolling, ambling, almost destination-less along the finely kept avenues of the brightest, most flawless stone in Scotland's golfing crown.

Great weather was set for the week of the 1984 Open and the town was awash with golfing humanity. Outside the ropes some holes looked like a mixture of Times Square and the Shibuya Scramble Crossing in Tokyo. As the players made their way around the Old, marshals unleashed armies of spectators at various crossing points, dust kicked up as if by ancient hordes marching across vast pre-industrial plains. A favourite spot was the tented village, where people could gather for a pint, some fast food (in mid-1980s Scotland this was a concept) and the chance to see all the latest golfing wares. Inside the Exhibition Tent all of golf appeared to have arrived. Stands promoted the many Spanish and Portuguese golfing destinations; golf wear like Pringle, soon to get quite a boost from Faldo's growing prominence; and the major equipment brands like Titleist, Spalding, PING, Mizuno, Wilson and Slazenger, not to mention Scotland's own John Letters, the clubs played by Sam Torrance, Bernard Gallacher and Lee Trevino. I always admired MacGregor drivers, the tools beloved of many top players, especially the quality strikers. To touch their pristine lines and feel their weight and balance felt almost mystical, akin to an expensive Japanese tea ceremony set, perhaps. The sense of a well-struck drive by quality persimmon was the feeling of the ball compressing on the head for what felt like a number of seconds, the feedback's duration, depth and resonance signalling the quality of blow.

The battle of the ball was taking shape, Acushnet's Titleist 384 Tour balata the ammunition of choice, giving the talented player the feel, control and distance – via 60 extra dimples – to move the ball whatever way they wished, and to get it to stop quickly, as if on command, albeit the Old Course, in fiery conditions, would not always comply. In the ball wars Dunlop had launched an offensive with their DDH, the abbreviation denoting the dimpling design, dodecahedron. They were leveraging the May release of *Indiana Jones and the Temple of Doom*. In June, Fuzzy Zoeller had used the ball in his US Open win at Winged Foot, and many fans in the tented village were sporting a badge with a round dimpled image and the slogan 'Indiana Fuzzy and the Dunlop DDH US OPEN WINNERS'. Sure, Zoeller was from Indiana, but to confuse the laid-back golfer with an action hero was a stretch. But, in a small triumph of marketing, I still have my badge. Merchandise-wise each Open seemed to throw up a favourite or two, something that went like hot cakes.

The prolonged hot spell of 1984 meant one very popular item was a free bucket hat with the Monarch airline and Sol holiday brandings. There were hundreds of them bobbing up and down as fan traffic snaked all over the course and town. For one contingent, the must-have item at every Open of the 1980s was the periscope. It always seemed bizarre to me, grown men (mainly) carrying a rectangular box around with mirrors in bottom and top apertures, allowing the holder to see above the crowds. Handy perhaps, but hardly as exciting as spying enemy vessels in the Atlantic. Another curiosity of the village was 'Lord Golf', a man dressed in an outfit that confirmed he was a cross between Darth Vader's long-lost cousin, a discarded Johnnie Walker label concept, and the really boring guy down the pub to be avoided at all costs.

I remember almost none of the practice days' golf as we'd be tearing about the place from hole to hole watching players famous and random, contenders and also-rans, most detail lost in the excitement, although one shot lingers, and it made the Wednesday morning papers. As I and my cousin, Derek, walked up The Links, the road to the right of the 18th, we heard a sharp crack, like the sound of a bullet; this was followed by a clack then a duller clop, and only then did we see the ball leaping on the tarmac. The drive had landed on the road not far behind us and other startled spectators, and on its final hop some yards ahead veered sharply left, danced over the fence, just shy of green high, and rolled down the right side of the sprawling, canted target towards the pin. Impressed by the luck and outcome, part of me wondered if this was some perverse bet between players to see who could whip their tee shot on to the putting surface. With no idea who the reckless driver was, we stopped and waited. As Chris Rea in *The Scotsman* reported, Tom Watson 'would not, however, recommend a repeat of the line he took from the 18th tee, his drive speeding up the Links Road [*sic*] before taking a left turn and finishing up 20 feet from the flag'.

The papers were full of Seve, Greg Norman, Watson, Nicklaus, Faldo, and just about every other golfer on two legs who might have a chance of winning traditionally, as well as those who might surprise and just shoot the lights out. The Open had that habit of throwing up a Bill Longmuir, a Nick Job, a Denis Durnian but already, even in practice, Tom Watson's play was making news. Driving that last green could be a handy trick come Sunday afternoon.

The 1984 Open Championship: Friday

Ian Baker-Who? – Seve and Tom Consolidate – Greg Norman Fades, Trevino Appears

THE OPEN'S first 36 holes often felt two-phased. As morning contenders brought rounds to a close, afternoon play cranked up. As one shaved the hole for par by the Road Hole, another was eagling the 5th. Others joined the hunt, the shifting sands of fortune amplified by the changing of tide and wind. The draw was part of the challenge, and Greg Norman was already conscious of his Friday afternoon tee time in his Thursday interview with the BBC's Harry Carpenter. Michael Williams of the *Daily Telegraph* noted that Norman contemplated his chances in the expected wind of Friday afternoon. 'Perhaps at that very moment, a seed of doubt was sown,' he wrote.

> 'There are three kinds of British Opens, all of them delightful and all of them distinctive. There is the one that is played in England at Lytham, where Jacklin won last year, or Hoylake or Birkdale, where it returns in 1971. Then there is the one that is played in Scotland, which is a little better, at Muirfield, Carnoustie or Troon. And finally there is the British Open that is played at St Andrews every so often, like last week's. This, indeed, is the British Open.'
>
> **Dan Jenkins**, *Sports Illustrated*, 1970

On Friday, Greg Norman was still the man to watch, with Faldo a keen favourite. But another Aussie was making the news when, as Harry Carpenter would remark on TV that evening, players 'were attacking the course all day long'. Ian Baker-Finch (also known as IBF), a 23-year-old Queenslander, had never seen the Old Course before the championship, but he'd practised with Peter Thomson, the last man to take out three Open gold medals on the trot, and holder of five jugs. In the first round he shot 68 to lie one back, and on the Friday IBF continued to showcase his Thomson schooling. He'd gone through the first 12 holes five under for the day and at the tricky 13th holed from 25 feet for a birdie three. He was into double figures below par, and only five Open Championships in the previous 20 years had been won at that mark or better. With his languid swing and silky turn he was a pleasure to watch, taken into the hearts of the Scottish and British fans while, upon seeing his name on the leaderboard, the initial response was simple: 'Who?' It was clear he wasn't Scottish, being just about the only player wearing a sweater on one of the country's finest golfing days. Playing partners Hale Irwin and Isao Aoki could only watch as the Aussie disembowelled the scorecard like a croc would a kangaroo. Again, the 17th hole would be a factor. It seemed to always throw up a fascinating concatenation of shots.

Baker-Finch struck a solid-but-safe tee shot down the left, on a similar angle to Ballesteros on Thursday. The flag was protected by Road bunker, although on Friday it was deeper into the green, perhaps ten yards beyond the trap. The angle, dead ground, slopes, humps and hollows meant there were a multitude of ways to look at the challenge, but not many realistic options for attack. A copybook approach was hit, especially after the BBC cautioned against a flier, but Ian was unlucky as the ball hopped left off a knuckle before the front of the green. A straight or slight kick right would have left him a birdie putt, while more juice on the line of the actual bounce would have left him very close to the hole. Instead, he was in Road bunker with a shake of the head. But he was equal to it, splashed out to about six feet and rolled in a sweet left-to-righter for par. It looked very easy for his first major. Up the last he nudged a solid drive just left of the centre of the vast fairway, but his approach was shy, landing atop the false front and rolling back into the Valley of Sin, that horrid swale. He would make par, pouring a solid putt of three feet into the cup. After a 66, Baker-Finch was ten under the card.

* * *

Ballesteros had not thrived in the clement conditions. Upon going to four under after the 1st, a birdie at the long 5th got him to five, but this was offset by bogey at the next, followed by a birdie at the 10th. Coming back home on Long Hole (14) Seve's tee shot was a strong attempt to move down the fairway as far as possible. He watched anxiously as the ball soared into the sharp blue of the Scottish late morning. He was considerably left, a long way from the out of bounds, the crowds, and the Eden course over the old railway wall that ran down the right side of the par five. He'd driven wide enough to be lying on the ridge of wispy rough between his fairway and the 5th. With a bit of thought on his stance and, once settled, with the ball above his feet, he *slashed* an iron, keeping it left, tracking along the border of the two holes, and well away from that diabolical crevice, Hell bunker. Seve was walking with a spring in his step as he raised his right hand to talk to himself about the trajectory of the ball while turning the club in his left hand to look at where the shot had left the face. The lay-up was ideal, flag open to attack and the player could virtually see what he had to work with to get the ball on to the small plateau hosting the pin. An early wrist cock and handsy clipped wedge later saw the shot into the air, sandy turf flying on the breeze. It landed almost precisely pin high, left of the stick. Perfectly measured, the ball came to rest about 18 feet away. Minutes later the player *rammed* in the birdie putt, ball hopping up in the air as it hit the hole then bobbled out of sight.

The gain was followed by a casual but direct stroll to retrieve his ball as he acknowledged the crowd with his putter aloft. He flashed a smile at playing partner Kel Nagle. Ballesteros was enjoying this and the galleries were right behind him. It was around midday by the time Seve was sizing up his approach to the 16th, Corner of the Dyke. He'd hit the pro's drive. The course guide by local bookshop J. & G. Innes suggested only the ambitious, confident or reckless would attempt to drive the ball straight down the fairway, but the safe tee ball brought other challenges. Alex Hay echoed this on the BBC.

Seve was facing a medium iron at the 382-yard par four and had to ensure Wig bunker was negotiated. To find it would be amateur and penal, but to go long and right would flirt with a tricky shot back, possibly from a swale. Seve stood just shy of his ball, swinging and sensing the shot. After two gentle, almost informal practice swings he took his stance. He swung smoothly and easily through the ball, perhaps not quite getting through it as much as he cared to, the ball leaking, landing beyond pin high but on a line towards the back right of the putting surface. He tapped down his divot with a hint of annoyance, as his ball had run 30 feet past. It was not as flush as some of his approaches on Thursday, but looked in control. Alex Hay: 'A nice lazy 6-iron, and not a bad shot.' After lining up his putt, Ballesteros took his position over the ball, settling in to the stroke after his routine touches. The sky was bright and clear and Seve's hair fluttered. He struck a confident putt directly at the hole and it ran straight in. Straight in. It was met by a hullabaloo of exclamations from the sidelines and Seve beamed, his putter high, thanking the gods for his extraordinary powers. It seemed for once Seve couldn't quite believe it. 'Well, the miracle man strikes again and joins Nick Faldo in second place,' said almost disbelieving Hay. The cheers and claps continued, and as Seve settled to watch his partners complete the hole, he raised his left hand; further thanks to the crowd. He continued smiling. It could have been Pedreña, with the sun out and the breeze freshening. He was now seven under par. Ahead, Nick Faldo, who'd just had a bogey at the Road, knocked his approach into the Valley of Sin at the last and was chucking his club in the air and spinning around in frustration and annoyance at coming up shy from less than 100 yards. He rescued a par with a looping ten-foot putt. Faldo had now completed 36 holes in seven under, 137.

In his playing of 17, Seve was not flirting with the right side. Faldo, about 45 minutes before, had driven right down the middle, hit to the green and run over the putting surface, ending against the wall, practically. A great chip and a mediocre putt gave him a frustrating bogey, as the young Englishman was turning out to be a key contender. The Spaniard's tee shot was marginally more favourable than Thursday, in a slightly juicier lie, but with a fairly obvious option, maybe his only option: play for the fat part of the green and make a four. As he was over his 6-iron, a police siren blared, the noise from the town bouncing off the solid walls and wailing across the links. Ballesteros put on the same backswing as his approach to the 16th, but his attack was more aggressive, into the ball with the minimum of grass between it and club. It sounded clean, and he was after it, walking towards the fairway, intently tracking the outcome. It verged on being a super blow but it was either a bit short, a tad left, or both, and the ball gathered on the same line as Ian Baker-Finch's. Seve was also in the Road bunker. It wasn't clear if he knew this, as he walked positively, club swaying rhythmically in his right hand as he looked towards his caddy, Nick DePaul. As Peter Alliss remarked, he'd be tested now.

Ballesteros had found the front right of the trap, toppling into the fluffy sand. Unlike the young Australian's, his ball had not run in at pace. Given the pin placement, the Cantabrian magician was going to have to play out but safe. Still, he was in his element, hunkered and bunkered, his knees bent to ensure a lower centre of gravity, the better to get in behind and under and through the ball to lift it up as quickly as possible. But he was constrained by the rear lip at his takeaway, denying the shallow angle of attack he *must* take. TV viewers could only see above his waist, Ballesteros poised like a hunter. He had a couple of practices on the backswing, testing the angle of wrist cock and descent into the ball. He made his swing and there came a solid clip. Some sand kicked up and fluttered in the breeze. The ball was still in the hazard. Like Thursday, Ballesteros was playing four from a dastardly position, a double bogey possible. He exhibited no frustration, just calm acceptance. He stepped out of the bunker, glanced at caddy DePaul, then started to focus on his shot. He didn't waste much time and hit a beauty, a lofted soft one that landed gently and rolled out, stopping five feet short of the cup. The stand behind the green was unified in approval, the dashing Seve responding to self-made woes. He rolled in the putt as if it was a bounce game. He picked his ball out of the hole and gave a half fist pump, half shake of the fist, delighted to save bogey and drop back six under. Seve made even the most mundane moments tense and exciting.

Seve was now behind Faldo, and with Baker-Finch three shots ahead, Greg Norman, Bernhard Langer and Tom Watson would all realise the chase was on. Severiano had been almost undone by the fiendish Road Hole as Friday approached the point in any drama when the plot and main players became more fully formed. One half of the draw were completing their second rounds and some contenders had carded their 36-hole totals. Despite his scare, the Spaniard seemed otherwise to be in total control. He hit the perfect drive up the last, left of centre, opening up the pin, which was middle-ish and in the front half of the green, seducing players like Baker-Finch and Faldo to flirt with the Valley of Sin. From 100 yards out Ballesteros hit a high wedge, landing it beyond and left of the stick, to 20 feet. His tempo was perfect, a controlled, artful swing by the shore. Also artful was his putt. He was faced with a slight downhill left-to-right breaker. Thousands looked on from The Links, and the packed stand right of the opening hole. Seve's putt was perfect, soaking up the break and dropping sweetly into the heart. With two feet to go Seve started to step to the left and turn away from the hole, putter in left hand, high; he knew he'd holed it. As the ball dropped, he was facing the crowds right of and behind the green, beaming and raising his right hand in thanks. He continued turning round, and walked towards the first tee, smiling into the camera, delighted with his work. He waved at all those cheering and shouting. Tramlined birdie putts at 14 and 16; a brave bogey at the Road Hole; and a closing, confident birdie putt at the 18th. Seve hadn't looked so energised and knowing since he'd chipped in from behind the 18th green at Augusta National in 1983.

* * *

Early-afternoon starters were initially shown the way by one player trying to stay in the hunt, Bill Longmuir, then by an American coming to join it, Trevino. The Anglo-Scot had driven the 10th and had a chance to get to ten under, joining Baker-Finch. Two putts from long range delivered a birdie and he was one behind. Then, at the 11th he made a classic error. Going long at the par-three hole is treacherous, so is being short in Strath bunker. Longmuir's tee shot dropped into the sand, falling shy of a pin cut over the trap's right edge. A par putt left short saw the air start to leak from the journeyman's balloon, a leitmotif of Shakespearean magnitude in major golf. At the 12th his drive flirted with the gorse down the left, a prickly grave for anyone. But Longmuir found he was not in trouble and knocked a delightful pitch that landed on the downslope left of the pin and ran out ten feet beyond. A terrible, weak putt later did not augur well, but at the 16th he made amends, running it in from 20 feet for birdie as a Scottish voice in the crowd encouraged the ball, 'Go in!', as it approached the hole. A massive cheer let out, perhaps aided by cold lager, in support of a fellow Scot. Both caddy and player were ecstatic. As Longmuir had faced his par putt at the 11th Bruce Critchley had fancied the player may have some interest in the Open right up until the closing stages. Upon the gain at 16 Mark McCormack joined with the gallery's enthusiasm: 'Right in the middle! Longmuir, after surviving a lot of catastrophes coming in has knocked it right into the hole for a birdie three at 16 to go nine under par.' Minutes later TV cameras showed a lonely ball lying in the garden of the Old Course Hotel.

A solitary white sphere in a bed of water-starved plants. Longmuir had carved his tee shot out of play. On such a brutal hole the immediate loss of two stroke-and-distance shots was as hard to stomach as the blow to a player's aspirations. It was bad enough, but at the Road Hole Longmuir still had a 461-yard assault course ahead. Not surprisingly his second ball was way left, down the 2nd fairway. This meant a wood to the treacherous target. Bill struck a lovely shot that flew too long, caromed off the wall and came back 20 yards to the path just over the green. On the Thursday, Longmuir's ball had smashed off the wall, come back on to the green and he'd secured a par. His fortunes had shifted. Friday was a seven, a treble bogey to become one of the 26 who made a double bogey or worse at the hole that day. Players struggled at the penultimate test, the stroke average 4.88 for the day. Afterwards, on TV, Clive Clark presented Longmuir with the ball that sailed out of bounds. It was the kind of interview stunt that today would earn the TV man a punch in the face and character assassination across the internet. It was a cheap non-joke, but Longmuir gamely played along. Perhaps the birdie at the 16th was the worst thing that happened – Longmuir told Clark he fancied hitting it left to right down the Road Hole, despite its danger. His moment in the sun was gone. Others were tackling theirs head-on.

Hardpan, sun, wind, fast-running fairways and greens formed precisely the diet Lee Trevino was reared on in Texas. A crowd favourite, his quick wit, down-to-earth approach and unceasing chatter were rounded off by his sponsorship from Scottish club maker John Letters. Super Mex, they called him, homage to his Mexican lineage and a salute to his skills. He could dazzle. To the untrained eye Trevino's action appeared awkward, but his fundamentals were solid, swing on plane and his line up perfect. Everything was played left to right, even his putting appeared to be a chopping or slicing action. Everything about his game was repeatable, a left-to-right metronome. His ball striking was pure and he was a master of control and his own line of artistry.

He thrived in wind and on tricky terrain. His tee shot at the short 11th was terrific Trevino. Feet pointing well left, backswing about 80 per cent to the horizontal and that sliding cutting action all belying the pristine contact. It was a rasping strike as he got in behind the ball and up through the swing to watch the flight, club twirling in his left hand in appreciation, a poker-like tell that he knew it was good. A flash of Texan brilliance, judged to perfection. The ball landed barely on the green, over Strath bunker, but still came to halt shy of the hole. The crowd whistled their appreciation. Scottish golf fans loved anyone who could play golf at the zenith of competition. Trevino had six feet for birdie and the chance to go to minus seven. His putt lipped out on the right, the low side, but got enough of the hole to lip up the green. It was a good putt but, by the tiniest fraction, not high enough. Trevino bent his knees as the ball tried to drop for him. He was in the hunt.

Any lover of Seve should be inclined to Trevino fandom. Both delighted in doing the most unnatural things with a golf ball, distorting the laws of motion and ballistics. At the 14th, Lee kept well left, then executed a glorious cutting wedge into six feet behind the stick, the ball rolling out but fighting the wind with plenty of spin. He made it and joined Seve on seven under the card. It was all starting to look like Seve's *fiesta* – Trevino was up there, Gonzalez was in the top ten, and although Cañizares had dropped back to three under by the end of the round, the conditions were greatly to their liking. Trevino played a crowd-pleasing masterly third at the 17th.

The stand behind the Road wall was a popular spot to rest and watch, where spectators could enjoy the perverse thrill of seeing the best in the world fouter about with a golfing combination few seemed able to unlock. Into and through the wind the Texan played a cutting, digging, punchy aggressive blow that landed at the base of the pin, hopped and sat immediately. He'd gone from 50 yards to eight feet in one easy go. On hard Scottish links any ball that stopped with spin had an air of magic, and usually attracted more than its share of applause. However, his putt touched the left side and stayed out, despite he and just about everyone else believing it had to go in. It would've been a superb par. At the last he made up for it, with a similar cut-punch approach into seven feet. Birdie. Trevino turned round to the crowd as if to acknowledge one person, gesticulating as if to say I told you so. He was challenging for a major and playing to the crowds, Trevino's natural habitat. His golf was that purist's joy in terms of control, quality of strike and ability to work the ball. He would play with Ballesteros in the third round.

* * *

The stage was set for the First Act of The Open to come to a close as Tom Watson and Greg Norman played out their parts in the three-act play of major golf – first two rounds; moving day; and the final 18. Champion Watson had started the second round tidily, birdying the 1st, parring the next four then making gains at six and seven. He was four under par in total as he made his way home from the Eden Estuary. At the 12th he had driven the ball straight down the middle and pitched from about 50 yards to ten feet right and pin high. He made three. This was the banner group for the Friday afternoon, Norman, Watson and young German Bernhard Langer representing the present and near future of golf's highest plane. Norman had hit a very sloppy approach to the 12th and came to rest in the swale at the rear of the green. Eventually a tweaked putt left for par meant a bogey and the big Aussie was not impressed. Like Tom, Greg had threes at both the 1st and 6th, and he'd also gained a stroke at the par-five 5th, virtually a par four for the long-driving Great White Shark. He'd reached eight under and was only two from Baker-Finch, but one ahead of Seve, Faldo and Trevino. But the bogey at 12 set off a bloodletting. Norman was still 20 feet away in three at the 13th, and although his par putt touched the hole, it stayed out. He parred the next but his approach at 15 was well left, and after three putts from 25 feet, and a first putt that was particularly misjudged, he dropped another shot.

The breeze stiffened and Watson thrived. To the educated, this was no surprise. Tom would beat balls all day, honing and trusting his swing to near-catatonic levels, and he didn't let the elements get in his way. In *The Quotable Golfer* he said, 'Wind and rain are great challenges. They separate the real golfers. Let the seas pound against the shore, let the rain pour.' No illusions when Watson was in the mix. At this Open the Missourian wasn't going to need his waterproofs, the wind was his friend, and he rose to meet it. At the 13th his second shot was down the pin but about a full club short. He two-putted to remain five under. At the 567-yard 14th Watson's third was only about 150 yards but a mid-iron was needed. He hit a missile, the ball coming to rest about six feet from the cup. Converted; six under. Watson's game was so well equipped for links golf, with the no-messing approach to play and course management, rarely lingering over the analysis of a shot or its execution, coupled with an efficient, classy action with a strong lower body married to forearms the envy of all Popeye fans. Peter Alliss's comment on Tom's approach to the 14th was apt: 'Bang. And you can see how hard he hit *that*; it was about a good 6-iron.' When Watson hit a ball hard you could tell. He knew in these conditions he had to stay committed through the shot and to believe in his club choice 100 per cent. This was cause and effect, effect and cause, total commitment, a swing like an engine. Same motion, just a change in pace through the ball. The benefits of long hours of practice and dedication, his fine play continued at the next hole.

A crisp penetrating ball to 12 feet and boom, another birdie. Seven under par total, six under through 15 holes today. As Greg Norman receded, Tom Watson grew in strength, knocking outstanding irons to tricky pin positions, and knocking in putts from everywhere. Four actors seemed to be in their element. Baker-Finch was playing the rookie, shooting the lights out and, most likely, not yet fully aware of the magnitude of what he would face. Trevino was responding to the conditions putting his shot-making skills to the test. Seve seemed to be in a home-from-home situation, loving the competition, his play and the reactions to it. While Watson seemed to be *at home*. At the 16th he had another birdie chance from 20 feet, and although he appeared to pull it and had no chance, the ball broke abruptly towards the hole at the end. It finished just short. Norman failed to get up and down, another pulled par putt from a yard signalled a bogey and, even worse, a putting stroke from close range that seemed to have developed a fault. If Norman was to be meaningful over the final 36 holes he was going to need to get rid of that nasty pull. 'Well, well, well. I think we may be burning a bit of midnight oil on the putting green tonight or on the bedroom carpet, things are not going well at all,' was Peter Alliss's candid assessment.

Watson was in joint second place playing the Road, but the hole continued to exact its toll, and of the contenders only Baker-Finch had notched up par. Watson had played flawless golf, his drives powerful and straight, irons lasers, putts true. Yet even he was reduced to the status of worse-than-ordinary. He didn't quite get his tee shot and was 250 yards back for his second, a long way into and across a now-robust breeze. He hit an iron that never really got going, perhaps a flier was expected, and it landed in Progressing bunker 50 yards shy of the green and around 80 yards from the cup. No doubt a local sadist had named the trap. The champ found his ball close to the face, but hit a pretty good shot on to the flat, front right side of the green. He faced a putt of around 100 feet, and although he ran it up decently to ten feet, he missed and had to settle for a double bogey. Such a cruel game. After hitting unmatched irons on the three preceding holes, Tom conspired to take five strokes from 250 yards at the Road Hole.

It was the kind of giveaway that could rankle for hours, maybe days. Give Watson ten balls from his second shot spot and he would not come close to making six. It showed why Seve was so happy to escape twice with just a bogey. As Watson struggled to double and Norman limped to bogey, Bernhard Langer hit drive and an iron into the Road bunker, splashed out to three feet and rolled it in for par. As the American and the Australian parred the last, the West German gave the crowds something to cheer about and made birdie. Langer had been virtually ignored in the UK media, with lots of attention lavished on the bigger names. But the German was already an eight-time winner on the European Tour and, among others, the men he'd defeated in play-offs included Seve Ballesteros and Bill Longmuir.

The Ballesteros Swing

Playing Real Golf de Pedreña – Young Seve – Maturity and Control

HONED ON the beaches and fields, Seve Ballesteros's young action was artisanal, designed to propel the ball great distances. Or to gently lift the ball with precision. Or to move it left or right with earnest aforethought. The early swing could seem agricultural, natural and raw. It could seem amateurish to the eye, but it could produce marvels. And disasters. His hands and arms were the arbiters of touch, sensory translations of form and movement at address, during the shot, and as the player felt the ball leave the clubhead at speed. After the ersatz golf club, its head fashioned on to a shaft of wood, Seve progressed in his next year to a real golf club. Genuine 3-iron, metal shaft. That first, proper club became an extension of his body and soul. 'Without it he could not exist,' said Manuel. When Seve began to steal on to the Real Golf de Pedreña course by night, the 2nd hole, La Rivera, 198 yards, became his benchmark. He wanted to match his brothers by reaching the green using this iron rather than borrowed woods, as his informal beach routines were precursors of the modern way of practice, varied to get the most from the game. His play of La Rivera was of another prototype – hit the ball; hit it hard, everything else can be learned. The indoctrination of Seve was not the cold monotony of same shot after same shot, regulated by loft and ball-flight expectations. Everything he did came from nature, from feel, vision and touch. Practising his art was Ballesteros's catechism, and his swing would become that undefinable thing, a moment of beauty or rage underpinned by an unknowable X factor.

John Jacobs, the teaching guru – and twice a Ryder Cup captain, first on Seve's debut in 1979, then when Seve refused to play at Walton Heath in 1981 – outlined the fundamentals of the golf swing at impact. The direction in which the clubface looks, direction of the swing, angle of approach to the ball, swing speed, the same things the young Seve's body and mind were grounded upon. Years later Seve would echo Jacobs, albeit the teacher would not sanction such abandon: 'The point is it doesn't matter if you are like a beast before or after the hit, as long as you look like a beauty at the moment of impact.' This was part of Seve's attraction, the enigma. Was he beauty or beast, when was he both? In his early day as a pro, Seve's golf could appear untamed.

Jacobs had a chance to see the 14-year-old Seve swing uninhibitedly in person, full of power, with an action flat enough to get as much as possible for the effort expended. How else to come out of bunkers or to cut through the grass of the Ballesteros family pastures with a 3-iron? Jacobs noted from photos, that having been so flat around age ten, Seve's swing was over-corrected and too upright by Birkdale in 1976, leading to some of the wildness. Then, talent and vision outscored fundamentals. Even in 1978 Seve's swing looked ungainly and natural, somewhat unschooled. Things were tightened up by 1979, but base instincts remained. This natural swing seemed to thrive in certain environments, seemed to thrive at certain moments. The swing of Severiano Ballesteros seems to fit two moulds, a powerful atavism born of desire and vision, or the power and the glory of controlled genius beyond our ken. The Seve Ballesteros swing journey all of its own.

The internet gives us the gift of near-perfect recall, arguments and opinions boiling down to the differences in how events and outcomes are viewed. John Jacobs was right about the Seve action in 1976. Was this part of the youngster's attraction? The takeaway was clean and clear and obvious. Straight back, up and to the top of the swing, flying right elbow set, before blurring in furious descent. It was a catapult, primed then fired. The quick-flowing beauty of the upright backswing generated such power. The drama was in the consequences. With that stance closer to the ball than would be taught, allowing the upright takeaway, the young player had nowhere to go inside or outside the intended plane when he got it wrong. Thundering drives, soaring irons, wild cuts and destructive pulls as synapses fired, near-instantaneous calculations in the space of microseconds understanding a mistake, the body, hands and arms shifting by infinitesimal amounts in an effort to correct any error. With tension and expectation, not every shot could be saved. In some sporting moments a rich seam of talent, vision and concentration provides only a veneer of control. In the early days the swing was held together by a passion so strong it formed a mighty bond between belief, desire and action.

In 1979 things were tighter. Although not by much. Maybe, built in 1897, 60 years before his birth, Lytham was made for a player like Seve. Undulating fairways, wispy marram grass, over 160 bunkers, and the wind meant that the attacking style of Ballesteros could at least hope to outlast the best Americans of the day – Watson, Nicklaus, Irwin and Crenshaw. The swing template was similar to Birkdale but the player had given himself more room, literally, for error. He could slash and pound with that less upright swing and still-dominant elbow. This was also the second time of asking. Lytham lies a mere seven miles due north of Birkdale, but in the three years between, Ballesteros had notched up at wins all over. The man could play and win anywhere. The attacking strategy of Seve was the key to his 1979 win, outplaying everyone from tee to green, disrupting the regulation norms – fairways and greens – for links golf. The spectator could sense that Seve Ballesteros saw his chance to win and was going to take it with both hands. And that elbow.

The swing and the action were more harnessed by 1980. The irons and woods came with more room at address, a bend at the waist with the straight back at 30 degrees. The hands were more arched and set, and the swing was starting to ally fluidity with the energy and visualisation acquired on the beaches. As Seve was picking up his second major, a nice jacket to go with his claret, his poise and moves seemed more trained, more – dare I write – professional. The inspired artisan was turning into the finely tuned craftsman. In taking out his second green jacket in 1983 the swing was yet more fluid. The hands were set a bit lower, creating the look of a golfer ready to strike. The takeaway was pure control and turn and synchronicity, every inch imbued with natural talent and finesse. Seve seemed able to hit 7-irons with the kind of balance and feel reserved for chips or bunker shots. By now the swing was a thing of natural, if not quite technical, golfing beauty. If it was artistic, it came with all the attributes of great art. Prone to flaw, incompleteness, but when it operated at its highest level it came with an aesthetic joy. The swing of the mid-1980s had a flow, a feel and a creativity, every shot felt tailored to its own challenge. It wasn't just about a shorter backswing or a slight change in pace, it was about every part of mind, body, soul and action together. Like a Swiss watch complication, it could provide great accuracy, but leading up to St Andrews in 1984 this delicately balanced mechanism was off. Timing and scoring were out, something was amiss. The advice of Vicente Fernández and Jamie Gonzalez gave him the confidence to get back in the slot and to rediscover his feel. When something is wrong with the golf swing, other dominoes collapse – touch, confidence, quality of strike and distance can all suffer. As frailties travel through the bag and through the shots, they devitalise. Approaching the third round at the Old Course, Ballesteros seemed to be in the groove.

ROUND THREE

'There are painters who transform the sun into a yellow spot but there are others who with the help of their art and their intelligence transform a yellow spot into a sun.'

Pablo Picasso

1983: The Open Championship, Royal Birkdale

Watson's Fifth Open – 2-Iron to Victory

THRONGING, EXCITED fans were jockeying to watch the decisive blow. The final-hole tradition in the race for the Claret Jug was a mad swarming, people rushing from the ropes, the leader's ball a sporting black hole attracting all spectating matter at a furious rate, and as Tom Watson was hitching up his grey slacks, analysing the challenge, spectators were at close quarters just behind him. He'd had an electric 45 minutes and a taxing day. The lead had changed hands numerous times and a raft of players had led, among them Faldo, Andy Bean, Irwin. The Englishman had come out hot, birdying three of the first four holes to wrest the lead from Watson who, in reply to Faldo's birdies, managed two early bogeys. Contenders jostled but Watson emerged with a battling back nine. He had not won at all since his 1982 Open victory at Royal Troon and a win at Birkdale would be only his third in 13 months, but every one a major. He had recovered from a poor front nine and an onslaught from others to birdie 11 and 13, finding himself coming down the stretch tied. He pulled his tee shot a smidgen at the 16th but struck a towering 8-iron to 20 feet. He rolled the birdie putt into the heart and led by a shot. He'd never won an Open in England, and in 1976 at Birkdale he'd missed the cut and the chance to successfully defend the title won at Carnoustie. After Troon in 1982, Tom had a successful defence in his grip. The week had already provided dizzying moments. The 1982 Masters champion, Craig Stadler, opened with a 64, and that same day the 1981 Open champion, Bill Rogers, flushed a 1-iron at Birkdale's 17th for an albatross, only the third in the championship's history. On the second day, Denis Durnian, a club pro from nearby Manchester, missed from ten feet to go out in level threes, 27, but 28 blows were still a record. As well as the sublime, the Open on the Saturday veered into the ridiculous when Hale Irwin went to tap in a one-inch putt and in a microsecond's loss of concentration missed the ball. A whiff! In a major. He momentarily looked up, internally registering what all watching immediately knew. He tapped in. But after three and a half days of slings and arrows a familiar scenario emerged.

Watson, the four-time Open champ, failed to birdie the par-five 17th and had no cushion as he faced the final hole. It was now (in 1983) a par four that asked for two solid blows in regulation. With the tightest swing in golf Watson had smoked his tee shot down the middle, the ball coming to rest 218 yards from the pin. Making his way down the fairway he was already thinking of the shot to come, the yardage, and the reception the turf would offer the ball down by the green. He faced a full shot into a target defended by two bunkers front left, and one right, and the camber of the hole and the direction of travel for an under-hit shot was towards the two traps Seve chipped and ran between in 1976. On TV the terrain looked flat and mundane, it was not. Watson selected a 2-iron. With steely focus, he stepped up to the ball as an expectant horde lined up behind him on the fairway, like an army of Visigoths prepared to unleash hell. Two waggles and a controlled flash. As Watson looked up he was engulfed by those who set off as if giving chase to the ball, the maddest of scrambles for a view of the final green and what would be the denouement. It wouldn't matter if Watson saw the result or not, in various forms he described it best: 'I busted that 2-iron as well as I could hit it.' He'd hit 2-iron into the last at Carnoustie to win in 1975. In 1982 he'd hit 2-iron at the 17th of Pebble Beach, before chipping in. The venue, the pressure, the moment, the crowds and the history. Watson was a five-time Open champion, like J.H. Taylor, Peter Thomson and James Braid. With one more Claret Jug, only Harry Vardon was better.

1979: The Open Championship, Royal Lytham & St Annes

Advice from De Vicenzo – The Art of the Attack – A Claret Jug

THE ADRENAL juices zapped round the Spaniard's system producing a very real physical sensation. Pressure. Pressure brought on by not knowing. It was what every golfer dreads, a mixture of fear and hope. Where is the ball, what lie will I have, is there a shot to the green? Can I make par or better? A maelstrom of the positive, the negative and the hoped for. These moments were unique to this game. The object of desire was struck into the distance to get to a point in space and time. After that object was hit, the player traipsed off to find it. These were the atavistic instincts and actions in what became golf, long before it was codified, long before 22-year-old Seve Ballesteros walked up Lytham's 16th hole to find his ball.

The Kid from Spain continued playing the way he had all week, defending only when he had to, when the drive or approach shot did not allow progress directly towards the green. When playing a practice round with Roberto De Vicenzo, the 1967 champion, it had been pointed out to the young man that the further one got up a hole at Lytham that year, the thinner and less penal the rough. Attack, attack, attack, and defend when required. The apogee of this strategy came at the 70th hole. He'd slashed and carved and wedged and chipped and putted round the tricky Lancashire links for four days and the end was approaching. In the final round he'd appeared in a hurry, like a man on a time-precious job. It had a youthful exuberance, with little to none of the analysis and soul-searching entertained by others. The wind was stiff and Lytham's bunkers were waiting, dotted all around its demanding turf. Ballesteros seemed at home. Often, he'd make decisions, prepare, hit and be off after the ball even as his swing wasn't yet truly finished. At the 14th he'd succumbed to a bogey, but at the 15th he was unabashed and pounded his drive – flying right elbow, club up and back and into a follow-through, club twirling, body contorting – way down the left side, once again in the rough. But the hole was right to left so he'd taken something out of the full regulation 468 yards. The ball was sitting fine, nestling in strands of wind-blown grass. He assaulted the shot and was away again, the gallery cheering their support and following as he marched after the approach that would come to rest 30 yards from the green. He'd then clip the ball beautifully, slicing under it and holding the wedge into that stiff wind, his lean to the left and towards the pin urging the ball ever better, ever closer. It landed about a yard shy of the hole and after a high hop came to rest almost immediately.

It might have been Lancashire on a typical unsummery summer's day in the north-west of England, but this was quite alien. Backspin. Seve acknowledged the cheers and cries and soon after tapped in for par. In many ways this seemed like the same Seve Ballesteros who'd appeared at Birkdale in 1976. He still pounded the ball, relentless in his quest to march holeward in the fewest shots possible, but all this was now fired by an inner maturity, as well as that belief in his ability to triumph. Since exploding on to the Open scene in 1976, Ballesteros had tasted victory over 20 times from Japan to New Zealand, in the USA, and across Europe with wins in Spain, Belgium, France, Germany, England, Switzerland and Sweden. It was a remarkable run that confirmed what many had thought upon first sight. He could golf beyond wildest visions, see ways round courses like no one else. Allied with that second sight, he could overpower, he was David and Goliath. By dint of his golfing will, he could dominate and take charge. In those victories since Royal Birkdale in 1976 he'd won by eight strokes. By six. By five. Many times, he'd won by three. He didn't just come to win and take a cheque, he played and won in style and with that most Spanish of qualities, gusto. Length gave him advantages. He could attack, knowing his powers of recovery were both in reserve and to the fore. Slashing one's way round a course could be physically and mentally exhausting, the hitting of shots from rough and the low-level anxiety about lies and ball locations a constant drain on energy over hours and days. But this is what Seve had done for hours, days, weeks growing up, battering his way round mental golfing assault courses unconstrained by ropes, crowds, fairways, expectations and having come to attention with that great chip at the 18th at Birkdale; a few miles south as the crow flies from Lytham, Seve must've felt on familiar territory. Ballesteros had leapt into the UK golfing consciousness manoeuvring and overpowering Birkdale with a near-perpetual smile on his face. The smiles were less frequent in 1979 because now there was an added intensity. Less obvious was the enjoyment and the fun, and instead those instincts were channelled through the vessel of winning. He'd learned to win and now was his chance to take out a big one, a major, and another shot was to urge him deeper into the global golfing consciousness.

There seemed to be a telling urgency about Seve. His goal seemed obvious, tee to green as efficaciously as possible, using

A young Seve splashes out of a bunker at Birkdale, 1976

Seve salutes after his famous chip-and-run at Birkdale

Seve celebrates his first Open victory, in 1979, with brothers Baldomero, Manuel and Vicente

Seve's first Masters green jacket, 1980, Augusta National, aided by Fuzzy Zoeller

A simple celebration after a dramatic chip-in to win his second Masters Tournament, 1983

Seve's famous 3-wood from the bunker at the 1983 Ryder Cup in Florida

A sublime up-and-down to make the 1987 Masters play-off

A first European Ryder Cup win in 1985, and Seve salutes the fans

Touch o' class, baby, touch o' class – Trevino, Ballesteros and Nick DePaul as Seve eyes up his famous long-iron to the 5th hole

Seve contemplating a final round putt at the Old Course, 1984

Tom Watson watches a last round drive in 1984

That lean, as Seve watches a final round tee-shot at the Old Course

Seve's penultimate shot, 1984

Ballesteros's iconic victory celebration

Seve hoists the Claret Jug

the traditional course routing more as a ready-reckoner than as a surefire mechanism for good scoring. The 16th is a 350-odd-yard par four that gently curves to the right. Downwind and by taking on the corner the hole would be a drive and a flick following the kinetic outburst that would be Seve's tee shot. On this final, blustery and challenging day the European held a two-shot lead, having held off then benefitted from the downfall of a host of chasing players, not least Ben Crenshaw and Jack Nicklaus, while Seve's playing partner and reigning US Open champion, Hale Irwin, was four shots behind and practically out of it.

On the tee Seve took his stance, ball at the front foot, started with an upright takeaway to the very top of the swing then savagely attacked, giving the ball what Peter Alliss described on TV as a 'tremendous clatter'. The sound of the club on ball was like the crack of a whip followed by a resounding thud. The educated ear would know all of the ball had been hit. By going straight at the green the Spaniard would carve out 30 or more yards from the playing of the hole, and afford himself a wedge back into the breeze. Arguably, going for the middle of the fairway and approaching more downwind would be harder. Seve whipped through the shot. At the moment of impact, just the pads of his left foot and a few of his right toes are on the ground, his head dips by about three inches and turns into the shot as he powers through the swing, in and out and up to the top, the force of ball sports' most complex set of movements carries his body out of the blow. Almost in the same movement he looks right and steps left as the ball sails high on wind. His power fade down the right has become a towering slice and it scatters fans, photographers, newsmen. In reality, he's about 70 yards right of convention, but maybe only 20 yards abreast from where he'd intended. On TV it appears the ball has gone into a car park.

Ten minutes later there are anxious moments as Ballesteros communes with an official. A British bobby, cape and traditional police helmet on, appears to have interposed himself as part of the conversation. Some in the Open field would like to see Seve arrested for failing to find the fairway or for planning the heist of some much-loved silverware. A free drop from the pride of dysfunctional British automotive engineering sees the Spaniard eventually rest on wheat-coloured grass with a clear vision, a wedge off packed turf, into the wind. A stiff breeze, hard, dried turf and a perfectly clipped shot was demanded. It must've felt like home. Again. Seve, poised and ready, looked as if he was in motion. In flight. With a wedge, hands high, slightly open stance, weight and body all designed to deliver the club into the shot with total confidence and optimal delivery through the wind, he punched the ball penetratingly into the middle of the green and it hopped and spun back. Minutes later Hale Irwin impassively looked on as the leader rolled in from 25 feet, bending at the knees signalling hope and sensing a birdie just as the ball toppled in. Seve pranced to the hole, acknowledging the appreciation with a raised right hand, precious ball held lightly in his fingertips. The briskness and spring in his step were still there, but he allowed himself a smile after flirting with the British car industry, the British police and a British rules' official. He had a three-shot lead in the British Open. The 17th was a notoriously difficult hole at which to record its par of four, and the final tee shot – arrow straight ideal, anything else could be penalised – was one to accelerate even the most confident player's pulse.

The penultimate test emphasised how quite brilliant Ballesteros could be. He advanced in two shots to the front right trap by the green and as the BBC's Clive Clark knelt down to watch the young maestro, a relaxed Seve showed how sand was in his nature. Although it was a bunker shot of some 15 yards, and although this was the closing stage of the Open, and although the long bunker shot was one of the hardest in golf, and although the pressure was at its utmost, he swung gently but with intent through the ball, chucking it directly to the target. It even had a glance at the hole before coming to a halt ten feet beyond the flag. He gave it the long look, expecting better. Probably every other player in the field but Nicklaus would have been delighted to just be in good shape, to have escaped danger and have a straightforward putt for par. But Seve was a demanding perfectionist. Not the absolutist, not the perfectionist like a Nick Faldo would become, but the perfectionist who demanded an unrelenting greatness from his own game, his own way of playing. He knocked the putt into the heart of the hole with a roll or two more than perfect pace. The confidence of a young man self-assured of victory. He smiled and raised his right hand, saluting the cheers. They were right behind him.

There was one hole left, barring calamity. Seve had played the last six holes in one under, a tricky stretch where consecutive holes played in different directions, where there was a par three, par five, long and short par fours. Where the fallen hopes of most US contenders lay strewn like corpses on a battlefield, the young Spaniard had taken on the wind not just by fighting it or holding shots against it, but in every way imaginable. Along with fighting and holding, he'd ridden the wind, he'd hit power cuts and tasty fades, as well as big draws and other right-to-lefters. He always seemed to be using the wind. He'd also hit bad shots, but the short sticks and the flat stick came to the rescue. He lost some control from the tee, but his power was matched by the strength of his irons and the luminosity of his imagination. After holing his putt at the 17th, he continued marching, eager for the next hole. He gave the impression that, were the holes limitless, he'd still be marching to the next tee, down a fairway, on to the green, right now.

He elected to hit a 3-wood for a bit more control and to get a softer landing, but this seemed to go out the window when he hit a draw and the ball went well left. Ballesteros would be excused if tension was creeping but once more the rough was to his advantage, finding himself well out of the way of the sand, and with a shot to – at worst – near the green. With a three-shot lead, self-control and simple golfing wisdom were required. The next two shots would not win the Open, but they could lose it. The home green was protected by sand, and from Ballesteros's ball the width of the opening to the putting surface was narrow to the point of choking. Some caution would be sensible. Seve and caddy, Dave Musgrove, agreed that typically it'd be a 4-iron for the yardage, but the angle required a crisp medium iron towards the apron; then the ball, elements and terrain could take over. Key would be a slightly more upright swing angle, taking as much rough as possible out of play, avoiding grass in the interface between grooves and balata. With a slightly open stance the strike on the ball was a clean slash and it was on its way. It landed and came to a halt quickly, resting just shy of the green. As lay-ups into the jaws go, it was perfect. Urged on by a Dave Musgrove bet with his fellow caddies that depended on Seve getting up and down to finish under par, the young man hit a majestic putt of about 100 feet that came to rest a yard or so just right of the cup. After a whole week of attacking and relying on recoveries and shots from the outer regions of some holes, Ballesteros had shown he also knew how to play safe, to lay up and then convert that brilliance into par.

Nine months later he'd hit the same approach shot – open stance, perfectly swiped mid-iron – into the heart of the lower tier of the 18th at Augusta National to win the 1980 Masters by four shots. At Lytham he was the youngest winner of the Open Championship in the 20th century, still only 22. His brothers ran to him, elated. Each knew the importance and joy of any win, but to win a Claret Jug was almost a fantasy. Pedreña cheered, too, as events were broadcast down the phone to Uncle Ramon. At the time, this was practically the absolute zenith of what a European could achieve, the only major they could be expected to play in as a near matter of course. When Seve slipped on the green jacket in 1980 he, Mark James and Sandy Lyle were the only European professional invitees to the Masters.

The die had been cast. Ballesteros's style, taking on the big shots when needed and seeing his way round courses differently from what God, 4.5 billion years of geology, and the course designers and greens staff intended was here to stay. The strategy was allied with prodigious power with the woods, great length with the irons when required. He had won at Lytham when the favourite had been Tom Watson. By denying Watson, Nicklaus, Crenshaw and Hale Irwin he had ensured that, still, no US professional had won an Open at St Annes. He was following in the footsteps of Bobby Jones, the all-round golfing exemplar, putting genius Bobby Locke, and sand-play maestro Gary Player, as prior winners on the Lancs links. Seve had much of what these players possessed in terms of tenacity and skill. Ballesteros's will and way to win, in the words of the BBC highlights programme, 'brought victory at Lytham in a manner that defied logic'. Some saw the defiance as pure luck, after wayward shot after wayward shot. Seve Ballesteros had practised on the beach unconstrained by the parameters of fairway and rough, green complexes and sand. In those years he placed or teed up a ball and played towards a target, and he did it time and again. In that boy's future, Royal Lytham & St Annes was already waiting.

The Art of Seve Ballesteros

Journey to Santander – Early European Golf – Seve's Skill, Seve's Art – America's Golfing Roots

THAT SPAIN might produce a sporting artist is no surprise. Goya, Picasso, Bunuel and others loom across the Iberian creative landscape. In *Art in History* Professor Martin Kemp tells us, 'We do not know how the first viewers of Diego Velázquez's *Las Meninas* reacted to his mighty canvas, but we can be sure they had seen nothing like it.' In 1857, a century before Ballesteros was born, Jean Delacroix wrote, 'The main source of interest comes from the soul of the artist, and flows into the soul of the beholder in an irresistible manner.' Seve's arrival in 1976 was irresistible, the world had never seen this most traditional of games approached with such free-flowing abandon. The USA had seen Arnold Palmer, but none talked of Arnie's art. For years I had been conjuring with the idea that Seve Ballesteros was an artist. We'd been fed this platitude so often we accepted it, convenient shorthand for his brilliance and flair, a shortcut to many forms of sporting imagination and daring execution. It also seemed simplistic – clubs, brush; brushstrokes, shots; golf course, canvas. Was Seve Ballesteros a *true* artist? I decided to travel to the source.

I arrived in Santander one late October day. A stern wind blew off the bay as riotous waves alternated between lapping and assaulting the promenade wall. Wrapped-up locals walked, water to one side, town to the other. I stopped for an intake of sea air, to feel the wind in my face. That it was classic links weather was not lost on me. After 15 minutes I walked from the water's edge back to my hire car and fought through the busy, mercurial traffic, rapid rush-hour jostling with the added tang of Spanish automotive impatience. It had been raining, the modern town felt drab, but when I popped out from those urban streets into a more residential section the history and wealth of Santander's bygone years was obvious. Headed east to the Hotel Real, I took in the pleasing Spanish architecture of the older town. The hotel was unveiled in 1917 as a summer residence for the entourage of King Alfonso XIII or Alfonso León Fernando María Jaime Isidro Pascual Antonio de Borbón y Habsburgo-Lorena as he was no doubt never known. The hotel boasted 114 rooms, almost the same number as letters in the King's name. He'd chosen the location well, atop a headland overlooking the port and the bay, down to the Magdalena Peninsula, home of the royal family's own summer residence, the Palacio de la Magdalena. As I got my bags from the car, I could feel something of the belle époque, but the Real was a wee bit tired, like a cake that'd been left out for a few days after the wedding party had departed. No glitz, not too much glamour, perfect for me. Inside, I found an old charm, like a rich, elderly person's house caught in a gentle time warp. I was not in season, so imagined the bustle in the summer, Spanish families milling about or heading out for the *paseo*, children screeching, wailing, having fun in the sun-washed halls, watched by proud grandparents dressed in their finery. A friendly señorita on the desk helped me check in. Room 114. On throwing my bags on to the bed then discovering the view I had of the bay, Real Golf de Pedreña and Seve's house, I felt the draw of my project, a sense of Seve and his home. Years after reading his quote on that ceaseless stream of ideas for non-fiction, I heard John McPhee on the *Los Angeles Review of Books* podcast. He continued the theme: 'Ideas stream by a non-fiction writer by the zillions. Why do you stick on one thing, why does it last for three months, six months, three years? It has, not always, but most of the time been something … a subject I was interested in when I was 18 or 16 … sport is definitely that.'

McPhee also wrote about 'the poetics of motion' and 'the art of sport', explaining the importance of drawing out the physical and athletic attractions. Seve did not accumulate the most wins and nor will he ever truly be regarded as the greatest, but his golf and entire way of going about the game created a chemical reaction that bonded acolytes to his faith. He possessed the undefinable. As art philosopher Arthur C. Danto put it, 'What makes art so powerful a force … There is really nothing like it when it comes to stirring the spirit.' All sporting heroes lift us from our seats and out of our minds. Seve had some of us hiding behind the couch, fearful of his failure. Many have better records than Seve – Harry Vardon, Bob Jones, Ben Hogan, Jack Nicklaus, Phil Mickelson, Tiger Woods – and Faldo won one more major, but the comparison between the two is the difference between a perfectly emulsioned factory wall and a work by Velázquez. Art and execution are two different things, although the medium is important. Faldo's final-round 2-iron into Augusta National's 13th in 1996, and his wedged third shot to the last in Oak Hill's 1995 Ryder Cup, were two things of inner steel and golfing beauty, like pieces of powerful standalone installation art, but we could argue that Seve was the last truly artful golfer, and Faldo the first modern one, his swing rebuilt to be machine-like. Art versus execution in a nutshell.

* * *

My journey to Spain had not been traditional. From Edinburgh I started with Manchester's Whitworth Art Gallery. I was there to see Pulitzer Prize-winning US author Richard Ford, a thoughtful, erudite man who does not misplace many words. By coincidence, he shares his name with an English chronicler of a much earlier Spain. The US Ford had previously written a classic modern American tale, *The Sportswriter*: 'Athletes, by and large, are people who are happy to let their actions speak for them, happy to be what they do. As a result, when you talk to an athlete, as I do all the time in locker rooms, in hotel coffee shops and hallways, standing beside expensive automobiles – even if he's paying no attention to you at all, which is very often the case – he's never likely to feel the least bit divided, or alienated, or one ounce of existential dread … His is a rare selfishness that means he isn't looking around the sides of his emotions to wonder about alternatives for what he's saying or thinking about. In fact, athletes at the height of their powers make literalness into a mystery all its own simply by becoming absorbed in what they're doing.'

Frank Bascombe, Ford's protagonist, saw athletes have a rare single-mindedness and outlook not found in us ordinary folk. Take all their qualities, outlook and vision, all their training and practice, and you have a 'rare selfishness'. In Manchester, Ford spoke with measured certainty and one question from the audience sought more detail on Bascombe – how did he come up with the character, what defined Frank? The response seemed to get to the heart of my thoughts on Seve. Ford didn't really consider there was such a thing as true character but that we judged and viewed people through the lens of labels and human traits. Every programme or article about Severiano Ballesteros told a story, often trotted out using the same descriptors – artist, genius, magician, legend, Spaniard. Although Seve was clearly, irrefutably Spanish to us, the notion of 'Spaniard' is also itself contentious, especially in Spain. I wasn't sure what I would find in Pedreña, but it seemed that just going there for a look would tell me something. What is our character but a series of events over time, and how they shape us? Seve was no different, all sportsmen and sportswomen are no different. The other Ford, the chronicling namesake, wrote of Spanishness in the mid-19th century, 'The general comprehensive term "Spain", which is convenient for geographers and politicians, is calculated to mislead the traveller, for it would be far from easy to predicate any single thing of Spain or Spaniards which will be equally applicable to all its heterogeneous component parts.'

From Manchester I flew to Paris. I had not expected to be so immersed in thoughts about my favourite golfer as the words of the American author brought into sharp relief some of my thinking. Paris, with its connections to art and freedom, seemed a wholly appropriate place to ponder Ballesteros, but in other ways it seemed about as likely a venue as Paris, Texas, but this was truly what McPhee meant. Once the germ of an idea appears, the references assault and antagonise, soothe and encourage. For centuries, before monetisation, media and mass consumption, ideas of art, beauty and aesthetics were wrapped up almost as one. For years, art – especially painting – was focused on religious themes, portraits, history, mythology. Velázquez broke some of the mould with *Las Meninas*. It wasn't just a portrait of a royal court, it was a statement on who was in that court and how it functioned.

Of landscapes, a dim view was taken by the French art establishment. This was never more obvious than when the Academie des Beaux-Arts' annual show, the Salon de Paris, began, in the late 19th century, rejecting the works of impressionists like Monet, Manet and Renoir. They didn't fit the idea of art, the ideas of beauty. Golf is full of rich, varied landscapes from Augusta National to the brown and golds and green of links golf scattered around the coasts of Scotland, England, Ireland, Wales and beyond. One shot of Seve's seemed to follow traditional notions of art. I'd considered it so often that I've watched it hundreds of times, it cannot be watched just once. Aesthetically, for me, it's the most fulfilling. It was on a hole of beauty and golfing lore, Azalea, the 13th at Augusta National. It was the 1986 Masters. Seve was the forefront of European golf and leading the year's first major by a shot from Tom Kite, with Jack Nicklaus ascending. On the tee, the power of the Cantabrian meant he could hit a 3-wood. It was cut and Ballesteros watched and leaned, a meaningless effort at keeping the ball left. Ballesteros always wanted more in the face of even the slightest chink. That lean was part of his method, his creativity, one of his imperfections. But the 3-wood was a tactical choice, keeping the tee shot shy of the rough. Going further right would constrict the angle of approach into the fat of the green, and the stance would make the shot that bit more difficult, less artistic, more Stakhanovite, more heft, less deft. Did Immanuel Kant not say that art was, along with taste, about beauty and pleasure?

When next we see Seve he's starting to address the ball, 195 yards from the hole. He takes his stance, the angles perfect. *Perfect. Everything is impeccable*, his black shoes, navy trousers and mid-blue polo shirt in contrast to the pristine whiteness of his visor and glove set against the verdant background of the Masters. The player's dark-tanned face and arms, his posture added a feline grace. This was an elite golfer, ready. Six-iron. Ballesteros strikes the ball. Everything in concert, connected, flowing: up to the top of the backswing, the club almost perfectly parallel to the ground, just a few inches shy, exercising maximal power, retaining enough control. The forged, strong metal of his muscle-backed iron perfectly attacks the compressed, highly wound rubber, the noise of club on ball a loud, solid crack reverberating in the loblolly pines of Amen Corner. Seconds into the ball's flight Seve's brother, Vicente, reacts: 'Fantastica,

Fantastica!' He knew what he was seeing and what he heard. The ball landed perfectly on the putting surface and ran out to about eight feet from the cup. Seve acknowledged the crowds as Vicente held his arm aloft, triumphal. If art and beauty were inseparable, that shot was art. I can never get beyond its absolute perfection, even the way it landed and rolled out. If he'd holed the shot it would not have been art, it would have been too perfect, too storybook. The shot was geometrically sublime as the swing exhibited an ethereal flow with a gossamer-thin balance of strength and technique, as if Ballesteros had squeezed everything he could from the moment, the surroundings, the opportunity.

Adding to the art, his father had recently died and Seve's golfing will was now driven by something extra, the desire to commemorate Baldomero, a vital rower of a man with straight broad shoulders and hands as big as the blade of his oar. He had shown Seve what it meant to compete. And to win. I watch this shot again and again, and think of Kant: *the mind itself is alone in life ... in union with its body*. Would a non-sporting viewer see this was not just a golf shot, but that it represented total unison of body, mind, passion and desire? Art is meant to be flawed, incomplete, full of tension. That Seve followed his soaring iron into the 13th with one of the worst shots imaginable into the 15th seems to emphasise his artistry. Anton Corbijn – Dutch music video producer, photographer, film director (*Control*; *The American*; *A Most Wanted Man*) – said of his photography, 'My work isn't quite perfect, maybe it still has something from life in it, because perfection often sucks the life from the work.'

* * *

Before reaching Paris, rivulets of John McPhee's ceaseless stream had begun to form. On my flight from Edinburgh, I had seen a gentleman well turned out in a suit and smart raincoat, an

R&A tie. I imagined him a member of Birkdale or Hoylake, returning from a few days at his St Andrews club. On the Friday red eye to Paris there he was again. Curious, I thought. On the shuttle bus at Charles de Gaulle Airport, I found myself standing next to him, and his Kilgour suit bag struck me as most uncommon. Pierre Bechmann, said the name tag; the captain of the R&A was on both my flights. Was he – as the first Royal and Ancient captain from Continental Europe – an inheritor of some of Seve's legacy? In the City of Light it was hard not to see Seve in every café creme, each pastis, every glass of Kronenbourg. Since Ballesteros passed away, I'd been conjuring with the question, could he really be considered an artist? How free was he to express himself, how free was he to create and redefine what we knew about golf?

Artistic similes and metaphors were strewn throughout Seve's career. Initial thoughts were telegraphed and anodyne, each golf hole the canvas, the ball the paint, and clubs were brushes, a spatula, whatever implement an artist might want to employ. A golfer chooses to get from tee to cup in any way they see fit, and this seemed to be how Ballesteros played. But would an artist adhere to rules? Surely a painter mainly has to render his art in some form of 'traditional' way? If you are an artist of portraiture, daubing paint on the floor, or pouring, is unlikely to achieve your ends. There are conventions in art, although modern artists have tried to break with those. In 2001, a Young British Artist, Michael Landy, destroyed every possession he had. This seemed to me extremely provocative, flying in the face of popular notions of modernity and what most Western people hold dear: things, possessions. What about expressing oneself within the confines of convention and rules? Could working within constraints perhaps, sometimes at least, demand more artistic expression? The *Encyclopaedia Britannica* defines 'Art' as modes of expression that use skill or imagination in the creation of aesthetic objects, environments, or experiences that can be shared with others. Skill. Imagination. The entry then lists so many forms of 'art' that it appears to omit only sex, sleeping, socialising and working. That art meant 'experiences that can be shared with others' suggested to me an international sport played at the highest level could be art. Surely anyone who'd seen Johan Cruyff execute a turn felt the same? Was to watch John McEnroe or Bjorn Borg hit a drop shot at Wimbledon not an experience of art deftly delivered beyond the comprehension of almost all common men and women, even if that art was executed in a microsecond, the waves of the brain firing a synapse, snapping sinew, muscle and bone into action? This also suggested that art was firmly allied with aesthetics. To the sporting cognoscenti, a Cruyff turn and a classic Seve swing were things of glorious joy. They had a flow and a richness, depths of feeling and understanding about the act and its outcome. Fritz Lang, the German auteur responsible for the classic films *Metropolis*, *M* and *Dr. Mabuse the Gambler*, said, 'The mediator between head and hands must be the heart.' That was Seve, alright.

Great sportsmen strive for so much, can be so daring or driven by such inner forces and demons that often their careers are littered with glory and pain. Was art really just beauty and aesthetics? Before travelling to Paris, I asked an artist friend what book I might read to understand all of this a bit more. He recommended the impressively titled *The Transfiguration of the Commonplace* by Arthur C. Danto, a US professor of philosophy at Columbia whose main beat was art. The book's title was not enough to kill my quest stone dead, to transfigure the hell out of it, and an early passage caught my attention: 'Heroes and heroines had to be cut down to size, made more like you and me [...]. The old heroes were too cosmic, their motives too exalted, too remote.' Deep down, Seve Ballesteros was one of us, this was his draw. The nature of his golf game allied with the power of his capabilities, combined with his personality and sense of self brought tension and drama. Even watching Seve on a typical day in a standard tournament often involved edge-of-the-seat stuff, never quite knowing what would happen next. At Portmarnock, in the Carroll's Irish Open of 1985, Ballesteros drained a 45-foot putt to defeat Bernhard Langer in a play-off. The ball raced into the hole, Seve threw off his visor and broke into a series of punches, mimicking a boxer at a punchbag. In that moment he transformed a long putt on a beautiful Irish evening into a sheer spectacle. For a few seconds – a hundred million miles away – the sun shone more brightly.

I read Danto, pieces by John Berger and Geoff Dyer, and Deborah Solomon's biography of Jackson Pollock, skirting the edges of the golfing Spaniard's artfulness. And then the gift of Robert Hughes's essay collection, *The Spectacle of Skill*. In his introduction, Adam Gopnik tells us Hughes saw the keystone of art as skill, the acquisition of dexterity and touch separate from, then intertwined with, thinking in the abstract. If this wasn't Seve Ballesteros, what was? Art isn't just about daring iconoclasm and self-promotion, the acquisition of skill requires effort, practice, repetition. Seve was gifted the head of an iron when he was seven. He took a stick, soaked it in water and attached it to the hosel. The wood dried and he had a shaft. Some craftsmanship and insight for a young boy. A year later he was given his first, fully formed club. Ballesteros himself dismissed notions of destiny and being born with a gift. He spent hours on the beach at Pedreña, on the family fields, and sneaking on to the golf course of Real Golf de Pedreña playing, practising, swinging, experimenting, wielding, feeling, watching and sensing. He saw no *el destino* for himself. Instead, he resolved to be the best. After winning four majors, just before collecting his fifth, Seve told us in *Natural Golf* he progressed via 'sheer fortitude'. With Ballesteros's skills, and his abstraction of the golf course, the disassembling of how to play certain holes, he was starting to feel artistic. We are not programmed to consider Picasso's or Mozart's acquisition of talent. Society and its mythmakers prefer that this be kept, to use Danto's word, cosmic.

We are taught to believe artistic geniuses pop from the womb ready for action. Or, in Jackson Pollock's case, action painting. Robert Hughes felt art without skill was like bullfighting without a bull. Jackson Pollock became enraged upon discovering critic Harold Rosenberg had compared action painting to being in an arena – like the bullfighter – suggesting the artist's abstract expressionism was simply a raw encounter. Pollock saw art as skill and underlying talent, not just reaction to paint and canvas. He saw some notions of art as shortcuts, lazy means of generating points of reference. We could consider Seve's great shots as reactions to the challenge, but they were founded on skills and experience which, in turn, allowed the Spanish golfer to see courses and holes differently. Ballesteros had acquired his talent, and it could be translated into sheer brio, the will and means to pull off dramatic shots. Severiano didn't care how it looked or what people thought he should do. He knew what he was capable of. By any measure of precocity, self-belief and desire to challenge the status quo, Seve was an artist. He burst on to the golfing atelier in 1976 as a total unknown who made an immediate splash.

Had he not been so polite, had he not appeared somewhat innocent in the face of possible greatness he would have surely been something of an *enfant terrible*. A real artist, surely, would've cocked a snook at all conventions and, having come second in the 1976 Open, declared it a victory, a triumph and win for Continental Europe, despite not picking up the winner's cheque. But this was golf, and Ballesteros was not yet established as a player or a personality; such brashness would not have been appreciated. Instead, it was the victor, California's Johnny Miller, who recognised the runner-up position would benefit the young Cantabrian's looming impact.

Long before Jesus bought his first sleeve of balls and rolled the rock, Plato saw art as an imitation of reality. Down the centuries art works were representative, then interpretative and impressionist, tending towards almost anything being art, as long as impresarios, collectors and critics judged it so. Driven by this and by the rise of art theorists and art schools, everything was in danger of being artful. Seve was authentic, that seemed evident. It didn't take an impresario or a pundit or a wave of online lionisation to realise this golfer was both basic and magnificent. Basic in his approach – just hit the ball; thrashed, if possible – but the outcomes, even the bad ones, were lavish. He was transcending the beautiful craftsmanship of, say, a Ben Hogan, and reimagining golf and golf courses, he seemed truly modern. He could force his ball so far down holes it did not seem to matter where it came to rest. What also set the Spaniard apart were his powers of recovery. When Jackson Pollock was asked if he worked from nature, he replied, 'I am nature.' Severiano Ballesteros was nature; he didn't just believe in ideas, he believed in action.

Into the 1980s

Spain Reborn, UK Decline – Seve's Open Wilderness – Dominant Watson

PART OF Ballesteros's allure and continued popularity in the UK was the timing of his arrival. And not just into blistering irons with those wide turns and crushing impacts. Appearing on the Open scene in the mid-1970s and winning at the end of the decade, plus his two Masters wins in the early 1980s, saw him as both the apotheosis of, and antidote to, the times. There was turmoil and change in Britain and Spain, and the irrepressible Spaniard seemed to both reject and harness the power of the moment, as well as the promise of what was to follow. He was an everyman fantasy figure, an individualist in the coming Reaganite and Thatcherite mould, while also rejecting the status quo and the standard golfing power structures. Seve suggested what was possible if one had talent, drive and a measure of confidence and gentle arrogance, the individualistic, all-conquering outsider who demolished old shibboleths and flew in the face of golfing convention. In him was the potential of society; and the iconoclast. Severiano represented many faces of a generation.

In 1975 Francisco Franco died, ending 39 years of fascism in Spain. In an uncannily smooth transition Madrid welcomed King Juan Carlos as an enlightened head of state, taking the frayed laces off the jackboot and exchanging them for the ermine of benevolent monarchy. When Seve complained of being almost unknown in Spain, suffering from a lack of appreciation in the press, this was, surely, a combination of solipsism and naivety, and perhaps a little ignorance. His country had many battles to fight. The transition to democracy, the rise of ETA, the forgetting of the Civil War and the ongoing national romance with football all meant that the country had much on its mind, much to get off its mind and much to consider while looking ahead. As if to emphasise this, the people's weariness merged with a sense of the Spanish dark humour upon the death by car bomb of the prime minister, Luis Carrero Blanco, at the end of 1973 in the middle of Madrid. 'One more pothole, one less asshole,' reflected the general sympathy the murder was met with. It's unimaginable today, and back then such a thing in many other countries would've set off a shocking chain of events. In Spain, golf and golfers were not high on anyone's list of priorities. In a verdant and often damp Cantabria the young Seve would be far removed from the concerns of the people on the arid, dry *meseta* and beyond. The country's constitution wasn't even passed until the end of 1978, and before that Spain was an idea, a series of beliefs and conventions.

The UK had its own struggles. Ballesteros's presence on the sporting scene took people away from their daily troubles and offered hope. It's a useful coincidence that Francis Wheen's book *How Mumbo-Jumbo Conquered the World* starts in 1979. I recall these times, albeit I could not always comprehend who was whom and what, exactly, was what – US President Jimmy Carter seemed to mess up a hostage rescue in Iran; some guy called the Shah of Iran appeared to be venerated by some, detested by others; a thing called OPEC controlled oil. I came from a generation where the prospect of running out of oil seemed real, and as a child you imagined life grinding to a standstill. In the spirit of the end of times, another popular myth at school was that eventually all the musical permutations for songs would be used up: okay for fans of Cliff Richard or The Osmonds. These topics, along with the four minutes left after the nuclear warning and how you would use those 240 seconds, were the kind of psychological terrors filling the daydreamscape for kids like me.

> 'Art washes away from the soul the dust of everyday life.'
> **Pablo Picasso**

From 1976, golf fans following Seve could be transported away from domestic crap and fraught global brinksmanship. He and other sportsmen and women were an escape from Arthur Scargill and Margaret Thatcher, Ronald Reagan and the Ayatollah Khomeini. In our house, anyone with a beard was treated with deep suspicion, so goodness knows what my parents thought of Khomeini. The brilliance of Ballesteros meant the UK had its own adopted son to relieve the strains of the everyday. He was redefining what we considered the proper way to play the game, and his young effervescence did not appear to be infected by any British stiffness. Severiano was knocking down the pins of golfing hierarchies ahead of his time. After the Open win at Lytham in 1979, *Golf Monthly* ran pieces featuring the views of Henry Cotton and Dai Rees. Rees expressed delight and admiration at how the young *golfista* deconstructed the course and the game, the Welshman witnessing some portal into an exciting, dramatic future. Meanwhile, Cotton thought of times gone by, of hitting fairways and greens in regulation. Rees saw the drama of scoring while Cotton adhered to convention. Convention was the very thing Severiano Ballesteros rebelled against or, given his background, didn't even realise existed. He wasn't brought up in a club environment, he didn't start golf by being taught or coached to play in a certain way. He watched his brother, his uncle, the members at Real Golf de Pedreña. He *played*.

The essays by Cotton and Rees are illuminating because one appears to look back in time, the other forward. It was clear Cotton was a fan of Seve – 'he has a great cavalier action' – but in saying 'Ballesteros can't flight the ball', the Englishman seemed to miss the very point. Seve was using every tool in and out of his bag to put together scores. This included using the wind, not fighting it, when the rough allowed. Dai Rees had another vision. The tenacious Welshman offered, 'Maybe this is where players like myself have gone wrong, and why we did not win championships. We used to fight the wind … Ballesteros simply rides it.' He notes Ballesteros's ball-striking abilities, playing from lies – he was there during the 1979 final round – he did not fancy one little bit. Dai's article was dotted with clues to the future of the game. So was Henry Cotton's. He had been pulling for Mark James to win, and the Englishman eventually picked up the cheque for fourth. Cotton finished with some thoughts on the home players, the men from the British Isles and Northern Ireland. He outlined how they seemed unable to handle the pressure, the expectation of the Open, the sense of occasion. He thought of his own playing days, 'We used to wilt, when I was young, when we saw a pair of black and white shoes, because black and white shoes meant Americans.' This was the same attitude Charles Lawrie's Walker Cup team shipped to Seattle in 1961.

Seve was to change all that. He routed the field in the 1980 Masters, reducing the course, its then Bermuda greens, and the field to supplicants, unfortunates coming to beg for absolution, but in the Open his form dipped. From 1980 to 1983 he finished 19th, 39th, 13th and then sixth. We can see 1980 as a natural outcome for anyone defending a title, and the vicious Sandwich links in 1981 would not be an obvious track on which Seve would excel. The early 1980s belonged to Thomas Sturges Watson, and after going head-to-head with Jack Nicklaus at Turnberry in 1977, the Missourian went on a tear confirming him as the best player on the planet.

* * *

Between his second Claret Jug (Turnberry, 1977) and the Open at Muirfield in 1980 Tom won 15 times on the PGA Tour, five times in each year. After Muirfield, he won the World Series in Akron, Ohio, in August. His win on the long and testing Firestone meant he'd triumphed at storybook venues – Riviera, Muirfield Village (still in its infancy but invested with Jack Nicklaus's imprimatur), Harbour Town (a Pete Dye classic), Pebble Beach and Pinehurst (where he eventually took home the title he'd denied himself in 1973). With victories in the desert, the hardpan, on the plains, by the sea, and a win in Japan, it was clear that Watson could win anywhere. He was by far the dominant exponent of tournament professional golf, no one else came close. Jack Nicklaus was still a great player, but by Turnberry, and half a generation older, the Golden Bear had notched up 64 of his eventual 73 PGA Tour victories. Along with his majors at Augusta in 1981 and Pebble Beach in 1982, Watson's résumé became mainly about links golf. He thrived and he plundered, and at the weekend Tom was just getting started.

The Watsonian purple patch was a glorious thing. For his first three wins, at Carnoustie, Turnberry and Muirfield, Tom shot 69, 65, 64 in the third rounds. These he followed with 72, 65, 69. From being the player who couldn't close, he became the man who slammed doors in faces. While Ballesteros managed tied 19th at Muirfield, Watson won by four from Lee Trevino. Given the high standards Tom was setting himself, he struggled in 1981, finishing tied 23rd in Royal St George's first return to the Open rota since Bobby Locke won in 1949. Adding victories at Troon in '82 and Birkdale in '83 meant Tom won three of the first four Opens to enjoy a Sunday finish. Not even third rounds of 74 and 70 could deny him. He realised in those triumphal years that being the hero wasn't required, and it wasn't about playing one's best golf. Patience and calm acceptance of the challenge counted. This and his ability to play his own game over all of the four days became the key to success. He'd become an Open weekend specialist. Watson recognised that, in winning the US Open at Pebble Beach in 1982, he'd played fine on the first two days, but on the Saturday on the Monterey Peninsula he was putting well and driving, in his own words, 'exceptionally well', and this set up his opportunity.

British golf had a near-total lack of glamour – a pale-blue sweater might be the most exotic thing you'd see on a course for months. The players coming through – Nick Faldo, Sam Torrance, Sandy Lyle – were exciting golfers and great players, but Faldo was seen by Scots as somewhere between miserable and dull, no matter what his golf might tell us. Sandy was known as a prodigious, natural talent, and it tended to be that if you were behind Sandy, you were certainly not for Faldo, who came across like a mummy's boy who's been denied his second helping of ice cream. For those born around my time, or earlier in the 1960s, the default hero was Jack Nicklaus. He was a dominant, steely, imposing figure who appeared to have the ability to hit the definitive shot at the right moment, or to grind opponents to psychological dust with Germanic consistency. Tom Watson would eventually sit on Nicklaus's throne. With his wins on the seaside courses of the Open, Tom was now surveying as his that rugged, bunker-strewn, undulating kingdom of links golf.

To Pedreña

Intrepid Spanish Adventurers – Cantabria – Towards the Horizon

EVENTUALLY, AFTER Paris, a train carried me to Hendaye, France's most south-westerly *ville*, and on alighting I jumped in a taxi to San Sebastián Airport in Hondarribia, hometown of José María Olazábal. Having picked up my rental car at a desolate terminal, an hour later I was in the centre of San Sebastián, a handsome resort for the royal and wealthy of Spain, its feel not unlike its cousin and fellow Basque, Biarritz. In 1887, the casino was erected, and eventually it became the city hall. Cultural life thrived in this period, and Donostia – the town's Basque name, *Don Stia*, literally meaning Saint Sebastian – developed into a fully fledged seaside playground. Following the outbreak of World War I, it became a draw for international figures of culture, politics and intrigue, Mata Hari and Leon Trotsky among them (an exotic mixed foursome pairing if ever there was). Across from the town hall was a pleasant, open space abutting the sea wall of the wide, impressive crescent-shaped beach at the head of the Bay of La Concha. Nearby was a sculpture of two icons of literature, Don Quixote and his faithful aide Sancho Panza. I may have been in the Basque Country, but I was now assuredly in Spain. Seve was still much on my mind. At dinner the night before, in Biarritz, I tucked into seafood while dipping into my book, Robert Hughes's autobiography, *Things I Didn't Know*, and I found this: 'It doesn't matter how often, or insistently, you are told an artist is great: unless you experience it for yourself the term will never mean anything to you, it will just be someone else's clanking superlative.'

I drove along the coast seeking, among the inlets and coves, hilly twists and turns, the ancient town of Getaria. Initially a small fishing village stretching to the sea, the old town was a collection of ancient, narrow streets and buildings dating back to the 1500s. The air was full of the smell of *pintxos* – Basque tapas, but with a much better Scrabble score – grilling outside bars and restaurants, reminding me of Ted Walker's sensations of Santander. This place had put its mark on history. A son of Getaria had been part of Ferdinand Magellan's voyage in 1519, a trip with its fair share of mutiny, intrigue, deaths by battle, malnutrition, and perhaps murder, all of which meant that by 1522, after sailing 82,000 kilometres, Juan Sebastián Elcano and his men on the ship *Victoria* became the first to circumnavigate the globe. Elcano and many others like him were the pioneers for the hardy, fearless Basque fishermen who'd venture far and wide from northern Spain and into and across the Atlantic to fish the seas rich in cod and other aquatic confections. After sampling the fresh local sea fare, I was in the car and a couple of hours later approaching Santander, having flown past Bilbao, knowing I would stop there on my return. Continuous rolling hills and valleys, gorges and swift, vertiginous slopes and proud peaks appeared, gazing down at sandy beaches and turquoise waters as I neared the Cantabrian city. It was October, the grasses a rich green, hills dotted with cattle. Anyone from the Celtic parts of Great Britain would have felt at home.

After a night's sleep in Santander, I awoke and looked out across the bay. Yesterday afternoon the wind had been a four-clubber, a drilled 7-iron to shift the ball 120 yards. Locals had struggled to keep their headwear on, hugging jackets as the bay sprayed over the wall near the town centre. The wind was fresh, not cold, but it howled and swirled. This morning it was calm and a bit damp. Spain sits on the cusp of so much history. Visigoths, Moors, Jews and Arabs, Spain's peoples are rich in their diversity. From food and wine, desert, coasts and mountains, to war and peace, the country's past is succulent, turbulent, laden with drama. One of the biggest economies in Europe now, it has seen radical changes since the 1950s. Could Severiano Ballesteros really have come from anywhere else?

The sky was as grey as an old British accountant, Santander soggy and sleepy as I drove through the solitary streets. I pulled on to the S-10, the roadside peppered by the detritus of modern economies, offices; car dealerships; and the port on my left, large containerships sleeping at the quay, cranes mimicking the mountains. It was not long until I came to my turn-off, looping round and heading north-east. I drive across a bridge where the south of the Bay of Santander becomes the Ria de Tiero and I make my way along a two-lane necklace dotted by quiet villages, Pontejos, Gajano, Elecha; and Rubayo, where Seve's paternal uncle lived. Gentle spits appear on the windscreen as the car weaves through the unassuming countryside.

The local radio station moves to a Rihanna song, and I begin to think of Seve. I feel slightly emotional, slightly awkward. From first hearing his name in the summer of 1978 I am now driving along a road solely to visit his birthplace, to try and connect with him in some way. Normally I would rage against everything this drive stands for as I try to conjure with an image, an idea, a construct. The Seve Ballesteros I knew and saw on the TV was not the real Seve. It was only a small part of the man. I continued my drive to 'Diamonds', the layering, energy and resonance in Rihanna's voice feeling fitting, if slightly clichéd for my own situation, accompaniments. I thought of some of

Seve's great moments – the blow into the 10th at The Belfry; the aggression and splendour of long irons at Augusta; and the scrambling and imagination of his play on classic links. There was nothing like him for a generation of golfers. Ballesteros and other sporting heroes, and those who have their single moment in the sun, represent the possible and the fantastic. For those who endure the daily grind, those men and women take us away from the stressful, the boring, the mundane. Now, whenever I hear 'Diamonds', it's not the lyrics or the singing that remind me of Seve, but its power, a passion that underscores over four minutes of pop music wonder. Maybe this is why, a few years later, when I was gifted the book *Silence: In the Age of Noise*, by Erling Kagge, I was delighted to read of the author's focus on the drop at the top of the song, the silence before the beauty of Rihanna's voice. That drop. Ballesteros at the top of his backswing.

These places I drive through have their own industriousness, mainly agriculture and its ancillary trades. I pass a few shops, some buildings scarred with double-glazed ugliness. The land is flattish and green by the water, the towns, hamlets and occasional dilapidated dwelling or outbuilding restful in the morning quiet. I notice a sign by a church and pull over. It tells me that St Peter's Church was built in the 1950s. Earlier, in Pontejos, I had also stopped. There, a similar sign told me the Church of St John the Baptist 'was built in 1946, to replace the former parish church in the Otero district which was burned down during the Spanish Civil War'. As I enter Pedreña it's like a gentle step back in time, closer to what Morris and Raphael and Walker and Pritchett saw. In *The Spanish Temper*, V.S. Pritchett said of early 1950s Spain, it was 'poor in body, stunned in mind, but not, as it seems to me, fundamentally changed'. I had a tiny glimpse of the old Spain – small, stone houses line the main road, a village shop appears, and the road drops down and round towards the water. The small harbour is full of boats, mainly small fishing ones, and the red ferry serenely makes its way towards Santander. I look out over the bay, the wind irritating my light jacket. The sun bounces sharply off the metallic, dark-blue sheets of the bay. The Spanish sense of place was something I took as a given, but Pritchett added some spice to the notion, and to the legend of Ballesteros, his house now just up on the hill behind me: 'Provinciality of the Spaniard is his true ground and passion. And with it runs a psychological passion. His town is not like any other town. It is the only town. And he too is not like any other human being; he is indeed the only human being.'

This seemed written for Seve, and his village was far from the humble place of my imagination. It had a connectedness. It was small and traditional but tantalised with potential. It was on the doorstep of Santander. Santander was at the door of the Atlantic. What delights did the young son of a local farmer imagine lay beyond? What trophies beckoned? The air was fresh, unpolluted. This was bucolic Spain with a view of the world. Pedreña in an isolated Spain was about community and family but it also seemed like a rustic suburb of Santander, and the city offered a gateway. Magellan and Elcano set forth across the seas not sure of what they would find, what encounters awaited, what hardships they would endure. They gazed across this same ocean, to the horizon, and, in their imaginations, onward. So must've a young Severiano Ballesteros, fuelled by stories from Manuel and Uncle Ramon. The entrance to the Bay of Santander reminded me of a mini Istanbul and instead of the great Topkapi Palace guarding the Golden Horn – majestic, dominant on Seraglio point, surveying and threatening all around, both a warning and a welcoming – Cantabria's main port was guarded by the city on the west, and Seve's house and the Real Golf de Pedreña sat to the east. Seve's gateway. And homecoming. Somehow, this place seemed ideal for production of a world-class golfer. Much more than, say, the middle of Missouri; and Kansas; and Texas. For years European settlers went to places like those in the US, they were destinations, or stopping points in journeys that only took their true shape when they came to an end, when people settled by the sea.

Pedreña was small and close-knit but also a place to look out from, to seek other places. As ABC had told us during the 1983 US Open telecast, in the middle of America were the places to produce powerhouses and machines, players like Jack Nicklaus from Columbus, Ohio; Arnold Palmer from Latrobe, Pennsylvania; Payne Stewart would come from Missouri. Texas was an embarrassment of riches – Tom Kite, Ben Crenshaw, Jimmy Demaret, Lee Trevino, Dave Marr, and one of the greatest athletes of all time, Babe Didrikson Zaharias, who won two gold medals in track and field at the 1932 Olympics, as well as three US Women's Open titles. If that wasn't enough, Byron Nelson and Ben Hogan were Texans. Power in numbers was Texas's key, and a desire to win. That was all of America's key. Seve shared the desire. Northern Spain's spirit was transoceanic, to faraway lands; middle America's pioneering spirit was towards the land horizon and beyond. Spain's spirit seemed to involve a homecoming, but America's was a spirit of continual change and new places, new homes. But, looking out from Pedreña I could see that Seve and the great American players shared the same fundamental lust to take on the challenges that lay beyond, lay in the unknown. They all wanted the sting of the battle.

The 1984 Open Championship: Saturday

Toucha Class – Watson Bursts Through – IBF Leads – Faldo Fades

ONLY 63 remained. Those who'd made the first cut at the Old Course in 1984 had almost earned their chance to walk up the 18th on Sunday to the adoration of the galleries. It would be the fifth Open to finish on a Sunday and the penultimate version to employ two cuts: one at 36, and after 54 holes. Some would sense the butterflies in the stomach feeling like pterodactyls, thinking themselves impostors, others would hear the click of a Harry Vardon niblick or the solid thud of a well-struck shot by a Tom Morris, Young or Old. In many ways the championship was not far from its early traditions, Saturday finishes historically designed to allow club professionals to return to their day jobs: the club, its members. Modern golf's Saturday third round meant jostling for position where every gain and every mishap started to feel more important as the players marched to the 72nd hole. Or beyond, if a play-off was needed. Newspapers were full of conjecture, but major golf was the most mercurial of masters, and round three would shape the final act.

Moving day was in full swing early, the possibilities of a jump up the leaderboard signalled by 66s from Bill Bergin and Sam Torrance. Jack Nicklaus – labelled 'The Old Campaigner' on BBC coverage, he was 44 years of age – posted 68. The proceedings were stacked with quality, established and emerging.

Ian Baker-Finch	-10
Nick Faldo	-7
Seve Ballesteros	-7
Lee Trevino	-7
Bill Longmuir	-6
Tom Watson	-5
Fred Couples	-5
Bernhard Langer	-5
Lanny Wadkins	-5

Of that group, only Watson, Seve and Trevino owned multiple majors. Lanny Wadkins had won the 1977 PGA Championship at Pebble Beach by overcoming a five-shot deficit in the final nine. He was streaky. But who knew when a streak would start? Or stop. Nick Faldo had promised much at Birkdale in 1983 but, by his own admission, didn't yet possess what it took to keep scoring in the biggest events. There were a dozen players within six shots of the lead and birdie chances were scattered throughout the narrow strip of raw golfing terrain. But a wind, fiery conditions and the Road Hole could wipe out a lead in 20 minutes.

By the time the leaders appeared on the 1st tee, the opening hole was downwind, and flying the Swilcan Burn and stopping the ball was going to be a challenge as the national flags on the main stands fluttered enthusiastically, looking more like those at a yacht club's regatta. The final group was home to the new guard, Baker-Finch playing with Nick Faldo. Both would sense the opportunity and danger that lay ahead. The difficulty of the examination and the class of touch and skill required were immediately apparent. Faldo's approach to the 1st came to rest just off the green, leaving a return of 40 feet across testing undulations largely unseeable on TV screens. In contrast, IBF generated some spin, his ball stopping about 18 feet past and just right of the cup. The vicissitudes of the majors were stark. Baker-Finch on cue – Hale Irwin told reporters the Australian on Friday had one of the most impressive putting rounds he'd ever seen – rolled in his 18-footer for a birdie as if it was a Saturday afternoon bounce game in Queensland to be followed by a few lagers, a barbeque, and waking up in an irrigation ditch. Accompanied by a quiet acknowledgement of the crowd, the Aussie retrieved his ball. It was back to remarkable business for Ian. Now, Faldo faced a simple two-footer. For birdie, he'd hit a well-paced putt but misjudged the line, the putt always being right. He missed the small mop-up for par. It was hard to tell if it was a purely technical error – surely not from that distance – or if he looked for it a fraction early, as his ball lipped the right rim, stayed out and ran two feet past. He rattled the next one in but walked off the green, head down, left hand massaging his bowl hairstyle.

Any Faldo fan or half-sympathetic golf lover would feel the Englishman's pain. Elsewhere atop the leaderboard, the day was starting to intoxicate. Tom Watson had made light work of the 1st, birdying, and although bogeying the 2nd, he'd signalled his intent for that sixth Claret Jug. Although maybe luck was going to be more important than intent. Watson's second to the 1st had landed shy of the burn, bounced over it and run up to seven feet beyond the cup. Langer was birdying the 4th to move six under, and Tom Kite had appeared at five below the card.

Lee Trevino and Seve shared common languages when it came to chit-chat and ball control, especially as the majors approached moments of truth. Into the 1st Trevino hit a punchy shot that saw one hop on a firm part of the target and his ball run out, coming to rest just off the surface, while Seve lofted a high approach that sat quickly – those magic hands – leaving about 18 feet for birdie. Trevino hit a great putt, almost holing it, looking away, averting from what was nearly an amazing start. Seve also missed, a well-weighted putt that was always on the low side. Glowering at the ball, he strolled up as Trevino had, and tapped in for par. They came to the 5th. Trevino was 'absolutely full of beans, full of fire' noted Alex Hay as Lee blasted his metal driver down the middle. Then Seve. Sheer white glove, white shoes and white shirt, mid-blue trousers and a primary red Slazenger V-neck sweater, Ballesteros stood out against the crowd as he watched the Texan cut his tee shot down the fairway. Trevino was speaking to himself over his shot but Seve, in contrast, was the model of concentration.

So much noise and praise were given to Ballesteros's talents in power and shot-making that the premium he put on concentration was ritually overlooked. He fired his drive straight, watching earnestly, fixating on what the next shot may bring. Hopefully a chance to get on the par five in two. One could sense the key players realising now was the time to keep up as a minimum and push on where possible. Elsewhere, Tom Watson was starting to glow. He'd given back his spot of luck at the 1st by bogeying the 2nd, but after a drive down the left side of the 3rd he hoisted a wedge five feet left of the pin. He rapped in the putt, birdie, and back to one under for the day, six under for the championship. At the 6th, after three birdies through five holes Watson lofted a pitch and let the wind and the terrain take their turn. The ball came to rest 18 inches right of the cup, a cast-iron gain for the defending champion. He tapped in, cheered loudly by the crowds who'd seen a move or two over the years. So had Lee Trevino.

Seve's tee shot had come to rest on an awkward downhill slope, and seemed to be lying 45 degrees to the level. It was bad luck for a middled tee shot, the kind of lie that encourages the player of almost any level to ask the same question, 'How did it stop there, why me?' One imagines Ballesteros may have uttered under his breath some typically Spanish maternal-centric obscenities. It was a tricky one, and the terrain in front did not assist. Hole O'Cross (Out) was protected by five bunkers, one right and four left, and there were two large hollows up at the green. Like most approaches at St Andrews, the shot on paper or initial analysis was straightforward, but reality differed. Seve angled his body to cater for the downhill stance and to ensure an angle of attack into the *back of the ball*. He shimmied a touch, feeling for the right position. He took a half-length swing-cum-waggle, testing the degree of descent. To add to the joys of the approach and the challenge, he had long iron in hand, a 3- or 4-iron Alex Hay surmised on television. In the distance one thing was in his favour: the flag was fluttering enthusiastically to the left, so the cutting action required by Ballesteros to lift the ball swiftly would work it into the breeze and act as something to hold the shot up against. Now ready, he took a full swing, right to the parallel. The sound of the shot to the educated ear was a thing of beauty, as if from a bygone age, like solid steel hitting leather, a combination of thwack and thump. It was flawless, and Seve knew it. His follow-through was quickly superseded by a seamless slide of the club through the left hand and the arm dropping to waist height, a classic Seve tell, the equivalent of Tiger Woods' club twirl or Jack Nicklaus picking up his tee without watching the ball. He'd hit a corker. Ballesteros's work was done, and now it was the gods in play. Super Mex tracked it and his appreciation was immediate.

'Touch o' class, baby, touch o' class,' rang his words, a clear expression of his own joy and appreciation of another master.

Trevino intimately understood the degree of difficulty for anyone to pick a ball off that slope with a long iron, propelling it 200 yards through a wind. The club player loved the passion, the tour player loved the quality, the execution, the nerve. The ball was launched into the dappled blue yonder. Seve had hit it so well he'd made it look simple but Lee's reaction said it all. It was the strike of the world-class golfer at his peak. This was the manifestation of years of practice on sand, of days spent in Pedreña hitting shots, conjuring up challenges. It was like clipping a 3-iron on a distant shore, and it was appreciated by a Texan who was a master shot-maker, who'd manufactured thousands on the hard and quick-running fairways of the Lone Star State. 'Gitup,' said Lee, still invested in the ball's journey, as was Seve. Ballesteros had catapulted the ball high in the air. It pitched just shy of the vast putting surface, and a bounce, skip and a roll later rested about ten feet from the cup. It was a stroke of power, perfect geometry, feel and touch. Perfection of the art of the angle of attack. To stand and know how to execute such a shot is one thing. To do it is another.

'Buena, Seve,' finalised Trevino.

'Well, that is pure magic,' said Alex Hay on TV, himself a golf professional of long standing. Would this be the fuel to truly start Ballesteros's engines? It was a surefire birdie for the Spaniard, possibly an eagle. He needed something, as Watson's tap-in at the 6th meant he went to eight under par, within clipping distance of Baker-Finch's heels. The champion had burst out of the pack and was now the Australian's main contender. The Defending Champion, a European Hero, a Young Pretender, the script was shaping up. Add Teutonic steel to the mix as Langer birdied four, five and six to get to eight under. The German and Watson were playing exhibition golf. Watson then birdied the 7th with a putt from four feet after a clipped sand wedge followed a big drive far enough down the hole that the approach felt like a pitch along the length of the double green. The American was nine under after but a single par. With five birdies already, Tom's game was all systems go, long drives and piercing irons forged by his putting. Ballesteros had his chance to go nine under with the eagle attempt. He had about ten feet to negotiate and hit the perfectly paced putt. The ball intently rolled towards the hole on a beautiful right-to-left course then declined to turn, straightened, almost breaking away. A dip of the knees in frustration saw Seve recognise the miss. But he was clearly not annoyed, he'd hit his perfect putt, it looked to be going in and was a good read. He exchanged a few polite debriefing words with caddy Nick DePaul, neither envisioning the ball taking that final course at the hole. He walked up, wind irritating his blue trousers, and tapped in. The crowd showered appreciation that Seve acknowledged with a polite smile and a nod.

Baker-Finch was also moving. As others pursued, he remained steps ahead, rolling in a 25-foot birdie putt at the 4th to get to 12 under. He started walking after the putt the moment he struck it, surely convinced he was missing. It dropped. He was a one-man bush fire. At the 5th he was just behind where Seve had come to rest and had 220 yards to the pin. He whipped a wood on to the green, beyond pin high. As Baker-Finch raged, the flames of Tom Watson's play steadily licked at par. Every shot Watson hit was on target, every swing the same, his action oiled to perfection. This was the five-time Open winner with number six in his crosshairs. He turned into the wind at the 9th and whipped a wedge into seven feet. 'Well, we are being treated to some scintillating golf this afternoon, this Saturday afternoon at St Andrews,' said Hay. It was a day when one of the ideal places to be was in front of the TV. The main actors were engaged in a full-on battle, golfing kung fu where everybody is fighting everybody else all at once. Turning back into the wind for the final seven-hole stretch was going to be the key that unlocked the top of the leaderboard for Sunday. Seve had a similar-length putt at six to that he'd had at five. He missed it, like other misses, on the right. 'And there's another one, he's missed alotta those. And those are the kind you've gotta make if you're gonna win this Championship,' noted Mark McCormack.

Ballesteros had holed some stunning putts on the first two days, but with Baker-Finch, Langer and Watson all simmering, he needed to keep up. McCormack was a good player himself, and after years in the sport management business he knew those long putts were part good fortune, part great play, but that true putting consistency and low scoring were typically founded upon the bread-and-butter ones, those Seve had missed so far today. To win any golf tournament you had to be at the top of the pack or near it when it came to putting stats, especially at the Old Course with its combination of subtle, historic breaks and obvious-yet-tricky undulations. On the same hole, the 6th, Trevino had half Seve's length for birdie – he also missed on the right. Perhaps the breaks on that line were too subtle for both sorcerers. At the same time almost, Watson missed his effort at the 9th and had to settle for being out in a mere 32 shots. At the 5th, IBF had about 40 feet for an eagle and he stroked a marvellous effort which, had it the full pace, may have fallen. He was a foot away and tapped in for birdie. Faldo had hit an even longer putt to a matter of two and a half feet past. He missed coming back. In the space of five holes Faldo was back at six under, and Baker-Finch was 13 below par and four in front. The Australian's progress was, given the venue, event and circumstances, remarkable.

Tom had one last hole to play downwind, the 342-yard 10th, named for Bobby Jones. The contact of the persimmon driver clubface on balata (from the tree known also as, aptly, bulletwood) sounded like a fighter jet slashing across the sky, a rasping surge of noise for a few microseconds. It sounded like it could later be bounding down the main drag in Kansas City. It came to earth just shy of the 300-yard mark, caromed 15, 20 yards before climbing over the ridge at the front of the green and resting about 20 feet right of the pin and a very makeable putt for eagle. The next 150 minutes of golf, as Watson turned into the wind and the other contenders made their way round the loop and into the elements, would set the scene for the final stage of this intricate drama. The fans sensed continued pressure from Watson, and further acts worthy of golfing greatness. Watson hit an eagle putt that for 95 per cent of its journey appeared in, and mostly in the heart, but the ball did nothing more than caress the left lip and stay out but he was now in double figures below par. As the players reached the turn and came back into the wind, you could guarantee some players would continue to experience moving day: backwards.

Faldo struggled, missing a succession of putts he should have made. He continued driving the nail into his own coffin, at the sixth, hitting a series of poor shots. A good drive left and a shot to a huge green would have set up a basic, soft, uninspiring par, but he was showing he didn't quite seem to have the mettle when in the major top flight. His putting – which usually cemented his good play – had utterly left him, and after driving into a small trap down the right and hitting a long pitch for his fourth, he missed the ten-footer and settled for double, a loss of more than two shots to the field. Meanwhile, at the 11th, Langer and Freddie Couples were entertaining the crowd. The German struck a penetrating iron into 12 feet below the hole, while the American flew his high into about five feet. Langer hit a firm putt but missed, remaining eight under. Couples holed his, and went to seven under.

At the par-three 8th, a hole of startling mundanity for the Old, Seve was hitting a mid-iron into the wind. He hit a tee shot of startling awfulness for anywhere, an astonishingly bad shot. Part quit, part uncertainty? He seemed to fractionally decelerate through the ball, or at the very least not drive through the shot as much as he should've. Perhaps an overcompensation as he tried to maintain his rhythm, especially into the elements. He immediately reared away, sand and some turf kicking up into his face. His ball ended – on the 178-yard hole – about 40 yards from the pin, left, and he was fortunate not to be in dense scrub or gorse.

It was a position in which we were more likely to see a 24-handicapper and the delusional duffer would've been disgusted. Seve at his temperamental worst, but every shot was a challenge. Blade open but aligned directly with the pin, and in behind a ball that was sitting down, Seve clipped it cleanly and the shot flew through the wind to eight feet shy of the cup, running past the hole, shaving the edge. He'd nearly holed it, and the ball came to rest three feet past. The response of the crowd was a small moment of quiet, a collective intake of breath, and then claps and whistles at near birdie. Forty-five seconds before, Mark McCormack had been remarking on Seve's worst shot of the week. His response to the pitch, 'Well, he's still got the magic.' He was truly lucky to have found a lie that allowed some finesse. It was a super shot any day of the week, but in the circumstances it was stupendous. Seve took a look at the putt, a step to the side, seeking hidden or too-subtle borrows. After his chip it was imperative that he make this. A bogey was bad, but following a great recovery it would be hard to swallow, especially with only two more holes downwind and then the final, dogged stretch. He stroked it straight into the heart of the hole, picked his ball out and walked towards the next tee, giving a slight tilt of the head, shrug of the shoulders – even he knew it was quite a par.

As Jamie Gonzalez putted at the 11th, and playing partner Watson looked on, the hunters and the hunted intersected when Ian Baker-Finch appeared. He was playing to the double green at the 7th and had walked up to eye up his approach. Watson had continued flag-hunting, hitting a medium iron into 15 feet at the short 11th. He hit a decent putt that threatened the hole initially, but rested right of it, and shy. He tapped in for par, trouser legs frantically flapping, a reminder of the march back to the Auld Grey Toun.

At the 9th Seve found his metier again. He'd only managed one birdie – courtesy of his glorious efforts at the 5th – and towards the turn his tee shot was followed by a mediocre approach with a wedge 25 feet right of the hole: he drilled the putt; it was aggressive and plunged directly into the middle. Cries of support lit up the air. It seemed Seve could hole almost at will outside 25 feet when it mattered, but anything less was painful. He'd arrived at two under for the day as Watson was converting for a birdie at the 12th from about 18 inches. At the dicey short par four he'd blasted a drive straight and true and almost holed his approach, the ball spinning to the right, just missing the cup. He continued to knock the pins out with robotic brilliance or, as McCormack put it, 'ripping the flag out with almost every iron he hits today'. One hole back into the elements for Tom, one birdie. The Missourian was two behind but 11 under par. As Watson's ball dropped, an early, gruff, Scottish roar led the fanfare.

Watson's round was a stark example of what Saturdays could hold in major golf. The trouble with a birdie blitz or run of good form in any sport is that it must, will, come to an end. It's part of the natural condition, and an important part of any sport where earth, wind and the player's fire are prime variables. The arresting of such progress brings a psychic challenge. This was facing Baker-Finch as the wind gained in strength. In the same way Seve motored away from the 1980 Masters field, Baker-Finch had to combat a lull and a mistake or two. The young Queenslander reached the turn in 33, 13 under par. Coming down from the psychological high, in the zone, giddy on the drug of invincibility, and the physical high – adrenal flow under control, increased power – was not easy to manage in new situations. In sport these things can stop as abruptly as a car hitting a wall at speed. He who manages it best can seize the day and from these reserves came the 'Big Wins'. Occasionally some came from behind to snatch a major, but that was not typical and, even then, the magnitude of *possibility* tended to weigh heavily on the shoulders of the unbaptised. Watson and Seve had both learned from being in the cauldron. It was these occasions when Ballesteros's loss in '76 and win in '79 were real strengths. Despite his five Opens, Tom knew what it was to lose and win the US Open at Winged Foot then Pebble Beach. Every victory came from the management of the fluctuations of nerve, emotion, aggression, optimism and pessimism, plus the distractions and challenges of the course's terrain, the weather, crowd interaction. One of the great things about sport is every player, from the average to the very good, can feel the emotion, turmoil and mental challenges faced by the greats. Those who embraced and harnessed the pressure often prevailed.

Baker-Finch first succumbed to error at the 11th, and playing on his mind would be the lack of birdie at the 10th, a downwind up and down expected by all 63 players. After a jarring bogey, he'd hit a lovely drive at the 12th and had a full wedge to the pin, but as the breeze got up the landing area between the false front and very real dip at the back was ever-decreasing. Baker-Finch was where every golfer would love to be. Every golfer. To smell and taste leading an Open. He hit a bold approach that landed well beyond the pin, hopped to the very top of the slope behind it and zipped back and to the right, leaving 15 feet for a birdie. IBF slammed in his birdie putt to get back to 13 under. The young Aussie seemed impervious to stresses and strains.

The first 12 holes had three into the wind, nine down, and Watson had reaped the benefits. Then the inevitable lull. Tom parred the next three, and at the 16th had hit another great drive, 'Position A'. But his medium iron to the pin was leaked a tad and rode the wind, finishing well right of the green, not far from the out of bounds. He hit a great Texas wedge putt stiff, just missing right. Par. In contrast, Langer was starting to play great golf on the trickiest holes, perhaps a function of his flatter, baseball-swing action keeping the wind's affects at bay. The German birdied the 15th to get to eight under the card and sit in fourth place.

As it stood, Seve and Langer would be in the penultimate pairing on Sunday. This was emphasised when Langer continued his form at the next. Following another solid drive and around an 8-iron into ten feet, the Bavarian boxed the putt, moving to nine under. The young player had a taste for the hunt. As his ball sped into the hole he was after it, raising his putter in the air in anticipatory triumph, a rare show of emotion from the endearing yet usually stoic man from Anhausen. He acknowledged the crowd as he strode to the Road Hole. Midwest solidity, Latin fire, German efficiency and Australian grit formed a rich amalgam. It was a perfect Open Championship Saturday in Scotland. A classic hard and fast course at a classic venue, ideal sunny yet breezy conditions giving the players both a test and the opportunity to use the wind on many holes. The world's best two players were battling, with a mixture of old and new opponents giving them plenty to ponder.

Alongside Langer down the 17th Watson was now steady, not electric. His approach at the Road Hole found an almost ideal lay-up, resting on the false front with a putt straight up the green to the pin. Although it was around 90 feet, it would have little break and the touch and feel would be similar to his long putt from the back right one hole before. He eyed it up, feeling the pace. A solid finish would anchor confidence for Sunday and, barring a three-putt or more Langer excellence, Watson could expect to be playing with Baker-Finch in the final round – five

Opens, two Masters and a US Open versus a win in the New Zealand Open: history knew the tendency. Watson hit a super putt, the ball breaking to the left, finishing stone dead. The crowds clapped and cheered. A lapse could have seen that putt well short or well past, but Watson was not about to relinquish his position. He remained six under for the day. Watson struck a sure blow up the final fairway, well over the road and right of centre. It was the perfect drive with the pin tucked on the far left of the sprawling, canted green. Tom could fire an aggressive shot right of the hole knowing the break would carry the ball towards the cup on landing. After a three-quarter swing and the clean clip of clubhead, ball then turf, Watson watched his shot intently. The whistles and cheering were sustained as the crowds were released to flurry across Grannie Clark's Wynd, and Watson strode confidently forward, saluting all forms of appreciation.

'That's pretty good, isn't it? That putt to equal the record. He's playing so well he's dazzling everybody,' came the BBC. Tom Watson had already compiled the round of a champion. He hadn't truly been in the mix, just lurking. Now he was the in-form player by some margin. He hit a near-ideal putt that pecked the left side and stayed out: 66, and 11 under par, firmly in second place. Others yet to finish were mainly trying to hold their positions. Langer continued to revel in his play, and let go with occasional bursts of emotion. His second at the Road left his ball tantalising, almost bizarrely, on the very right edge of the bunker. Standing fully in the sand and with his club about 45 degrees to his body he held a pitching club at the very bottom of the grip, almost on the shaft. He played a deft pitch on to the side of the swale and as it hopped over the crest Bernhard lifted his arms up, striking a Biblical pose. The ball came to rest just in front of the hole. Stiff. Langer remained nine under. Meanwhile, back at the 14th the young Australian had been making life difficult. Baker-Finch ran up a bogey, his primary sin being the knocking of his driver left into the Beardies, the complex of traps protecting the flanks of the fairway. The player could blame the wind and the lengthening of the hole for the 1939 Open – the tee being moved back around 60 yards – for his sandy disposition. Three shots later he still wasn't on the green and did well to only surrender one shot to par.

Seve was on the final stretch. He'd again hit a lovely tee shot down the 16th, and had a great angle from the left side into the pin cut right and towards the rear of the putting surface. He struck a beautiful iron that flew just left of the stick, landing 20 feet shy and rolling out to seven feet. A bold, accurate shot. The crowd whistled and clapped. Ballesteros eyed up his putt with customary intensity. He stroked it – perfect line, perfect weight – into the heart. The birdie was met with a unified crowd saluting the conversion. Ten under par. He acknowledged the gallery with a raised putter and nod, the look now assuredness, he wasn't smiling. He looked up at the Road Hole corner as he walked to the tee, perhaps already visualising the shape of his drive. Another test. Baker-Finch was at -12 and as Seve surveyed his pending drive past the Old Course Hotel the leader was clipping an iron into 15 feet at the 15th. In the final arena Langer almost kissed the right lip of the hole for birdie, but it was a tad off.

In symmetry, virtually at the same time, Baker-Finch did the same two holes back. Bruce Critchley remarked that while before they had appeared to be dropping, now they were missing. Still, IBF was 12 under. The Aussie surely would've given all the water and sand at Bondi Beach, all the beer in all the eskies, all the snags on all the barbies to have been in his position, but top-flight sport plays real mind games. He'd gone from invincibility to just missing, maintaining his lead but maybe feeling it very slowly ebb. This is also why the lucky golfer is not what he seems. The intense psychology of the game, its playing fields, hazards, and the art and science of competition mean negativity can creep in from the most positive circumstances. The challenge is player reaction.

The examination provided by the tee shot at the Road Hole was once again beyond the Spaniard. If 50 per cent was the pass mark, Seve once again scored below what was required, as if some doubt entered his mind every time he faced the corner of the dyke by the Old Course Hotel. Perhaps that doubt was the clear imprint of his wild drive in 1978, or the fact that once Ballesteros let the ball start to go right, that was it. His swing seemed fine but the shot was tweaked, and it came to rest in virtually the same position as Friday. Seve hit another 6-iron in, left. After hitting a pitching wedge just shy of the green, the Cantabrian was not on the putting surface and double bogey was a glaring prospect. Again.

Saturday was another round when up and down was good enough for a bogey. He had to negotiate a severe hump while avoiding undercooking or going too far left into a swale, both of which could've carried his putt into Road bunker, like one of those treacherous tracks along a South American hillside, the valley below dotted with cars and buses who'd previously misjudged the challenge. The degree of difficulty was matched by the length of Ballesteros's backswing followed by a firm strike. The putt raced up the slope, across the flat of the main green and was being greeted by caddy DePaul with a gesture, thumb and index finger forming an okay sign. He was impressed, and the putt almost dropped. On the BBC, Critchley felt the miraculous now commonplace. The demeanour of Ballesteros seemed to have changed. No longer the waves, smiles and small gestures of possible feigned surprise at his own touches of brilliance; just steely determination accompanied his thanks for the fans' appreciation. He knew there were only 19 holes left. He also knew it was just a bogey and he'd lost only a tiny fraction of a shot to the field. In 24 hours, fractions would cost a championship but for now a bogey was far from problematic, especially after his usual machinations towards a six or worse. Seve had one hole of the penultimate round to play; Baker-Finch had just teed off behind him.

Baker-Finch	-12
Tom Watson	-11
Bernhard Langer	-9
Seve Ballesteros	-9

Like Watson and Langer, Ballesteros's approach to the final hole was left and below the cup. He hit an aggressive, game putt but missed. He tapped in for a 70, a decent round that at times promised much more.

Baker-Finch made hard work of the last few holes, a bogey at the Road hardly breaking news. A mediocre tee shot and a second that, by his own admission, he was afraid to fully commit to saw him come up short, followed by a chip and two putts. Up the final expanse, while others in the leading pack had nestled their seconds below the hole, IBF didn't quite get far enough on to the green, and his pitch drew back into the Valley of Sin. Again. He managed to two-putt but the approach, with a wedge, needed to be further up the green and ideally anywhere 20 feet left of where it landed. His next competitive wedge would be from the 1st fairway on a warm and dusty Sunday afternoon in the boiling pot of the final round of the oldest, greatest major.

ROUND FOUR

'Let's not force things, but let everything arrive at its own moment, in its own peculiar manner, fusing its rhythm with ours.'

Juan Ramón Jiménez

1983: Ryder Cup, Palm Beach Gardens, Florida

Seve's Superpowers – A 3-Wood and a Driver – Victorious in Defeat

ON THE flight home from that single-point loss in the Sunshine State Ballesteros declared the 1983 Ryder Cup result a victory: a vision of golf's near future, a message to America and the Europeans. Save the difference of two halves or an additional game's win in Europe's favour, the overall result would have seen a then-unique triumph on the turf of the USA.

The USA team in 1981 at Walton Heath is recognised as one of the strongest of all time. At career end, only Bruce Lietzke would not have a major. Even non-playing captain Dave Marr had the 1965 PGA Championship won in Arnold Palmer's backyard, at Laurel Valley, Pennsylvania. The 1983 edition saw a shift. On tour, Gil Morgan, Bob Gilder, Jay Haas and Calvin Peete were all good-to-great players, but superstars and intimidating they weren't. Not for Severiano Ballesteros. Change was afoot for the American Golfing Empire. Bernard Darwin in 1932 bestowed that name upon the behemoth begat by Francis Ouimet's win at Brookline in the US Open of 1913, and there was a moment in the 1983 Ryder Cup Saturday afternoon when the golfing planet wobbled on its axis. On defeating Bob Gilder and Tom Watson, Paul Way and Seve ensured that going into the singles in an away match with the USA, scores were level for the first time. In 1979 the away side had lost 17-11 at The Greenbrier, West Virginia, but come Florida the Europeans had truly arrived, not that many noticed. 'I remember the 1983 matches in Florida. There weren't a thousand people watching. It all changed after that,' Curtis Strange noted on the McKellar podcast in 2020.

* * *

Ballesteros was a hero to those who loved his passion, but in the Ryder Cup he became a superhero. He bestowed powers upon others, channelling his confidence directly to playing partners, galvanising the whole team to elevate their games and beliefs around what constituted the possible. Seve did not allow received wisdom of American invincibility and greatness to infect him, and he encouraged others to draw from this philosophy. Like all greats, it was in times of struggle and disappointment that he showed his mettle. It is easy to look wise in times of victory. In modern mythmaking the superhero has a burden to overcome, a setback to recover from. Seve's Ryder Cup origins were dark, anti-hero-esque. He'd refused to play in 1981 over wider squabbles about money – this would appear *very petty* in the eyes of the golfing establishment – and only turned out in Florida after talks with captain Tony Jacklin. Jacklin himself played a massive part in subsequent triumphs, only taking the European job after guarantees of top-class treatment on travel and lodgings. As twice a major winner, he understood the need for positivity.

In almost all Ryder Cups post-World War II until Ballesteros and Jacklin emerged, teams this side of the Atlantic started as inferiors and went backwards. Any sense of victory or chance of it was displaced by the kind of belief system that went the way of the Raj. The GB&I teams were stodgy dumplings to the sweet, sumptuous mom's apple pie of the USA.

In 1981 Ballesteros had already won his first two majors, but along with the murk of refusing to play, his Ryder Cup tally was inauspicious, four losses from five in 1979, all defeats involving the self-educated hands of Larry Nelson, who'd notched up a perfect nine in two transatlantic clashes. Despite the flawed anti-hero's individualist refusal to play, Ballesteros's powers would eventually become super. I recall vividly watching some of the 1983 matches, but I would be lying if I said I could remember *the shot*. Apparently, it was never filmed, yet a legion of people claim to have seen it on the telecast. The magical wood from the bunker in the first singles match of the final day has passed into the mythological, slipping into a wormhole of space and time. Maybe this is the zenith of fandom, claiming a part of the moment for ourselves.

For golfers of my age – 12 in late 1981 – the Ryder Cup was nothing more than a skirmish, but the next edition, 1983 at PGA National, was different. A pal's dad, who worked as an engineer for Air Canada and therefore no stranger to North America, attended. I sensed the idea of the event but had no feel for its true potential, and then US golf on British TV was almost a curiosity, gaudy Warholian colour splashed over the screen. The lingering miasma of defeat was a big factor, although the players clearly cared, wanting to win each game. As the finale approached, Sam Torrance hit a superb pressure-laden wedge at the 18th stiff to keep Europe's hopes alive. Two games later, Lanny Wadkins did the same, his punched wedge all over the stick to retain the Ryder Cup, his post-shot swagger an exhibition of great insouciance. One shot of Seve's has remained lodged in my mind for 40 years. When people talked generally of the amazing wood at the 18th, I was convinced I had seen it. And I had, except it wasn't the shot of popular legend. On one of the first two days, Seve had pummelled a tee shot down the 578-yard final hole's fairway. He then pulled a driver, a blend of bravado, the diabolical and madness. He took his stance, his feet a bit wider for extra foundation, and swung at the shot with an anger that seemed powered by every Ryder Cup disappointment stretching back to 1921. A motherlode of fury.

But in these days, not every shot or nuance was unpicked, analysed and overblown. I searched newspapers and reports for a titanic driver up to the final green. *Perhaps* I did slightly misremember the club, but out of Florida *The Palm Beach Post* carried, 'Ballesteros, who seems to be followed by drama wherever he strides, again went all out for birdie on the par-5 18th hole.' *The Tampa Tribune* rounded it off, 'At the 578-yard 18th, Ballesteros gave his team a halve [*sic*] with two gigantic wood shots to the back of the green.' Seve would pitch and putt for his four. *All out. Gigantic. Striding. Drama.* Those words will do me: in my mind, it remains a driver.

A superhero needs enemies, arch-villains. With the power of Superman and the agility and fun of Spiderman, Seve also seemed to possess the darkness of Batman. He could be serious, brooding, intense. This was never more obvious when he played with or against Tom Kite. When Kite missed a putt by about a millimetre to force a play-off in the 1986 Masters, and as Kite legitimately agonised over his tantalising brush with greatness, Seve was right in his peripheral vision, starting to line up his own putt, now that the American's hopes were extinguished. To me, this seemed like a silent message; Seve did not give two fucks that Kite had missed. Tough luck, his movements said. It was strangely exhilarating, like watching Quint being consumed by Jaws, coughing up blood. Grizzly. There is no delight in taking solace in Kite's pain – he was a superb golfer – but that was the power of having a hero, their enemies became yours. There was no shortage of villains in Seve's sphere. Lex Luthor was Deane

Beman, and other villains were mainly the US players who he felt didn't give him the respect he felt he deserved. For Seve fans, Beman, Kite, Strange and Azinger seemed to represent a cabal pitched against Ballesteros and Europe. But throw just half a dozen competitive exponents of something, anything, into a room and sparks fly, regardless of nationhood or other affiliations. None of these men advanced by paying too much attention to others, unless it was in their interests. It made for great TV. Every year the Masters felt like Seve against the field, and himself. The other villain was, of course, Seve's own desire to win, allied with inner demons, perceptions of slights and conspiracies, all the while targeting high standards for his own golf. It could be no other way.

When Ballesteros played like Seve, his game and entire demeanour had a special kinesis, a current of defiance and ambition. Through the shots, watching him watch the ball, he'd lean this way and that, wishing it to come back or not continue going away. He could spend whole tournaments doing this, leaving the supportive viewer in a near-perpetual state of unease. I recall it most clearly from the final holes of the Masters in 1987, a form of non-life-threatening torture. Seve made his own play and capabilities, his own hopes and villains of many a piece.

In the movies, villains seem to play dirty, by a different set of rules, push the boundaries of fairness or appear outrightly dastardly. In golf this was not the case, but the US players came from such a different place, such a different culture and golfing set-up that they were in sharp contrast to the artistry of Seve or the workmanlike-yet-natural abilities of, say, Nick Faldo, or the pure natural skills of a Sandy Lyle. Golf in the US seemed to produce golfers like the Evil Empire in the Star Wars films had stormtroopers, a never-ending stream of playalikes. They were great, great players and to see them and watch them play in person was exciting. I particularly loved the height they hit their full irons and tee shots, so grand and impressive. They played a different game and appeared to have it all. Their gilded golfing lifestyles were not what the everyman saw in Scotland, the rest of the UK and Spain. Theirs was a sense of entitlement. Sure, they were entitled to feel they could win every week – they were the best players – but when that entitlement came to running down our hero, belittling his play and calling it luck, or resenting his arrival on their shores, it wore somewhat thin when they didn't even turn out for the Open or started to bleat about losing the Ryder Cup. The supervillains for Seve came from a different planet and held a different set of values. For Europeans, the new Americans did seem less worthy, less like winners and the players we knew of old.

We'll never know if the arrival of Seve and the European Army on the major scene stopped the USA in its tracks, but perhaps the USA was on the wane anyway. The lineage of Ouimet to Hagen, Jones to Byron Nelson, to Hogan to Palmer to Nicklaus, to Watson – and involving Johnny Miller, Lee Trevino and Tom Weiskopf – appeared to be at an end. Those great players and individuals were being replaced by money-making machines who could reap cheque after cheque but rarely had anything of interest to say. Many seemed to be just golfers, little more. I liked Fuzzy Zoeller's relaxed play and I enjoyed Curtis Strange's mild-sway action; Craig Stadler was good for the occasionally incendiary moment; and there were the class and skills of Ben Crenshaw. Once they properly materialised as major threats Fred Couples, Paul Azinger and Payne Stewart brought a mix of obscene natural talent and fire-in-the-belly golf, but that was about it from an army of post-college superstars. Greg Norman stood alongside Seve in offering real daring, that feeling of never quite knowing what would come next. Greg was the sometime abrasive hunter in the Outback compared to the temperamental Goyaesque artistry Ballesteros brought to golf's easel. Did Seve, Greg and others capitalise from an erosion of the American Golfing Empire, or did they make it crumble with their own ambition? It was probably appropriate that the first US golfer to become official #1 in the Sony World Rankings was Fred Couples, a naturally gifted player who golfed like no one else before him, or since.

Seve's powers allowed others across Europe to believe they were as good as or better than the next man or woman. This didn't just raise the quality in the biennial fight against the USA, it raised the competition and determination levels week in, week out. The signs of one of his greatest superpowers – belief – manifested themselves in the Ryder Cup when, in 1983, he partnered Paul Way, then just a 21-year-old, in the foursomes and fourballs, encouraging him every step of the way. This he would take to new heights with José María Olazábal. Way, Olazábal and others were European heroes, sidekicks to the superhero of Ballesteros.

1982: The US Open, Pebble Beach

Watson Wins the US Open – Another 2-Iron

LIKE OTHERS with a true thirst for the big moments, Tom Watson could use the negatives to reinforce his play. The man with three Claret Jugs and two green jackets missed for birdie from about two feet at the 7th hole of the final round, then assured himself that was not going to be the difference between winning and losing the US Open. Elsewhere on the front nine the player felt he'd only hit one solid putt. Tom packed that all away and focused on the holes ahead. Standing on the tee at the penultimate exam he was in a tie with Jack Nicklaus, who'd already signed his scorecard and was now waiting at the last green, anticipating a play-off. After the challenger's tee shot, Jack was being congratulated by some on a win and a historic fifth national open.

The target at Pebble Beach's 17th makes the Postage Stamp at Royal Troon look welcoming. The monkey nut-shaped green almost flush with the ocean on the Monterey Peninsula sits at a 45-degree angle and, apart from the entrance to the front right, was well protected by varied traps. It wasn't unlike the puzzle faced by players at the 17th at the Old. The green was angled, protected by sand, and the only 'easy' option was to aim for the opening to putting surface and to let the ball run out somewhat, at least leaving two putts for par. Like the Road, this ocean hole became more difficult when the player fancied his chances. The short 8th at Royal Troon seemed like a sprawling, warm embrace of love and affection in comparison. At Pebble the margin for error tended to zero. Its 210 yards demanded a long iron or, as Tom's playing partner Bill Rogers hit, a 4-wood. In the US Open of 1972, Nicklaus had hit the greatest 1-iron of all time. By his own admission he almost tweaked it left, but years of golf and millions of synaptic firings allowed Jack to control his swing as it went infinitesimally awry, and he sent the ball flying right at the pin. It landed a yard from the flag and clattered the stick. It came to rest two balls away. In truth, the greatest 1-iron of all time was about an inch from leaving the already two-time champion, at Oakmont and Baltusrol, in a terrible spot beyond the green. Maybe Jack was a bit lucky. Maybe we accept golf as a game of millimetres.

The flag fluttered as Watson watched Rogers fade a 4-wood into the heart of the target, the ball coming to rest about 30 feet away, right and shy of pin high. Playing this hole running back directly towards the ocean, almost perpendicular to the famous final hole that snakes along the rugged coastline, Bill Rogers – the 1981 Open champ – was two shots off, still with a chance. Watson had already made two birdies and a par at the hole but he watched his playing partner's ball intently. He was pumped up, considering a 3-iron. He envisaged a bold shot, drawing it off the TV tower behind the middle of the green towards the flag tucked in the back-left third. But there was that breeze. Watson selected 2-iron; decision made. In Jim McKay of ABC's words, Watson was the game's greatest star seeking to win the US Open, the major that had 'so far eluded him'. Tom did not let this factoid linger. He struck a timely good shot, the sound of ball on club solid. But halfway into the ball's flight he asked for it to get down, it was drifting off the pin. Tom had drawn it a fraction too much, and although the ball came to rest about 20 feet away, it was slightly past hole high, left, and in the rough. Slightly downhill to a fast-running US Open green, with 12 feet of USGA rough to negotiate, life suddenly looked very difficult. As Tom and caddy Bruce Edwards walked, and then as Rogers putted for birdie and missed, eliminating himself from the running, ABC outlined that while Watson was a brilliant chipper and putter, getting up and down for par would be the tallest of orders.

In his favour, Tom's ball was not sitting down, otherwise he'd be in a terrible jam. Instead, it was sitting on the USGA rough, allowing for control of the line, and at least some hope of controlling pace. He would have to slide the club under the ball, lofting it on to the fringe, letting the gods do their work. It was the decisive shot of the championship, possibly. To get up and down would allow victory to come from a birdie up the last. Maybe this took some of the heat from Watson's shot. And his expectations. Tom played a delicately thrown pitch, his educated hands landing the shot just on the putting surface, sliding silkily under the ball. He'd allowed the clubhead and gravity to take over, it was all the player could do. It landed after about nine feet and hopping a bit forward on the putting surface it gathered speed, and a last-minute aiming adjustment appeared to have provided the ideal line. Watson bent his knees, an urge for the ball to not speed up too much and he stepped to the left, where he could see the direction was perfect. It went straight in. Tom, Edwards and all onlookers went crazy. In an instant it seemed as if Tom had done it again, a dramatic takedown of Nicklaus. Big Jack barely registered a response as he watched on a portable TV near the final green.

That chip by the sea wrote Tom Watson's name into the US Open record books, giving him that trophy besides two pieces of Masters Tournament silverware and three Open jugs. A month later he'd win his fourth Open Championship. He'd admit later that perhaps the luck of the chip at the 17th at Pebble meant if he dropped another 100 balls, he wouldn't come close. He'd waited for the moment, he hadn't forced a thing.

The 1984 Open Championship: Sunday

Early Golfing Notables – Mounting Tension – Missed Chances – Two Players Emerge

FOR CONTENDERS, the final round of any Open Championship is as much about fighting marauding thoughts of victory or defeat, both fatal if unchecked, as it is about playing well. Stay focused but relaxed, concentrate on routine. Championship Sunday, 22 July 1984, dawned around 5am, the warm promise of the day emerging as the Saturday had barely been extinguished. It was to be a dry, hot, sunny affair in golf's grandest arena. Set betwixt the natural dunes, grasses and rugged beauty of the West Sands and the Auld Grey Toun, the Old Course and the Open approached an enthralling climax. Tom Watson was seeking to match Harry Vardon's record tally of six wins. Playing in the game ahead, Seve was looking for his second Claret Jug.

Only the sociopathic would have slept well before such a date with sporting beatification. The denouement is a chance for the emerging and the established to etch their names into the sport's ledger of greatness. Every single player who's won a major owns a line in that great book, but the greats want to reappear time and again. Ballesteros had ended his press conference on the Saturday night by telling the throng that he'd see them on Sunday. By implication he meant as champion. The final 18 holes would be a topography of fear, doubt, confidence, control and calm, and the victor on this uneven golfing and psychological landscape would come from the top four, surely:

Ian Baker-Finch	-11
Tom Watson	-11
Seve Ballesteros	-9
Bernhard Langer	-9

The nearest chasers – Hugh Baiocchi, Lee Trevino, Lanny Wadkins – were five shots behind the Europeans and would need that elusive combination of low score and impressive collapses by all of those above to win. A play-off was not beyond the imagination, but tended to be – in the intense pressure – rare, as most players were likely to fold amidst the fog of golfing war. It envelops the sporting mind resulting in all kinds of egocentric and physiological short circuits. That fog and those singed fuses of the psyche had been most evident two years prior.

At Royal Troon in 1982 a 22-year-old American pro of less than two years, Bobby Clampett, burst off the 1st tee, shooting opening rounds of 67 and 66. Five shots ahead. After the 5th hole on the Saturday, it was seven, he was pulling away. On the long par-five 6th on the classic but understated Ayrshire links, Clampett drove into a bunker, took three to get out and virtually was never heard of again. The baton of fate was then handed to a young Zimbabwean whose sole victory had been in the 1980 Swiss Open, not an ideal grounding for major intensity. Nick Price went into the final round one behind a wounded Clampett, then found himself in front. Price opened with two birdies, one courtesy of a 40-foot putt from just off the front of the green at the 2nd. Much later, Tom Watson hit a majestic medium iron into three feet at the 11th, yielding a classy, important eagle. But the reigning US Open champion's challenge seemingly petered out with an uninspiring finish, including a bogey at the 15th and pars elsewhere. With six holes to play, the young man from southern Africa was three shots ahead. Then the mental fog crept in. Price bogeyed the uber-linksy 13th and two holes later a weak chip contributed to a double. At the tough 223-yard 17th he dropped another. Nick then needed birdie to force a play-off against the three-time winner, Watson. He pulled his final drive left on to spectator walkways, then hit a fine iron on to the green, but it ran 30 feet past the cup. Price hit a valiant putt, but it tailed away on the contours around the hole. Tom Watson was the victor again, joining the Toms Morris, Willie Park Snr, Walter Hagen and Bobby Locke as a four-time winner. He also joined the illustrious club of Trevino, Hogan, Gene Sarazen and Bobby Jones who'd won the US Open and the Open Championship in the same year. In 1982, after that Pebble Beach chip in and Nick Price faltering at Troon, maybe Tom Watson was the luckiest player in golf.

The end of the 1983 Open at Birkdale saw Watson once again make records, but that time he was the one who weathered the fog and played gritty golf, grinding down the stretch. Triumphing in 1984 would have Watson the first three-in-a-row winner since Peter Thomson, who followed Bob Ferguson and Jamie Anderson in that feat from the 1880s. Both achieved the then-Scottish Slam, winning consecutively at Musselburgh, Prestwick and the Old Course. Courtesy of having won the 1977 Open at Turnberry, then the only Open to have been played by the lighthouse, Watson had the chance to win a unique modern Scottish Slam. Could he follow his wins at Carnoustie, Turnberry, Troon and Muirfield at the Old? These venues' victors included Nicklaus, Jones, Palmer and Hogan, a disgustingly great ensemble.

The tension and unfolding of recent Opens showed what was possible and, for most, impossible. Those lying on three under, including Irwin, Couples and Faldo, probably needed a miracle. They had nothing to lose. The intensity of the leading pack would result in some great stories if any one of the players was to triumph. Watson would make history. Again and forever would he be in the firmament of the golfing Scots' imaginations. Baker-Finch would become the third Australian to have won the Open, all on the Old. The tall, slim, handsome and sweet-swinging Antipodean had already played his way into the UK golfing hearts, and aged 23 would become the second-youngest modern winner behind Seve. A Spanish win would further ingrain Ballesteros as the number-one player of his generation, someone on the road to greatness. Bernhard Langer could fire another revolution – the second modern European to win a major, and a victory over Seve would signal that golf's global battle had seeped into Northern Europe and taken on another Continental dimension. The last act of the dramaturgy would play out in a theatre around 100 yards wide and 380 yards long, bisected by Grannie Clark's Wynd. The final hole at the Old Course is the most generous in all of professional golf and by the green the Royal and Ancient clubhouse waits, judging all who pass. At the summit of the game, a win at St Andrews carries extra golfing cachet, but an Open triumph in the Auld Grey Toun is the zenith.

Good golfing weather in Scotland must never be counted upon, the conditions a series of variables intricately woven into the fabric of the links game. But when the sun does shine and a cooling breeze takes away the heat's edge, golf and life seem so much better. Seve had come to the fore in the hardpan and blissful summer of '76. And 1977 was the exemplar of great golf played in joyous conditions as Watson stared down Nicklaus. As the final act in 1984's play got under way and the leaders gathered themselves for a long day of staying focused, we lazed about. We'd had our fill of all-day golf, and while we looked forward to the conclusion of an already thrilling week we were in no rush to see more than we felt necessary. For the umpteenth time we watched the latest Bond movie video, *Octopussy*. The late return charges on the tape would be a horror story, but I didn't overly fret as we mused over Maud Adams and Kristina Wayborn. Surely winning the Open would secure a dinner date with either? Or in Seve's case, probably both. This Open was the first time Seve's mother had come to watch her son play, and she was accompanied by Carmen Botin, Seve's girlfriend. Further incentives, if needed, for Seve to pull out all the stops.

I had been staying at my uncle's, on Nelson Street, a mile and a half from the course. Here and there were signs of the town's heritage. A few streets away were Tom Morris Drive, Freddie Tait Street, Allan Robertson Drive and Bobby Jones Place. Robertson was a St Andrews hero and one of golf's first professionals, often playing challenge matches for money, with the great worthies of the day watching and betting. In *Tommy's Honor*, Kevin Cook recounts how, in 1843, Robertson became the golfing cause célèbre of the town by defeating Musselburgh's Willie Dunn Snr over ten days' golf and 20 rounds. Elsewhere Cook describes Robertson as 'loud, cocky, full of mirth and wrath that could switch places in a blank, he was a grinning, muscular elf. Not quite five and a half feet tall, Robertson had mutton-chop whiskers, an off-kilter smile, and the wrists and arms of a blacksmith. His strength and pickpocket's touch helped make him the best golfer of his generation.' Like an angry Ian Woosnam starring in a period tragi-comedy, Allan Robertson was the first player to break 80 on the Old Course, at a time when many good golfers could barely break 100 there.

Freddie Tait was also a legend. He was from the fairer side of the tracks, born in 1870 and schooled at two of the north's finest independent schools – the Edinburgh Academy, and Sedbergh School in Cumbria – and then at the Royal Military College, Sandhurst. Territorially, the British Empire was still to reach its highpoint, and Tait was at the vanguard along with legions of others. He was a prodigious golfer, winning the Amateur at Royal St George's in 1896 and at Royal Liverpool in 1898. In 1899 he lost in the final at Prestwick on the first extra hole (the 37th) to the legendary John Ball, an eight-time winner. Months later, in February 1900, Tait was dead, cut down at Koodoosberg while serving in the Black Watch in the Second Boer War. In *The Great Boer War* Sir Arthur Conan Doyle wrote, 'The Boers were seen to be assembling on the north bank. By next morning they were there in considerable numbers, and began an attack … The Boers made excellent practice with a 7-pounder mountain gun, and their rifle fire … Poor Tait, of the Black Watch, good sportsman and gallant soldier, with one wound hardly healed upon his person, was hit again. "They've got me this time" were his dying words.'

As in death, Tait was a battler in life. In 1893 he drove the green at the Old Course's 13th, then 341 yards. Everywhere in St Andrews the spirits lurked. Streets in the name of Tom Stewart (a famous club maker: some claim he made the first set of matching clubs) and James Robb (1906 Amateur champion and twice the beaten finalist) were also nearby. But this was Scotland, and to keep any enjoyment in check were memories of bygone religious days, namely John Knox Road. We turned our back on John Knox and made our way into town, determined to see our own worshipping play out its Sabbath sermon.

Walking up the long and winding way, the town teemed with people: a few locals out for a Sunday stroll and thousands of Open spectators, many on their way home to sit back and watch the golf on TV, the best way to guarantee a view of all the action. Most thoughts were around Tom, Seve, or whether the young Baker-Finch could hold on. I was dying for a Seve victory. The Spaniard was my sporting hero, and I was still smarting from a slight directly at the hands of Watson. Two years before, in 1982, while crossing the 7th fairway during a 1982 Open practice round at Troon, I came face-to-face with Tom, intersecting on the crosswalk as he came down the hole. I was so close to him he might have been expecting me. I asked him for an autograph. He fixed me with something of a smirky smile and said, 'Nope,' and continued on. For a soon-to-be 13-year-old it felt like a simple kick in the family jewels, with possibly a knee to the face as I fell. I just didn't understand why someone who seemed bestowed with greatness and modesty, and when there was practically no one around – this was the Open in 1982, before the world had monetised the shit out of everything – he would refuse me. I now realise, because he was at work, certain psychological barriers had to be in place, and no autographs during any play was probably a rule; and a good rule. To a young me, it just seemed cheap.

Almost atop the hill we passed the Whey Pat Tavern, St Andrews' oldest bar. Reputed to have dished out beer near the site since the 1100s, many of the local caddies looked as if they had been patrons ever since, only popping home a couple of times for a wash and occasional shave. Across the road, the stone-arched gate to South Street was awash with all the colours of the rainbow as fans swept in and out of the ancient thoroughfare. By the time we got down City Road, jinked into North Street and then on to Golf Place, people and anticipation were bursting in all directions. By 11am 30,000 spectators had entered the course, but it made sense for many to be departing. This was the first Open where the BBC televised all 18 holes. Two hundred BBC staff, 35 miles of cable and 20 manned cameras did the trick for the TV viewer.

Turning left at golf's most glorious intersection, rounding Golf Place on to The Links, we'd usually be offered an instant view down and across the opening and finishing stretches of the Old. Now we could just see people and grass and hear the hum of humanity, that indeterminate bubbling of quiet conversation and anxious chats on what to do next and where. Our timing was perfect, almost. The final group had just teed off, and although we'd missed that particular moment, the beginning of the end, we hustled down the street and found ourselves abreast of Tom Watson and Ian Baker-Finch as they walked towards their balls. My cousin Derek and I scuttled between the oncoming masses and stationary faithful who were watching that final procession. Almost at the end of The Links, just as it kinks, with the Swilcan Bridge to our right, we stopped. Others continued, many heading for the exits, some stretched for a view as the breeze brought hints of sea and hamburger. Baker-Finch stood out in his bright-red sweater and dark slacks alongside Watson in his white slipover and pale-blue shirt. It felt as if all 30,000 spectators had assembled. Half a mile to the south-east was a scene redolent of *Lawrence of Arabia*, the kind of thing that Wilfred Thesiger would've licked his lips at, quite literally, as sand and dust hung in the air, kicked up by the spectator movement hither and thither in the tented village, the lunchtime rush, those heading for the car parks, and others making their way to the middle of the course.

A faint, golden sheen awaited the final groups. The two players chatted, belying the pressure of the situation, and a response to it, the small talk freeing up the mind and the lungs, a pleasant diversion. If there was a time to chat, it was now, both as a way of easing oneself into the stifling heat of the moment, but also to steel oneself for the pressure to come, four hours of highs and lows where giddy emotion could often meet stomach-churning concern. The Australian had struck a nice tee shot down the right side, and had a pitching club to the hole, cut beyond the middle and slightly to the left of centre. He made a smooth, efficient pass, opening up his stance just to ease the shot forward, a crisp punch, his hands to the left of the target. The ball climbed, a combination of the pure strike, loft, and light headwind, and landed on the green. I tracked some of the flight from my position, about 100 yards away. I saw the shot land, followed by the frenzied hop of a ball sucking back, sucking some of the air out of IBF's lungs as he watched. In a replay of his last competitive wedge the night before, his shot coming back into the Valley of Sin, the ball drew back, over the edge of the burn and into the drink. Initial claps of appreciation turned to utterances of shock. Peter Alliss felt the player desperately unlucky. Baker-Finch was not the first caught by the sheer flatness of the second shot. Even I knew it was the clipped wing on the first bend of a Formula One Grand Prix, a puncture in the early stages of classic cycle race. The Aussie gave a quizzical look and quickly accepted his fate.

In contrast, while Ian had repeated his final wedge in the third round, coming up shy, the experienced Watson was not about to repeat his opening of the third round in hopping over the Swilcan. The American's approach came to rest pin high, and while he missed his birdie putt after a mildly weak effort, he opened his account with a nerve-settling, solid par. Baker-Finch showed his grit by dropping under penalty, chipping virtually stiff and starting with a bogey. Not what he wanted, but the best he could expect after getting wet. It would seem that the definition of luck or bad luck very much determined upon whose side you were on. The final skirmishes had begun. As one player retreated a touch, two advanced.

At the 1st, Lanny Wadkins, in the diamonds of his Lyle & Scott sweater, had done what he was so often good at. Saunter on to the tee, hit tee shot; saunter down fairway up to ball; hoist wedge on to green; foot and a half; stride to green; knock ball in for birdie: six under par. Was Lanston Wadkins going to tear up the Old, and the field? Dressed in the black-and-white football colours of his native West Germany and playing with

Seve, Bernhard Langer had knocked his tee shot down the left, essentially the 18th fairway, and pitched to a foot. If the steely German felt any nerves, they would have evaporated with that blow. Seve – white undershirt, white golf shirt, cream, woollen slipover, navy trousers – also started efficiently and had a ten-foot putt for birdie from left of the hole, just below pin high. Hands delicately on the putter grip, he rolled the ball nicely. It took the right lip, finishing just behind the cup. He looked around and up, turning away and almost staring across to the Road Hole. The angst of a missed opportunity. There would be few easier chances and now only 17 remained. His makeable-but-missed putt continued the theme from Saturday.

A main difficulty of the Old lies in the pin placements. One can studiously avoid bunkers all day, but that does not translate into lots of easy chances and pars. Finding sand adds an extra dimension. Bunkers from the tee at the 2nd are all hidden from view, and Cheape's has ruined many a score early on. Watson would commit the other sin – the Open Programme had pointed out that 'anyone underclubbing with his second is left with a horribly difficult approach'. For his third, Tom putted up and across fiendish undulations, plenty of break around the hole, running over six feet past. He missed the return and dropped back to ten under. Baker-Finch steadied his ship with a par. Elsewhere, Greg Norman was laying down markers. The Great White carded four birdies on the front side, birdied the 12th, and was now patrolling the shores of the leaders. He was just three behind second place, although he still faced the challenging stretch back to the town.

Watson had surrendered that early lead and was again tied with Baker-Finch. The pin at the 3rd was cut left, and in an effort to get close Langer had found the front bunker guarding the approach to this double green shared with 15. He hit a lovely bunker shot that ran about 12 feet too much, then missed.

He'd had the benefit of watching Seve's missed birdie putt, but couldn't convert, and the German had given back his opening gain. What was going through the players' minds was anyone's guess, but corralling one's thoughts was paramount, as was the processing or abeyance of frustration. How does the fighter who's lost a couple of rounds box his way back without opening himself up to a knockout punch? Patience can be bitter but the fruits of it are sweet. Ballesteros had missed three opening opportunities; Langer had made one then given it back; Baker-Finch would still be feeling the sting of that early mistake; and Watson had dropped a shot when he would've known a safe shot to the middle or right portion of the 2nd green would have delivered a par. He responded to his bogey by smashing a lovely tee shot down the middle of the 3rd. Although he had a short approach, his ball and stance were on a sharp downslope. Avoiding the pot bunker that caught Langer out, the American snipped a lovely wedge full of spin that landed at the front of the green and skidded pin high, 20 feet from the hole. As Tom settled over the putt, Bernard Gallacher watched alongside his caddy across the double green. Watson boxed for birdie, the Scotsman smiled in admiration, and the American succumbed to the wry look of someone back in control. Leader again.

At the 4th hole – Ginger Beer – Langer responded immediately to his bogey, knocking his iron from 150 yards into eight feet. Seve's frustration continued. He'd hit a lovely shot pin high, with 20 feet for a birdie. His effort slithered along the left edge of the cup, and finished behind it. He let go of his putter in frustration and put both hands behind his head, a great chance lost at the 463-yarder. Yesterday's strand continued with plenty of birdie opportunities, few taken. Still, four pars to start. Langer's chance of regaining some impetus was lost with a poor putt that started outside the hole and was never going to come back. Making their way to the Eden Estuary the players were tacking in a wind that was not always in their favour, and the 564-yard 5th was no easy birdie. Although missing chances, Ballesteros had holed a good putt for par at the 2nd, and the par five was a fair opportunity to record his first gain. He'd struck a beautiful drive down the middle and was left with a fairway wood. Off a slight downslope, open stance, he cut it beautifully, but it was as little as five yards too far left and landed short, scarpered up the slope at the front of the green, tailed left and came back down, leaving him a long pitch. Back at the 4th the leaders were creating their own problems. IBF had missed the green to the right and, described by Alex Hay, played 'a little Scottish chip-and-run', which ran seven feet long. Watson struggled and paid the price for not being up to the pin. He hit what probably seemed like a perfectly acceptable second just right of the pin, but it landed on the green, checked and broke right, leaving a tricky putt of 30 feet. He rolled it up to six feet short then missed. Already Watson had used the putter twice too often and was one over for the day, ten under. Baker-Finch also missed. Lanny Wadkins continued his casual wanderings below par. As relaxed-looking as ever the Virginian had followed his birdie at the 1st with a birdie at five followed by a sweet three at the 6th from six feet. Unfazed, coming from the rear, Wadkins could be free and easy.

Ballesteros was eyeing up his third at the par five. He had to come over a bunker and a steep slope, but had plenty of room, about 60 feet, on the baked, fast-running green. His educated hands sliced the ball from the turf. He peered over the ridge but would see nothing, instead the stirring cheers and occasional wolf whistle told him his pitch met with the approval of the Open crowd. He was ten feet beyond the pin, lying right of it as one approached from the front of the green. His easiest chance yet. Putting, the weight was good, verging on perfect and it dropped in the right side for a four. The congregation roared as Seve was quick to pick the ball out of the hole. He walked towards the side of the green where the next tee was, a gentle smile and a wave of his Anser putter in his right hand. He was ten under, joint leader. With Watson. Seconds later, Langer took, in the circumstances and for any good player, never mind an elite pro, a brutal bogey six, and dropped to eight under. He weakly missed a five-footer, seeing his ball break sharply across the hole. And Watson's putting woes continued. Most unlike him, given the last two days and the entire decade before. He found the front of the green in two at the 5th, but left his long first putt short. He missed the next narrowly on the left, the ball breaking slightly. But it was a par, and he was still in a share of the lead. He and Ballesteros remained to the fore but the heat of their putters seemed to confirm events on the greens would decide the outcome. The dynamic was the classic final-day tussle, with the mix of established stars looking to stamp their authority, the up-and-comers trying to hang in there and find their rhythm, and, sadly, the newcomer fading. Down the 6th Baker-Finch succumbed to that classic Old trick, finding a pot bunker from the tee. He only advanced halfway towards the green, then contrived to take another four shots to get up and down. Double bogey. His chances were extinguished.

* * *

As the Australian and American made their ways towards the 7th then the loop, that circle of crucial holes that might yield birdies, we sat in the stand alongside the 1st. After watching Baker-Finch zip it back into the burn we'd crossed the wynd and found a spot three quarters of the way down the stand, nearer the middle of the last hole than the green, affording us something of a view of the Road Hole approach, and our vista of the 18th was uninterrupted. It was time to let the golf come to us. It was warm and bright and the expectations and temperature rose in equal measure. Like everyone nearby, we monitored the scoring on the iconic yellow scoreboard behind the final green, and the galleries reacted as the under-par tallies undulated with bogeys and birdies. It looked like the outcome would be decided by Watson, Langer and Ballesteros. IBF was receding after three days of valiant play, and others had too much ground to make up. The prospect created some tension as we cheered and clapped all the players who came that vast final expanse, a simple thank you for being at the centre of the golfing universe for a few hours, a few days.

At the 8th, Ballesteros struck a crisp 5-iron through the breeze at the 178-yarder. The ball appeared to almost land in the hole. A seven-foot putt later he was 11 under and in front for the first time. Ten holes left and his first Open lead since 1979. Around the loop, roars were let out, matching the delight at the Spaniard's move. Seve released a gentle smile harnessed with the fixed look of determination. This kicked off an intense 45-minute spell. Langer had missed from just outside Ballesteros so stayed in the hunt but towards the periphery. Back at the closing arena, a further, louder cheer went up when the big yellow scoreboard signalled Seve's move. Wadkins made a further advance, birdying ten to get to eight under, just two behind Watson, and three behind the Kid from Spain. With a mistake from those at the top Wadkins still had a chance. Seve and Bernhard both parred the 9th, and had chances at the 10th. Langer chipped and putted for a birdie, but although Seve had a putter in his hand for his second, he three-whacked and remained only one ahead. Watson played seven to nine in regulation figures but drove the 10th, smashing a driver on to the front of the green. This time his putter did not fail him, rolling his eagle effort to a foot. Watson and Ballesteros were now tied for the lead on minus 11. Then errors reappeared. Seve misjudged his tee shot at the 11th. Opting for an 8-iron he'd underestimated the wind, coming up short on the slope at the front of the green, running down the hill back on to the fairway. He chose to putt and didn't do much better than his tee shot, coming perilously close to not making it up the slope, although by the finest of margins a bit more pace would've seen his ball slide down towards the cup. His next shaved the hole. Bogey. He fell behind Watson virtually at the instant Tom had made his birdie on the 10th. Ballesteros had made two errors in two holes. Further misery resulted as he struck a majestic 9-iron to five feet left of the stick at 12, but missed another chance. Did anyone want to win this Open Championship?

Tom made his par at the 11th then came the strangest mistake. After an easy par on Thursday, he had recorded back-to-back birdies at the 12th. Was he buoyed by this and almost holing his approach on Saturday or did his drive on to the 342-yard 10th encourage him to have a go? Was he pumped up by being in the lead? What happened to waiting patiently? Watson pulled his tee shot into the Scottish golfer's nemesis, gorse. Thick, tangly and prickly with brilliant yellow flowers, it added splashes of colour to courses throughout Scotland, Wales, Ireland and England, but any such bush was a horrid spot. He had the jaundiced look of one who'd made a rudimentary error. A shorter club from the tee would have left the American well away from the trouble and in a fine position, but it seemed Watson was chasing a birdie. A birdie and solid play down the tricky final gauntlet might have been all that was needed. The man from Missouri took a penalty drop and played an excellent pitch into around 25 feet, but the putt for par was too much. He and Seve were once again joint leaders. Six holes remained, some of the most thrilling, most watched, most revered in golf. And in the Road Hole's case, the most dangerous.

* * *

Anticipatory thousands lined the avenue to the last green; roars, shouts and the occasional collective groan marked the scoreboard changing with the frequency of a stock-market ticker. Warning: the value of your player can go up as well as down. Seve's birdie at eight, his bogey at 11; Watson's gain at ten, and his inexplicable bogey at the short and outwardly simple-but-dangerous 12th. What was going on out there, we wondered? Imaginations meandered then ran riot as tallies changed then changed again. We continued to watch some great players end their championship. First-round leader and dominant player Greg Norman had finished with a flourishing 67. His first and last rounds were stellar, but the 74s between were his undoing. He would have his time, soon, surely. Lee Trevino hit a crowd-pleasing wedge into 18, the ball biting, spinning, skipping, skidding to a halt. All were edging to the moment when there would be one victor, many losers. For almost two hours we'd watched the good, the great and the admirable play the last with easy drives and simple approaches. Some made the error of ending in the Valley of Sin, others compensated, finishing too far up the green for comfort, leaving themselves in Doug Sanders's country. Player after player holed out, the hole cut again more on the left side, like Saturday, another tantalising invitation to flirt with the horror of coming up shy and rolling back into the Valley of Sin, or going long, leaving a nasty left-to-right putt down the green that could get away if misjudged.

We'd entered into a psychological battle with a lady sitting down a row. She wasn't too keen on our pro-Seve chat. It visibly irritated her. We hypothesised on positive Spanish outcomes and negative American-related events when she eventually remonstrated, turning round with quite a snap. We were taken aback, but as teenagers we found it mainly amusing and, of course, she'd now signalled that we were getting under the skin of a Watson fan. None of the chat was nasty, it was just the enthusiasm of teenage sports fans, but it showed that with our excitement and her annoyance, anxiousness was on the prowl, even for the spectators. For these few hours Ballesteros and Watson were the epicentre of golf, that peculiar moment in sport when they existed in a singularity, all other golfing masses drawn towards them. No matter what else was going on at courses and golf clubs around the world, these two players were atop the game's highest peak, vying for supremacy. Here, strange things happen to the golfing mind. The swirling, twisting vortex of pressure and expectation infects the thinking, floods the body with adrenaline. The great players thrive in these moments which demand control, presence, and the confidence to settle their thinking, settle their bodies. The great dig deep, mining for added drive and sense of purpose. The very good players lust after going to that dark place where the demands ensure collapse and humiliation may never be far away.

After his travails turning homewards, Watson showed his mettle. The 13th is a dastardly, classic links hole. The drive feels like a shot to nothing, and the player can choose to go straight or rightish, or veer well left, allowing for more latitude on a poorly struck shot, but bringing the Coffins (those bunkers whose purpose is betrayed by their name) into play. Watson smashed his shot well left of even the fiendish traps, opening up the pin for a medium-iron attack. The flag was cut right, guarded, especially from a straight tee shot, by Hole O'Cross bunker. With the breeze now straight into his face, the defending champion and man-on-the-verge-of-further-Open-greatness striped his iron into ten feet. It was majestic on any day, and Watson knew it as he gave a subtle smile to caddy Alfie Fyles. Seve was also galvanising himself, concentration wrought across his Latin features beaming in the sun. This was now a fight, one mistake could mean lasting damage. The 14th has been the scene of many a calamity. At 567 yards its name shows little imagination beyond that Scots trait for saying it as one sees it – Long Hole. With dynamic poise Seve took his stance, steady, then launched himself through the shot. He gave it a tentative look as it catapulted towards the Beardies; however, it was perfect, running past the three small bunkers that formed the latter part of the sandy quartet. Ballesteros then flung himself into his second, the flat-out power familiar from 1979. He now lay beyond Hell bunker, about 70 yards from the pin. The Spaniard flighted a lovely wedge up into the breeze that landed then sat swiftly 12 feet left of the hole. Langer had played down the 5th fairway, played a long iron for his second, then an iron into the same distance away as Seve, but right of the cup.

The two protagonists were now in unison, a hole apart. Watson eyed up his putt at 13 and knocked a beautifully paced ball, that never looked anywhere else, into the heart of the hole; Ballesteros rattled in his birdie putt at 14. As he retrieved his ball he acknowledged the crowd with a look of piercing concentration, right hand meeting the gallery's applause. Scotland's dream scenario, two adopted golfing sons were going at it, toe-to-toe. As Watson threw a hook, Ballesteros jabbed ferociously at the American's ribcage. Walking from the hole a handsome smile shot across Ballesteros's face, acknowledging the appreciation of Langer's caddy, Peter Coleman, who, in the early 1980s, had spent time looping for the Spaniard. Seve seemed at ease, confident. There was little tension in his form or demeanour. Langer made a gallant try at his birdie but the ball ran stiffly past the left side. The two leaders were back to 11 under par, trending one better than the lowest-ever mark at St Andrews, Kel Nagle's 278 in 1960.

Playing the 16th, as the wind gathered a touch and early shadowing appeared, Seve now appeared in his talismanic navy Slazenger sweater, the white slipover discarded as his Spanish blood demanded a bit more heat in the late Scottish afternoon. Ballesteros had safely parred the 15th and at 16 he took the pro's line once more, going further left than the Principal's Nose and taking out of play Deacon Sime bunker. Negotiating Wig bunker guarding the flag, Seve hit a sweet approach into the green and was around 12 feet from the target, facing a putt of relative straightness. He struck it purely and it rolled towards the hole. And it rolled. And it rolled. And it came to a halt on the edge, tantalisingly close to a birdie and a one-shot lead. A rueful Seve made a playful swipe at the ball, bemoaning the slight lack of pace. As Seve parred, Watson hit a lovely 30-foot putt at the 15th, then tapped in for a par. And now the players and the spectators had reached the denouement, the holes of the Old and the part of the Open where the winner would be decided. Watson had the 16th to negotiate while Seve eyed up the forbidding Road Hole. At the 18th Wadkins and Torrance had already recorded Sunday birdies, as had Fred Couples. In his first visit to the Old he'd notched up a par, two birdies and an eagle at the final hole. In the next 45 minutes anything could happen.

The 17th was the ultimate puzzle, the golfing senses under siege as the player contemplates the blind drive coupled with the angle of attack to the green. The right-handed golfing body repels at the thought of the fade ideally needed off the tee, and a draw into the green. The entirety of the golfer prefers a shot moving away from the trouble off the tee and, if anything, a gentle fade or baby draw on to the top tier of the green. Not a hole for the faint of heart. Ben Crenshaw had remarked that one reason it was the world's best par four was because it was a par five. The possibilities were almost endless on this stretch of links land, great shots usually rewarded, poor ones almost always punished. The Spaniard surveyed the 461-yard challenge. The educated onlooker would imagine Seve must at least be trying to eradicate notions and feelings of the first three days. How could he not be, he'd struggled most desperately for a player of his calibre and in 1978 the hole had been the difference between a run at the title and the undoing of lots of nice work over 68 other holes. A four today would give nothing away. Seve pulled the driver. He looked at ease with the club in his hands, testing its weight, feeling the shot. This was an extreme golfing scenario, managing tempo and expectations of the tee shot at the Road Hole while leading the Open. It was perhaps the ultimate golfing scenario, the chasm between glory and disaster. Stomach churning for the uninitiated. The Spaniard took his stance, looked across the corner of the sheds at the Old Course Hotel, pulled his left trouser leg up a tad and swung swiftly – perhaps a bit too swiftly – but the ball was off and flying through the dry, warm Fife air. It seemed he'd hung the ball a bit left of his intended line. Driver in hand, right hand dangling as he walked back, Seve stepped to the left, watching, mildly demanding a small correction in the ball's flight. He gazed down and over the edge of the sheds. 'Probably okay,' said Peter Alliss. Ballesteros had taken a cautious route, but he was safely in play.

Contrastingly, and still with the chance of a win if he could net the rarest of birds, Langer swiped his tee shot down the right side, his flat swing delivering the ball into the perfect position. Ballesteros looked to have set himself up for the chance of a par. The German had set himself up for the chance of a birdie. Sitting in the stand abeam the final stretch we gazed towards the Road Hole and for the first time in three hours we saw again the main actors' entourage. Having tracked the scores up to now, we could see a few groups of inside-the-ropers walking up the 17th. I felt a palpable sense of tension as our hero would soon appear, chased by Langer, challenged by Watson. We'd soon be ringside. The big yellow scoreboard told us Seve Ballesteros and Tom Watson were deadlocked.

Now, perhaps, some small luck was in play. Ballesteros's ball had come to rest in almost the same position as Saturday's blow from the 17th tee. In turn that drive had been similar to Friday's, and not too different from Thursday's. A 4-iron and two 6-irons had so far delivered three single-putt bogeys, but while the line and type of shot were telegraphed, the lie would determine the player's options. In theory the play was obvious and the player could choose to draw strength from the fact the approach was similar to the final iron into the 18th at Lytham in 1979 – from the left to a pin well protected, in this case by the contours of the green and the Road bunker, with the road protecting a shot that went too far. The pin was tantalising but the guts of the green were the target. As he walked to the ball Seve would know much would boil down to the lie, how the ball was specifically sitting and what grass encircled it.

In 1978, the Golden Bear had hit a 9-iron from 134 yards at the 16th to record a birdie and take the lead after New Zealand's Simon Owen had been unlucky with a flier and overshot that green, resulting in bogey. The 17th hole that year was Jack Nicklaus at his measured best. He took 3-wood from the tee and found the middle of the fairway. With the pin tucked left of centre, protected by the bunker, Nicklaus's thoughts were make par and let the others follow. Jack felt par was paramount. The modern player's equipment and control might see this approach as over-cautious but Nicklaus's opting for a 6-iron, allowing him to hit up to the green in a way he felt took the bunker almost totally out of play, took real balls. He would two-putt from 60 feet. In *Jack Nicklaus: My Most Memorable Shots in the Majors* he preached 'cool analysis' – in the heat of a major afternoon! – and the section on this shot, one of just over 50 to make the book, was entitled 'Play for Your Score, Not Your Ego'. Let's not force things, but let everything arrive at its own moment, in its own peculiar manner, fusing its rhythm with ours. Back on the tee, Watson waited. Seve eyed up his second. Langer was ideal down the right and went first, hitting a high cut he spun out of early, perhaps a reaction to the cavernous trap. The ball looked destined for the tarmac, but it checked and sat abruptly. We heard the gallery's appreciation but in the sunny haze and from the stand at the 1st could not make out where Bernhard had finished. Then it was Seve to go. Only the insanely reckless would attack the pin or think of going near it. The Spaniard pondered. We could see on the scoreboard that Watson had completed the 16th: in par. This was Hemingway's *Death in the Afternoon*, playing out the final act. Who was the bull, who the matador? Ballesteros pulled another mid-iron from the bag, took his upright position over the ball and prepared. The lie was fine – that's all it was, fine – but on TV the ball could not be seen, meaning there must be complete accuracy of strike to propel the shot up and away squarely to the well-protected target. How much of 1978 was in his head and had to be shaken off? How much of the first three rounds in 1984 was lurking, seeking to distort the thinking, and had to be dismissed? It could all have been there, but the greatest players know how to deal with these challenges.

With a slightly more upright swing than usual, the better to attack while minimising the grass between clubhead and ball, reducing the chance of a flier, Seve struck a controlled 200-yard 6-iron, making a full swing but focused on the strike, delivering the clubhead into the back of the ball, exploding through and launching it into the late-afternoon ether. He held the shot up, fighting against it turning over as a result of the lie or the tension of the moment. When the club hit the ball all four days' efforts could evaporate in an instant. The clean blow was heard to those nearby, the ball flew high and true. Perhaps Seve had opened the clubface a bit, adding height to counter any shot catapulted by grass on the clubface. The shot landed directly on line for the middle right of the green, bounced and hopped up on to the putting surface, almost too far. It came to rest beyond the pin high, almost at the peak of the slight slope at the top of the green. From our seats at 18 we heard some gasps, a sharp collective intake of breath and then a rumbling roar of approval as our hero's shot came to rest. We could not see it but the response from the crowd told us that most certainly Seve had not repeated the mistakes and misjudgements of previous rounds, he was on the green, we hoped. The crowds cheered and whistled, clapped and shouted and we could hear loud ripples flowing from the Road Hole. On TV, BBC commentator Bruce Critchley called it marvellous, a great shot under the gun.

Poise and control. Pure Ballesteros. Now Watson could drive. His powerful swing rifled the ball from the tee peg, but it was right, possibly flirting with the boundary. The defending champion stood back, both arms raised, asking the question, part hope, part anxiety. His ball was struck on the perfect line, but cutting. However, belying conventional wisdom, there is plenty of room on the right for the longer player, and Watson had clocked it. The ball came to rest well down the fairway. 'Position A+'. Tom Watson had set himself the perfect test coming into the green. As the final 30 minutes of the Open approached it looked like a busy, intricate ballet from faraway, or a large film set where all the extras were moving *en masse* into their next positions as the key players sought out the marks from where they'd shoot the next scene. Watson was walking round the corner at the Road Hole, making his way to his perfect drive, as Langer eyed up his 55-foot putt along almost the same line as Seve's but which, if holed, would throw the Spanish-American dogfight into utter disarray.

If Langer birdied, the shock to the top of the leaderboard and spectator expectations would be thunderous, rocking the foundations of a Spanish or a US champion, undermining three days of news and TV reporting. Langer had truly been given a bit part by the scriptwriters, but now he had a chance to change the ending. Studious as ever, the German surveyed his putt. He sweetly rolled the ball and as it made its way to the hole Seve walked to his ball, taking in Bernhard's pace and direction. It passed Seve's marker by a few feet and made its way to the cup, hanging left of the target, the break left slowing as it approached the slope of the bunker. The ball came to a halt two feet away. Langer would get his four. It was good fortune – pure luck? – for Seve that the stroke had been on a similar line to the one demanded of him, and it was ideal that Langer had hit a good one. Both length and line had been admirable, excellent mental data for Ballesteros to process, giving the Spaniard a great view of his own challenge.

A putt with the correct weight and even approximately the correct line would be almost stone dead, as the ball would gather towards the hole and start to correct itself as the slope of green started to level out towards Road bunker. Weight would be everything. An undercooked putt could leave a nasty breaker right to left, and a nervous, over-hit putt could leave something testy coming back. Seve's hands were delicately on the PING Anser, that trusted tool of many. He struck the putt crisply three feet right of the target, all the time tracking towards the hole. For a few seconds it looked as if it may go in, weight and line both looked excellent under the pressure of the moment, the venue and the championship. Eventually the ball came to rest three rolls shy and would likely have missed a few millimetres left.

It was a class attempt as the tension rose and now rested squarely on Watson's shoulders. He still had half of the 17th's conundrum to solve. Ballesteros had passed his test but the American was on the verge of redefining the modern Open. We watched Seve and Langer walk on to the 72nd tee, the German's bright-red sweater standing out, allowing us from the stand up the final stretch to pick out Ballesteros as he blended into the darkening shades of the worshipping multitudes. Minutes later Ballesteros had clocked a beautiful drive.

* * *

Seve had played 274 shots since lunchtime on Thursday. It was now late afternoon, minutes before six o'clock on Open Championship Sunday. The delirium of the crowds was founded on intense expectation. For Ballesteros a few more shots would be the difference between a win and a loss, four majors and three majors. Another Claret Jug was within reach. Or perhaps Tom Watson, as he eyed up his second to the 17th hole on the Old Course, could already taste the full-blooded Bordeaux as it glugged into his sixth jug.

The Spaniard walked tall and upright across the Swilcan Bridge, his long arms and big hands relaxed at his side, a confidence in his step. The calm seemed to belie the opportunity he faced. Opportunity also faced the American: winning an Open Championship on the Old Course at St Andrews, golf's primal playing field. As they marched up the 18th towards his tee shot, Seve told caddy Nick DePaul that if they made birdie, the championship would be theirs. Ballesteros sensed *el destino. Everything you can imagine is real.*

* * *

Tom Watson was around 190 yards out and had a variation on the Nicklaus-Ballesteros dilemma to consider. He pondered his options. Patience and quick decision-making did not seem obvious bedfellows, but since 1975 Watson had married the two beautifully, winning eight majors of three different flavours. The PGA Championship had eluded him, coming closest courtesy of a play-off loss to John Mahaffey at Oakmont in 1978. There seemed to be some indecision at St Andrews as Watson toyed with the clubs in his bag, fingering a few sticks that could deliver the right shot to the green. On his line probably everything from a long iron to a 7-iron could feel correct, depending on the shape and power of the shot, and how the player sought to use or counter the breeze.

Spectators could almost sense Tom conjuring with Henry Longhurst's view of the Old's lingering challenge – *what exactly is it that I am trying to do?* Surely the minimum was to knock the ball on to the front part of the green, letting nature take its course, while avoiding the fate of Road bunker, leaving two solid putts for par. Two days prior, Tom had three-putted from long range, and maybe there was a compulsion to manage the shot closer than a lengthy two jab. Eventually he pulled an iron and settled on it. A 2-iron, the club that had been the foundation of major denouements at Carnoustie, Pebble Beach and Royal Birkdale. It did seem like an awful lot of stick for the terrain and the moment's adrenal nature. It seemed the oddest of choices. Commentators were also bemused, Peter Alliss suggesting indecision as Watson backed off his shot and returned to his bag.

Or was he, as Jack Newton suggested, waiting for the cheers for Ballesteros to subside as the Spaniard prowled the final fairway? Sitting in the stand, Derek and I roared on Seve. We had waited three hours and had been gifted. Given we were at St Andrews, a small place on Scotland's east coast, it was almost difficult to take in, to appreciate the sense of luck and privilege. For thousands of golfers Seve Ballesteros was their Muhammad Ali, Bjorn Borg, Pelé, Joe Montana, men at the peak of their sports who grabbed headlines as well as titles. We considered them brave, entertaining, they were revered. It was hard to imagine a more perfect ending as the evening sun showered the scene and Seve walked up that final, golden parade towards his ball. He'd powered a 3-wood up the middle, giving him plenty of club through the breeze and up to the green; this wasn't the time to be cute or inventive, artistic or magical.

Tom Watson then made a possibly fatal error. He would later say he tried to hold the shot up into the breeze; but surely it was at least two clubs too many for that one moment in space and time? His second shot sailed over the front section of the putting surface, over the main plateau, totally cleared the green and almost came to earth directly on the tarmac behind it. Anywhere around 25 yards shorter would have worked for Watson, depending on the ball's trajectory and pace. Instead, it bounced on the dirt path just before it hopped, caromed, skittered, shuddered and came to rest in a near-calamitous proposition at the base of the dyke, a yard away from the stone, having clattered into the bottom of the wall almost as it met the ground. We peered through the dusty haze, the gasps and groans signalling all was not well, the gallery reaction the opposite of what we sensed from Seve's second shot into the penultimate target. We couldn't detect quite what had become of Tom's approach. A fellow spectator with binoculars suggested he was on the road. Our expectations for Seve spiked, very quickly tempered with the knowledge that Tom Watson was the greatest exponent of Open golf in modern times.

We were in that typical spectating mindset, glorious hope underscored with enervating stress and worry. There was much to-ing and fro-ing at the Road Hole as marshals, media and officials scuttled around while spectators at the wall peered over it to review the grim resting place for the American's approach. Unlike the practice round of Tuesday, the tarmacadam had not been kind to Watson, and now the thousands of spectators up most of the final and first holes were watching Seve. The stands were packed. Behind the green and alongside the 1st fairway spectators were jammed in between the stands and fence about ten deep. The road up the right side of the 18th was decorated with the eager, the impassioned and, occasionally, the sozzled after some long summer hours in the beer tent. Spectators watched from roofs and balconies of the various St Andrews golf clubs and apartments, and the Rusacks hotel was mobbed with onlookers. Seve had about 100 yards to the pin, the flag cut front-ish and left of centre on the large canted green sweeping from the right, the target protected once more by the Valley of Sin. The biggest danger for any player in this position would be a breakdown of routine and thinking. Ballesteros was almost directly in front of us, on the fairway below, about 120 yards away. Tension hung in the air. He clipped a wedge, turning through the shot, neatly and squarely at the target, kicking up the grassy powder of the ever-drying turf. His only concession to the circumstances was to step to the side to avoid the small dust cloud.

* * *

As I write, it's not entirely by chance that on my wall hangs a Getty Images' photo of this precise moment. It's not colour. Instead, it's more grey-white-and-greyer, with one exception. Almost in the middle of the image, Ballesteros appears darkly resplendent like a dangerous man in black, his navy sweater and trousers rendered sable-like, topped by his white shirt and white shoes. The shot is framed at the top by a Search crane and below that and to its sides thousands watch. The heads of the fans are like small beads but it's clear that while many in the stands and by the wall are looking down the 17th at Watson, many, many are taking the opportunity to watch Ballesteros hit up to final green. Seve has punched his wedge, the follow-through is abbreviated, hands and arms to the left and through the ball, grip aligned with the middle of his torso. Nick DePaul looks at the shot heading towards the green and in the fractional milliseconds after the strike Seve looks up intently, poised perfectly it seems, as a million dusty golden sand particles rise in the breeze like the thinnest of muslin sheers, momentarily obscuring the view of the player. The shot was the culmination of 20 years of golf. Seve's ceaseless stream began with thousands and thousands of shots hit on the beaches of Cantabria, leading to this one moment upon the firm links' turf of Fife, Scotland.

* * *

Attacking and out through the shot Seve hops to his right to avoid the dust and to keep his eye on the ball. The approach lands 20 feet shy of the hole, hops forward about five feet and swiftly comes to a halt. Only four players remain, two with a chance of victory, and the crowd claps and shouts, stands and cheers their praises for Ballesteros's shot and to mark the Spaniard's and the German's procession. Europe was united as the thousands raucously commended and encouraged the exploits of Seve and Langer. As the Bavarian hit his final approach shot a Glaswegian female was heard to shout, 'Come on, Bern'ard.' Those thousands would also be delighted to see Watson win, as the quality of the competitive spirit was what mattered, what galvanised all as golf lovers and fans of sport played at a level beyond the ken of mortals. Seve received the adulation of the throng behind the final arena, gently waving his right hand, then left, again and again, a determined smile on his face. Having sat for hours watching player after player putt out and finish their Open, we had a sense of what Seve faced, what lay between him and possible triumph. As Ballesteros and Bernhard made their way to the final green, we stared back down to the wall at the 17th.

Watson analysed his shot, choosing one club and then another, testing his thoughts and motions against the limited room between ball and wall. In 1926, while playing the hole as part of the USA Walker Cup team, the 1913 US Open champion, Francis Ouimet, found himself in a similar position. He had a bit more room to play with and rifled the ball on to the wall, finding the green. Tom did not have that luxury, and this was stroke play. He barely had a backswing so the play was almost a feverish stab, the sort of shot that often goes too far but that can travel almost nowhere if not committed to. A phalanx of photographers ran perpendicular to the dyke, forming a near-orderly line to the player's right. Could Watson produce more major 17th-hole chipping magic, was that in his mind? Anything within ten feet would be the greatest of tricks. He optioned various clubs, back and forth with his caddie. The type of shot was not in question, but the combination of loft and punch was key if the ball was to get the tiniest bit of airtime and get on its way efficiently. Once he'd chosen, what looked like a 9-iron, Tom took half a dozen swings, testing the stroke, the angle of attack, the length of an albeit very short and jabby backswing. Bruce Critchley described the perfect shot, but surely that was a fantasy – across the road and path, up the bank, then trickling, rolling down to the hole. Like a truck attempting a handbrake turn on black ice. The slope up to the green ran at about a 60-degree angle, although the commentator did earlier recognise Watson needed a miracle to get up and down. The miracle required was not Biblical but the odds, in this cauldron and at this stage in the championship, were not in the holder's favour. After steadily getting his mind in gear, Watson executed the quick, positive jab required, and did hit a good shot. The ball hurried up the bank, ran past the pin and broke up the slope at the bunker, tending towards the town, its final resting place about 25 feet beyond and to the right of the hole from his angle. Tom would face a putt that would break off the bunker, make its way up the gentle slope to the pin and fall to the right. A double breaker, over and down a gentle slope and then up another to the hole. He turned his attention to the 18th.

I won't forget the shroud of hushed anticipation that enveloped Seve. The scene had gone from controlled pandemonium, people scurrying hither and yon, to a pregnant calm, masses focused on the final green. Seve stalked his line, studied the hole, steadied himself. It was a putt the length of which for most of Saturday and some of Sunday he'd missed, watching them slip past the hole by a hair or two. Over the ball, putter toe in the air: a single practice stroke, and then … as the putt rolled, we could see from the faraway stand the pace was about correct, instinctively knowing where the hole was and when a ball should disappear. It tracked smoothly across the putting surface as we all waited for the moment of truth. The small white sphere began to slow and appeared to stall. To stop. From the stand, thousands took a deep breath. For the briefest of perceptible moments, the ball seemed to halt, to ponder whether or not to accede to the powers of gravity, to perhaps rewrite the laws of physics at that very instant.

This was all two or three seconds of action, the putt's journey. Did Ballesteros have the will to make something happen? Did the energy of the crowd's anticipation emit waves of hope? We'd sat and watched putts all afternoon and literally, for a second, the ball appeared to have come to rest. Then it fell in. Our stand erupted into panicked joy. The whole structure tectonically shifted as some roared at Seve Ballesteros while others cheered at one another; some hugged and a few sought validation of what they had just witnessed, glazed in an elixir of disbelief and astonishment, all as Seve pumped the air, elation scored across his face, part matador, part boxer, part golfer, part you, part me. A pure triumphal outburst of raw emotion, unbound relief and a complete purging of tension. I recall a riot of deep joyous emotion. Joy at Seve, at his putt, the joy of having lain in wait all afternoon and to have it so justly paid off. It was easily the most intense feeling of my young life, flooding my entire system like a narcotic. All were caught in a wave of primal human emotion and ripples of delight from the player himself. In that moment thousands upon thousands of spectators were spellbound by the brilliance of the Spaniard. Birdie. Two hundred and seventy-six shots over the four days. There was no time to think, just react, Seve had won the Open. Surely. At St Andrews. Against Tom Watson. This was action painting, genius, charisma, daring, imagination and belief all bundled into a single explosive moment. This was a million golf shots struck on the beaches of Cantabria. The turn of a couple of dimples on a golf ball created a shared experience of a kind of glorious, disbelieving outrage. As we would say in Scotland, it was magic.

Death in the Late Afternoon

Invoking the Matador Cliché – A Gift to the Camera – Seve at Turnberry

AS THE matador kills with a plunging of his sword between the bull's shoulders, so Ballesteros's winning thrust ended Watson's challenge. Coming minutes after the American's scrambling the Spaniard's putt was the deadening blow. Tom, with the weight of history, pride and expectation on his back was reliant on holing out for eagle at the last to force a next-day 18-hole play-off and another chance to win, as he had at Carnoustie in 1975, in extra time. Just after Seve's birdie at the last, Watson missed his par attempt at the Road, defeated by the subtle break from the remnants of the slope behind the bunker. The Open was closed.

Almost two years later my life intersected with that Sunday in 1984. My school reached the 1986 final of a Golf Foundation event to be held at the Old Course, with lunch in the R&A clubhouse afterwards. Post a filling repast we were given a tour, and in the secretary's office we looked out from the balcony and through the binoculars so powerful you could almost see the underwear of the players putting out on the double green by the Eden. As others surveyed the links, some milled about, and I turned my attention to a table, noticing a photo album. I opened it. There was Seve. Navy sweater, white shirt. He'd been photographed from the top of the stairs. Standing near the bottom, he held up the Claret Jug, surrounded by members and officials, every single one of them delighted with their winner. Ballesteros's voltaic smile beamed, shining across golf and its future.

Ballesteros was a gift to the lens, a tempest with sharp lines and a comportment that suggested an inner desire and restlessness. Dashing looks and primary colours delineated him, all reflected in David Cannon's introduction to his book of photos, *Severiano Ballesteros* (1986, with an update and reboot in 2021). Cannon recounts how, in the Spanish Open at La Manga, he saw a young unknown full of fire who, at one point, admonished *The Guardian*'s golf correspondent, Pat Ward-Thomas, 'You mustn't talk when we play!' It was, said Cannon, 'A composure and a self-assurance that this youth, without achievement or experience, really had no right to possess.' Seve was born for golf, his belief system based on almost zero competition beyond his own headspace. He had developed his power and vision without feeling the shock of stroke-play losses and head-to-head match-play defeats. His golfing education had the purity of play. He didn't measure himself against anything but his own grit, his own vision. Of course, this was flawed. All of us are flawed. How much of his single-mindedness led to unrealistic reactions to authority or decisions that went against him? How much of his fire and ire was the intense pride of a Spaniard? Seve could appear narrow-minded, unflinching, even selfish, but it was underwritten by a single thing – the desire to play golf.

The cover of the Dave Cannon book features a post-action shot. Seve holds a 6-iron almost vertically, watching the ball with intensity; his coal-black hair rests neatly; a pair of charcoal grey trousers topped with a pale-blue Slazenger golf shirt with a narrow stripe. He is absorbed in the outcome of his 6-iron. His eyes and the lean to the right suggest the shot has gone slightly left. The close observer would note the overlapping grip and the delicate balance of the right hand on the club, perhaps a nod to the fact that Seve saw golf as a right-sided game. The closest observer would note the club is forged, muscle-backed, and has that piece of lead tape affixed to the top of the toe, controlling shots tending to the left. The book features Seve in many moments so typical – annoyed, delighted, disappointed – and at every point in the swing. It's an archive of golfing fluidity and power. Page 15 features a near-symmetrical shot of the Swilcan Bridge, the Old Course Hotel out of focus in the background as Seve strides across the burn, caddy Nick DePaul behind, Bernhard Langer trailing. The world knows what happened next. Another photo, from the 1985 Masters, has Seve in head-to-toe mid-blue, white leather golf shoes and a white, Masters visor. He's right at the very end of his follow-through, position held at the top of the swing, almost straining. A blurred crowd of Augusta patrons watches. The colours of the photo delight my eyes but, as a golfing document, it is meaningless aside from its subject.

Phil Sheldon's book, *Seve* (1986), also hallmarks the classic Seve swing positions, the highs and the lows, and the Spaniard's foes. In an innocuous photo on the back cover Ballesteros is shown through impact on his tee shot at the iconic 9th at Turnberry, lighthouse in the background. Playing partner Roger Chapman and his caddy look on. It was the final day of the 1986 Open and Seve and Chapman were both well off the pace. The Spaniard had carded 76, 75, 73 to find himself 13 shots adrift of an indefatigable Greg Norman. Amazingly, Turnberry was the third major of the year on which Norman had led by the end of Saturday night. At Augusta National and the Shinnecock Hills US Open he had capitulated. At Inverness, Ohio, he would do the same in the PGA Championship, the undoing of his hopes a holed bunker shot by Bob Tway on the final hole. At the Ayrshire links in 1986 Norman would dominate, winning his first major.

I'd gone down to the Open early on that final Sunday in 1986, catching a bit of golf before heading home to watch the unfolding on TV. I recall little of what I witnessed – I cannot even recall who I was with – but for a few minutes I stood at the 6th green, then the long-short Tappie Toorie at 222 yards, and watched Seve hole out for par. He was already two under for the day and striding off the green. Ballesteros appeared to be a golfer on a quest. He walked right past me, fleet of foot, directly to the next tee. Perhaps he was in a hurry to get home or to the next event: he could not win, and this was just months after the bruising 1986 Masters Tournament and Nicklaus's greatest major Sunday of all time. An impatience marked Severiano. In navy Slazenger sweater and bright-red trousers, it was unmistakeably my hero. He marched on to the 7th tee, pegged up his ball, looked down the fairway and pulled his driver from the bag, all in one long, single motion. He did not pause, took his stance almost immediately, and after a slight tug on his left trouser leg and a look at his target made a swing that was about two things and two things only: power and unwavering confidence. The white ball fizzed through the Scottish summer air against the light-blue backdrop, fading about a yard and a half as it descended into the valleyed fairway. I had almost the same view as Ballesteros, standing as I was about four yards away. I watched every inch of the flight. If Seve had been aiming for a target the size of a matador's cape, the *muleta*, the ball would have come to rest smack in its centre, right in the middle of the fairway, just through the corner of the dogleg, affording the perfect approach over 200 yards up to the green.

It was a mesmerising fusion of the meaningless and the intense. He could have hit any shot he wanted. It would not be recorded or commented upon for prosperity, it would not be captured, sold, poured or fawned over. It was just another golf shot at another major. As a golfing document it is meaningless, aside from its subject. It was not in the heat of any battle, it was not seen on TV by millions, it was a shot to nothing. In spite of its nothingness, it was executed *perfectly* with an absolute minimum of fuss. It was glorious. Every time I play that hole, I see Seve's ball in the air and where it rested. If Seve had pulled it into the trouble left, or come off it and left a longer shot in, it would have made no difference. Maybe he was proving a point. He'd complained the course was too difficult and it had been splashed across the papers. The course wasn't too difficult on that day. He birdied the 7th from that drive and, although he bogeyed the 9th, gains at 10, 14, 16 and 17 saw him tap in from 18 inches at the last for a 64. Seve waved to the crowds and threw his ball to them, smiling. Peter Alliss, on the BBC, said, 'And that is one of the great rounds.' It was a beautiful habit of Ballesteros's – turning the quotidian into something special. Sometimes it was just a shot, or a look, or a moment, or a round put together in otherwise ordinary circumstances that stuck in the mind. Once seen in full flight, never forgotten.

Shades of Augusta, Real Pedreña's 6th hole

Real Pedreña's 17th, 1st, 2nd and 4th greens

Real Pedreña's 3rd hole

Real Pedreña's 2nd hole

Back to Real Pedreña's 5th green, and the church where Seve's funeral service took place

Real Pedreña's putting green across to Santander

Montage in the Salón Seve Ballesteros, Real Pedreña clubhouse

Engraved key to Seve montage

Seve's honours board

Seve's house atop the hill

Seve chatting on 1st tee at San Roque

Seve's opening drive at San Roque

Seve at a corporate day, on Royal Troon, trying to find his swing and test it on a links for the '84 Open

Seve mobbed by fans at a tournament in the late 1980s

Seve's house

Lush landscape behind Santander

Somo and Santander ferry leaves Pedreña

Rowing photo in Bar Paqui, Pedreña

Pedreña rowing club mural

A beautiful villa on the main drag displays the importance of rowing to Pedreña

ONE-CLUB CHALLENGE

'I know there is no straight road
No straight road in this world
Only a giant labyrinth
Of intersecting crossroads'

Federico García Lorca

1984: The New Course, St Andrews

Seve Again – The Power of Heroes – Ballesteros's Legacy

IT'S HARD to adequately explain what being there to see Seve Ballesteros's final putt in 1984 means for me. It means a lot to others, too. I've met them, they've told me. Of all the other places I might have been, I was all afternoon waiting for the finale. It was an encounter with sporting greatness, a vision of euphoric madness and complete abandon, thousands of people united in celebration of a denouement that, looking back, barely seems plottable in a credible way. Seve's putt seemed to have missed. Stayed out. Rested. Stopped. Was it the intake of breath from the galleries down the 1st, the elemental power of the sportsman himself, or was it the slow astronomical turn of the earth that shifted one more dimple towards the centre of the cup, creating a catastrophic imbalance, allowing the ball to drop? Sometimes things are just meant to be.

The late US sportswriter Frank Deford wrote, 'Athletes are the touchstones of our memory,' echoing John McPhee. I have replayed those Seve moments thousands of times in my head. The hot glow of joy I feel goes beyond the norm. A trace of that putt and Ballesteros's reaction rushes through my veins, floods my system. It makes me feel better. For years I had a 30-minute walk to work, and usually I would listen to some music as I considered my first meeting of the day or a sticky problem to be resolved. When certain songs came on, I could imagine Seve preparing for a shot before flying into it with everything, every ounce of him part of the strike. These images of Seve, crystallised in my mind, made me feel good, lifted me, readied me for the day. It doesn't rest entirely easy saying that as a grown man, but these memories and our heroes aren't about men. Or women. They are about boys and girls and the dreams we had as children and teenagers. Sporting heroes represent the dream or some kind of ideal life. How things might have been or could be in some alternative universe. Many others there that day in 1984 have similar feelings for that final moment, how it turned them to golf, committed them to a social and playing life on and around the fairways, how Seve became *their* hero.

One writer's stream is another's giant labyrinth. About 40 hours after Ballesteros's final putt and commiserations with Tom Watson at the prize-giving, my stream once more flowed. I don't recall anything special about my 15th birthday on the Monday, and no doubt warm greetings would appear when I got back home from my Open week, but after six days watching the world's best it was our turn to play, and we headed for the New Course. We did it again on the Tuesday on another sunny day as the heat, for Scotland, was rising again. We walked down The Links and cut across the 1st of the Old, the course still closed to the public. As we headed towards the New there was Severiano Ballesteros. Right in front of us. And Nick Faldo. And Isao Aoki. Trevino, too. And Greg Norman. Hal Sutton, as well. It would be impossible now without the deepest of pockets, this calibre of golfer having a fun knockabout for the Epson Trophy one-club challenge for BBC Television. It was a time of sporting innocence. In papers the next day, Seve said, 'This is good for my game. It makes you think your way round the course more.'

Hard to believe we didn't stop for long. The last few days had left us hungry to exercise our own skills. Having stopped for a few minutes to take in a scene that included two of the most talented players to ever wield every golf club in the bag, we walked over to the New Course, waited our turn and played away. Odd that we did not linger and soak up the one-club play for a few hours, but this was the impact of sporting heroes and watching others in the furnace of world-class competition, you wanted to try it for yourself, find your own bit of magic, or sense something those players might sense, might know. One shot from my rounds on the New I still recall. A beautifully struck John Letters 3-wood into about 15 feet at the 221-yard 17th, with a green that falls away to the left while protected by traps on the right. It felt like the kind of thing Seve would do – conjure up a fairway wood into close range, the ball struck from the middle of its persimmon face, its time on that face a fraction of a second longer than usual, the feel solidly resonating up the shaft, through the grip and into my hands and body. A properly good shot feels good, too. Severiano Ballesteros informed my golf for years. It was fun, it was awful. It was wayward, it was embarrassing. Sometimes it was great, the warm sensation of pulling off what felt like the impossible was a drug. One that should not be taken too often.

For years I putted with my putter toe in the air, just like the Kid from Spain. Golfers tend not to recall the terrible shots or the ones they really should not have taken on, wrecking the scorecard or giving a match-play opponent a lift at the wrong time, but other shots stick in the memory, like the bounce game 7-iron I aimed out over the railway for fun and drew the ball 35 yards into a foot. You could draw a balata ball like that. Or one-club challenges with pals, once knocking two raked 6-irons very close to the green at the course's hardest hole of around 450 yards, before bumping and running then holing out for par. The second shot Seve hit stiff to the 16th at Lytham in 1988 stayed in my bag for over 20 years. It wasn't until the advent of everyday video streaming on the internet that I realised my vision of the shot was wrong. That beautifully struck, clipped 9-iron was, in my mind's eye, more of a backfoot trap. It was a go-to I hit with a blade pitching wedge for two decades, effectively, in the main. In truth it was more Trevino or Wadkins, but in my mind's eye it was Ballesteros. I've expunged all the terrible efforts at recovery, the silly shot too big to reasonably take on, the charged first putt followed by two more. What Seve Ballesteros did for me and thousands like me was make golf exciting, it felt like a contact sport.

Even in some of the darker moments of Seve's career there was a twisted brilliance. A fan would say that. In the 1995 Ryder Cup at Oak Hill, he clashed with Tom Lehman on the Sunday. The Spaniard's game looked laboured, forced, the sense of timing and flow obviously way off; in truth, lost. His swing looked as clunky as his nasty mallet putter. Outwardly, this was not the Seve Ballesteros of yore. Inwardly, it was. He scrambled and chipped and putted and kept himself in the match. Although Lehman eventually won easily, 4 and 3, Seve never stopped trying. Seve hit not a single fairway on the way out. On the 12th hole Ballesteros invoked the rules to request Lehman replace a four-inch putt he had tapped in out of turn. Although part of his competitive make-up, this was part desperation. But he knew no other way against the USA in the Ryder Cup. His desire to win took over. Come the end, Ballesteros looked exhausted and Lehman looked haunted. Lehman felt that if anyone else had been hitting the approaches off Seve's tee shots, he – the American – would have won 8 and 7. As the American novelist Norman Mailer told us, 'Ultimately a hero is a man who would argue with the gods, and so awakens devils to contest his vision.'

This book has unashamedly focused on Seve's great times up to and around the mid-1980s. By his own admission, 1984 was his greatest moment, yet in his autobiography it's given six pages. Did it not deserve more? The rich story of Seve led entirely to that moment, but our lives are nothing more than a stream of events, people, happenings, serendipity, coincidence, luck, chance, good or bad, the collision of things in the universe, and billions of these collisions happen every day, every second. Those collisions are abundant, sometimes notable. As I was initially writing this chapter, a friend – who knew nothing of this book – sent me three articles from *The Times*. Two caught my eye: one about Ernest Hemingway, and another was by David Mamet, America's pre-eminent playwright. I had been considering Mamet in the context of Seve for years. In 1999 I saw the playwright in conversation with Jonathan Romney of *The Guardian*. Mamet took the stage, sat down, and in answering Romney's first question on how he might be remembered, responded along the lines of, *for someone like me, a career is a post-facto consideration*. An opening line so punchy it was like a jab to Romney's ribs. The playwright went on to say how an artist sets out to create, and it goes from there. There is no real target or roadmap or mission or grand unifying vision. Was this not similar to what the American writer Richard Ford said about characters, that basically we are a jumble of events and influences? Maybe characters aren't important, maybe it's the story that counts.

Ancient and modern mythmakers like to present the lives of the famous and notable as gilded existences or triumphs over adversity or insurmountable odds. No one charts a path of existence and follows it, uninterrupted. Most cannot curate their life, control their destiny, timing is everything. In 1976, Seve appeared just as global connectedness was starting to accelerate via TV, film, air travel and package holidays. In the autumn of that year, the first VHS video recorder was manufactured. The Sony Walkman appeared on 1 July 1979, 20 days before Ballesteros won his first Open. A week before he won his first Masters, in 1980, Post-it notes began sticking to meeting papers, desks, fridge doors, and drunk people's heads at parties. The Open Championship of 1984 was the first to produce an annual, an account of the week, venue, the history, notable players. The R&A's timing was perfect, golf was changing. So was the United Kingdom; it was in a dire economic state. The UK and Europe could do with a golfing hero. So could the USA, although they didn't yet realise it. As Tom Watson was dominating, Seve drew alongside him. This was all assisted by a fading of the American Golfing Empire's light.

As late as 1988 *Golf Digest* celebrated Seve's second Lytham Open win with an article, 'Super Seve', by Jerry Tarde: 'In case you didn't hear, a 31-year-old Spaniard just may have saved golf. You didn't know the game needed saving? Well, he did it by winning the British Open, playing golf the way Tyrone Power played Zorro.

'What does his victory really mean? It means everything. It means that megabucks haven't relaced megatalent and megaguts. It means that a golf tournament can be won by somebody you've heard of … It means that the great championships can still identify the great players. It means a superstar is out there somewhere.

'What we didn't have before July 18, 1988, the day he won at Lytham, was a living, breathing, practicing superstar.'

The article was four years too late. The Open in 1984 represented the turn. As Tom Watson was to fade from the majors, Seve's greatest moment represented his individual zenith, and thereafter the Ryder Cup became his stage. There he was a superstar as the Europeans won the cup and tried to save golf from the mundanity of the making-the-cut merchants who confused great scoring with great golf and entertainment. That tension, the struggle between golfing cash and golfing spectacle, continues today. In truth, Seve didn't save golf, he made it, in the 1980s, along with Tom Watson. As the latter waned and a host of collegiate golfing machines invaded the planet, every European player who pulled on a brand-new, pristine white leather glove or laced up and felt the soft embrace of a pair of Footjoy Classics drew on the power of Seve's unstinting belief in his own abilities. Yet Seve was not a genius. He saw that the skills which made him stand out were crafted for hours and days on the beaches and land of Cantabria. His parental bloodlines and his brothers undoubtedly gave him a head start, but who would ever have imagined what the boy from Pedreña might achieve. Swing timing was everything, too, along with deep powers of concentration as he practised his tricks with imperfect equipment, and Seve Ballesteros the boy started to become Seve Ballesteros the golfer. There was a will, and Seve created his way.

Looking back on his life, I find some of the most telling tributes come from his direct adversaries, men the Spaniard seemed to actively dislike at times. Paul Azinger and Curtis Strange have spoken openly about their memories of Seve. Azinger was a very tough competitor and doesn't get enough credit for birdying four of the last seven holes to make a play-off with Greg Norman and win the PGA Championship at Inverness, Toledo, Ohio, in 1993. Curtis Strange took out the 1988 and 1989 US Opens at The Country Club then Oak Hill. His game and record promised more, but we only get one chance at life. A contemporary of Strange's told me a decade ago that when Curtis and Jay Haas turned pro, having been dominant college players and team-mates at Wake Forest, they had 'absolutely no doubt they would make it on the PGA Tour. No doubt whatsoever.' All these men were the hardest of competitors who ran into Seve Ballesteros at his most unforgiving.

Seve felt he wasn't given the recognition in his home country, but Spain had been in the wilderness for 40 years and golf was a privilege. In the new Europe, the wealthy and the upper middle classes played the game. Seve benefitted from Spain's emergence, as did a wave of great Spanish golfers. What if Ballesteros had appeared five years earlier, would a 1971 Europe and UK golf scene really have been ready? Could TV and the newspapers have embraced him so? They might have embraced him, but perhaps not many would have been paying attention, he'd have been up against Trevino, Miller, Nicklaus, Player and, eventually, a younger Tom Watson. What if Seve had emerged in 1981? Perhaps Greg Norman would've become the dominant force in the majors. Seve's story is not wholly unique in terms of humble or inauspicious beginnings for a golfer of renown. Read a book on Lee Trevino's life and marvel about what he did and how, and where he came from. And Greg Norman. Everyone has a backstory and a tale to tell. But Seve seemed special. He emerged in 1976, won in 1979 and set the sport on fire. For Europe, for Spain, for golf, his emergence was perfect, born at the right time to the right family playing the right game. Emerging is one thing, punching through and capturing imaginations another.

Seve was a kind of magician. He practised his tricks repeatedly, producing glorious surprises at the most testing of times on the greatest stages. Magicians are amazingly well-practised showmen and prestidigitators. The hands of Ballesteros aligned with his mind and body to envisage some of golf's most joyous creations – the power of The Belfry and Palm Beach Gardens, the touch of Lytham, St Andrews and Augusta National, and the imagination and recovery skills exhibited on so many courses dotted around the world. But was Ballesteros really an artist? If the late Brian Sewell could say some of the contents of the Guggenheim in Bilbao were 'intellectual jokes' and that art had replaced religion, then become entertainment, the definition of art is no longer clear. Like modern sport, art has been engulfed by the flames of glamour and privilege. But Seve seemed to live, walk and breathe what he did on the golf course, his game vitalised by his entire sense of self. On the beaches and golf course of Pedreña he'd literally trained his mind and body, from his head right down to the soles of his feet to understand how a ball was lying, how a shot felt, what it would look like exploding from the clubface. He created shots full of daring and vision that challenged our understanding of the game and how it could be played.

Art critic Andrew Graham-Dixon saw that Goya 'lit the fuse of modern art'. Seve lit the fuse of European golf. Robert Hughes saw Goya as 'truly up against the irrational', and Seve flew in the face of golfing convention and a British belief system steeped in the glory of defeat and the stiff-upper-lipped justification of post-imperial second-bestness. Better to lose than to win wearing a pair of unpolished shoes. Picasso saw the portrait painter as someone who essentially painted himself. As the opposite of an automaton, a po-faced dollar-accumulating machine or plucky runner-up, Ballesteros seemed to invest himself in every shot, the powers of concentration and the years of ingrained play fundamental to how he went about his golfing business. The golfing artist from Spain exhibited his works, surprising, delighting, challenging and disappointing by turn. His game was beautiful, flawed, exciting, enervating. His art challenged and exulted. He wasn't just a magician and golfing savant, a creator of beautiful shots and terrific drama, he was also the whole, imperfect package. He had grace and a sense of style, a feline vision of beauty and stealth.

I have long been obsessed with Seve's second shot into the 13th at Augusta National during the final round of the 1986 Masters. Somewhere in my loft I still have the BBC highlights on VHS. I used to return often to Seve's blow leading to his eagle: the set-up, swing, strike and reaction were so pleasing. I would watch it repeatedly. I've consumed a lot of Seve's play, repeatedly, during this journey. Not all of it is pretty or creative, but does not every painter create a work on canvas before obliterating it and starting again? The beauty and the art come from the flaws and demand for what feels like perfection. Does great art not require repeated examination? I had visions of some of Seve's shots being hit very hard – and certainly many were – but many of his shots were played with a swing speed I think others would not attempt. He could complete his turn and full physical execution with about 80 per cent of his power. Watch his second into the 15th at the Masters in 1986, the 4-iron that broke his spirit. Then watch his third-round iron to the 8th at St Andrews in 1984. The uncertainty of his art created a legion of followers. Those skills and the uncertainty of some of his golf gave the media, golfing public and his fans riveting storylines with twists and turns others could not deliver.

Seve tapped into our human needs for play and storytelling. In his book about how stories work, *Into the Woods*, John Yorke tells us, 'Art is born out of as well as encapsulates the continued battle between order and chaos.' Sometimes, when I think of Steve McQueen trying to jump that fence on his motorbike in *The Great Escape*, I think of Seve. Perhaps, somewhere in another universe, time or reality, McQueen leaps over the border to freedom, and Ballesteros hits a beautifully controlled 4-iron into the 15th at the 1986 Masters. I like to think, somewhere, both those realities are possible. Seve created dramatic tension. His swing could misfire or he could make an outlandish decision and be penalised for it. He was a mirror of our own golf, albeit at the extreme level of world-class competition. He reflected our own golfing fears and hopes, the worst and the best, and his inner golfing life represented the clash of opposites within himself

– the power player, the hands of a fine artist, the charming modern European, the unforgiving competitor. His complexity as a man and a golfer drove him and the drama that surrounded him. It was fascinating, infuriating, frustrating. It doesn't take a genius to create works of genius. Above all, Seve was a man, a human being with imperfections and impulses that both drove and rewarded him, while on some days they worked against him, showed his feet of clay. 'At the heart of all great art is an essential melancholy,' said Federico García Lorca.

Severiano Ballesteros played the game as we wished we could, dazzlingly flawed, married with the brilliance of his imagination. We witnessed plot lines unfold in unthinkable ways. Bobby Jones, Ben Hogan, Jack Nicklaus, Tom Watson, Nick Faldo, Tiger Woods won more majors and have better records, but no one played the type of golf Seve played. What other, single golfer could hit that chip at Birkdale in 1976, dismantle Lytham in 1979 and hole that chip at Augusta in 1983 – and that putt at St Andrews in 1984 – all the while being the sole European to undo the status quo. He cleared the stage for others to learn, follow and believe in their own talents, believe in their own golf games. To believe in the art of winning, time and again.

2007: The Masters Tournament

Pedreña – Some Seve Tricks – Ballesteros's Last Majors – 1984 Redux

THE CA-141 runs the length of the main drag in Pedreña, the local road names changing and eventually becoming, at the start of the bend downhill towards the small ferry port, Avenida Severiano Ballesteros. Not that you'd notice. Pedreña is low-key, and if it wasn't for the golf course or the ferry, one might pass it by like all the other small towns and villages on this slither of tarmac east and across the water from Santander. Along that strip, which eventually runs along the bay, past Real Golf de Pedreña and into the beach town, Somo, are dotted small bars. Not that you'd notice. Some are obviously bars, others appear like adjuncts to the shop next door, or as speakeasies some thirsty hombre may have set up in his front room. And at certain times throughout the day, men, almost always mainly men, gather to talk loudly and enthusiastically on the topic of the day.

I sat at one of the more obvious hostelries, Bar Paqui, utilitarian within, and somewhat spartan outside. Enterprisingly, the tables in the sunshine had been sourced from the Valderrama Masters, the tournament's logo at one table corner, and Estrella's at another. Inside, the walls are dotted with photos of events and crews from the local rowing team beloved of Baldomero Ballesteros and his sons, Sociedad Deportiva de Remo Pedreña.

The bar appears full of regulars, some talking passionately with the staff, while others all seem to know each other, conversing ebulliently. In my ignorance, with most of my Spanish lost through lack of use, I know not of what they speak, but bursts of laughter and the friendly chatter signal all are having a good time. I finish my coffee and sandwich, and stroll towards the port, the checking of tomorrow's ferry timings an excuse to saunter to the water's edge. I pass a mural, its middle section a long rowing boat, the oars raised, and on both sides of the image are six other oars, elevated, the outer ones with an asterisk on them, and the ones between reading SDRP from left to right, the team's name abbreviated. Further along, La Trainera restaurant has, on its gable end, an image of a rowing boat and its crew hard at work. Nearby, a very attractive, caramel-coloured villa sitting well above the road simply has two pristine white oars on its road-facing wall. It was clear socialising and rowing were among two components that bound this small community, connected to Santander by the regular ferries and near-constant views across the bay.

The day before, I had played at Real Golf de Pedreña. No wonder the Ballesteros family loved their sport. It wasn't just their proximity to the course, but the glorious vistas across to Somo and El Puntal, that long spout-shaped spit of sand, vegetation in the middle, where Seve photoshoots of his beach golf took place. Sweeping westward from El Puntal one was faced with the majesty of the Magdalena Palace, the Real Hotel, and the bay, promenade and grander homes of Santander. I was in shorts and a light golf shirt, so warm was it. It did seem quite magical. Strange one could follow a player for a lot of one's golfing childhood and, 40 years later, be standing on a spot that inspired that man who touched millions.

I knew the weather could, at times, be forbidding, with rain and wind more Scottish than typically Iberian. And, although the course at Pedreña has changed, it too seemed imbued with a sense of magic. Much of the front nine felt terraced as the golfer plays along, through or up some gentle undulations, before most of the back nine played atop a higher ridge, offering views of Somo, Santander, Seve's house and the Ria de Cubas. The bunkers held a shimmering white sand, smacking of Augusta National, and perhaps my favourite hole was the sixth, a par four of around 420 yards from the tips. A fairway bunker lay to the left, but further up the hole a diagonal of three gleaming traps framed the approach to a green itself framed by trees at the rear and three bunkers at the front and right side. Into a breeze it demanded a drive and a 7-iron, and when I went long, I found myself staring at a nasty, too-delicate chip to a very fast putting surface, a false front awaiting. It all felt like the Masters in microcosm, a fitting tribute to Europe's greatest golfer. It reminded me of the very last time I saw Severiano Ballesteros.

* * *

We'd been sitting in the stand for a while watching the players skip balls across the pond at Redbud, and Henrik Stenson, Charles Howell III and Retief Goosen had just passed through. Now we had the unexpected bonus of two past Masters champions, a special invitee – a past US Open winner – and 2006 US Amateur runner-up John Kelly in the next fourball. The young college player from Missouri was treating himself. In front of me once again was Seve Ballesteros. Twenty-three years after seeing him beat Tom Watson at St Andrews I was sitting in the small stand left of the 16th tee at Augusta National faced by my hero. He was days shy of his 50th birthday and seemed dulled by the passing of the years. But he had shone so brightly. The glow of Seve's star was now a light from another time, but still visible. Someone called out and Ballesteros turned round, arms open as if to say, what do you want? The crowd and his young playing partner were entering into the spirit, albeit Kelly had his hands on his hips, smiling, perhaps not totally sure how to react. Ben Crenshaw was laughing. Jerry Pate looked somewhat curiously at the Masters patrons cajoling Ballesteros. They were enticing the players to skip their balls across the pond, but the Spaniard wanted better. Seve proceeded to hit some shots standing on one leg, others on his knees. I had only ever read about these in magazines, back in the 1980s. It was great to witness; these shots and routine were part of the golfer, Severiano Ballesteros. From 1964 he'd fused their touch and vision into his blood, into his bones, on the beaches and grasses of Pedreña. I had seen Seve at Royal Liverpool during the Open of 2006. His son, Javier, was caddying, but the player looked like something of a lost soul. At both Augusta and Hoylake, quite possibly the brain tumour that would cause his collapse and untimely death was there, enervating.

At Augusta, nearby Rae's Creek had commingled with that ceaseless stream of John McPhee's. Kelly was from Missouri and two years before had been runner-up in the Missouri State Match Play, an event Tom Watson had won four times. Crenshaw had won the Masters twice. His first: 1984. And Jerry Pate won his US Open at Atlantic Athletic Club with one of the greatest closing irons of all time, a 5-iron over water and into two feet. In 1976. His iron might be better remembered had a young Spaniard not hit a glorious chip-and-run at Birkdale in the same year. The motifs – Seve Ballesteros; Missouri; 1976; 1984 – were right in front of us at Augusta National. Surely the Good Lord was playing tricks.

In 2010 I had the opportunity to attend a function that was to celebrate the 150th anniversary of the inaugural Open Championship in 1860. Rumour had it that Seve was the first former winner to reply, accepting his invitation. I was amazed that I was going to finally meet my hero and that, after all the memories and moments he gave me and golf, I would be compelled to hug him, like an old friend, like someone who needed all the hugs in the world, given the struggles with his health. I wanted to hug him like someone I felt I knew. Of course, I knew little of the man. I knew the golfer, a near-facsimile of the man born in 1957 as Severiano Ballesteros Sota, son of the sea, boy of the beaches, niño of nature in the fields and on the fairways of Pedreña. I never did meet him. He had to withdraw from attending the 2010 Open and the function, his doctor advising he was too weak to travel.

I am lucky to have seen Seve's art in real time, to have felt his magnetism, to have witnessed the power and the feel, to have sensed the attraction of the man and his golf game. The lavish draws, the electric cuts, the exquisite bunker shots, the glorious chips and the wonderful putts, I hold them all dear in my memory. When I need a boost, I am that boy sitting in the stand at St Andrews. Seve's putt rolls and rolls and rolls; and seems to come to rest. As the ball drops, I rise to my feet with thousands of others. We shout and we scream and we roar. Seve Ballesteros erupts with pure abandon at his birdie, his face flashes with a glorious smile as his fist pumps the air. He punches the air, salutes the crowds, hugs his caddy. The Kid from Spain is consumed with elation. So is the Kid from Scotland. Ballesteros walks off the final green, seemingly assured of victory. The minutes before were a whole career in microcosm. The heat of competition, the chance of victory, the taking of that opportunity. A moment of wonder and tension and the chaos of celebration. The power and potential of the hero was the golfer who challenged and changed golf, who created beautiful and outlandish golfing images.

* * *

The putt topples in. Seve rises on his toes and punches in celebration across his body, as if to ensure the putt remains holed; four quick, joyous punches downward follow as he starts to realise what is unfolding; he turns and punches upwards, towards the stand behind the 18th green, exulting in the sweet taste of victory; his smile is lit by a thousand Cantabrian suns, the white light of his joy a beautiful contrast to the beaming tan of his handsome features and the solid navy blue of his iconic sweater. He turns again towards the crowds down the side of the green, punching upward, driven by years of Spanish fire and a million grains of sand on the beach at Pedreña. The watching multitudes shout and celebrate with the player, crying and laughing and shaking their heads at this competitor elevated to champion in a crucial instant with the simple turn of a small white ball: that was, and is, Seve Ballesteros.

Acknowledgements

THANKS TO all who assisted; projects like these are a team effort. Russ Fothergill sent me his precious VHS tape of all the 1984 BBC highlights, a real fillip for my project. A bit more randomly, he also sent me the book of Jack Nicklaus's greatest shots. Thanks to Raymond Russell for putting me in touch with Nick DePaul via Edinburgh Jimmy, the late European Tour caddy. Thanks to Hannah Fleming and Kieran George at the World Golf Museum for their time. SJR for his hospitality, allowing me to spend days pouring over many US books I wouldn't have considered. To Ross Cowan, thank you for Ronnie's 1970s magazines and John Jacob's *Practical Golf*. Two Spaniards – Cantabrian and Basque – Mario Ruiz-Capillas Ramos and Javier Lopez Uriarte discussed with me northern Spain and life there.

Many provided gentle encouragement and help with my scribbling. A lot of thanks to Dougie Brown for his writing insight and thoughts. To this manuscript's genesis, Douglas McCreath provided encouragement from the sidelines, and I must thank some personal reviewers: having people like Dougie, along with Iain Robertson, Andrew Lochhead, Craig Harrow and Graham Fox spend time and effort in reading one's words is hard to repay. I should also thank Foxy for helping out with a few days of old newspaper research. Thanks also to Edward Thomson for his time reading, as well as our discussions on

Seve's swing. Calum Callan's forthright views keep me in check. Thanks to Ewan Thomson for the serendipitous gift of Hughes's *The Spectacle of Skill.* To Tim Newton for guidance on Spanish usage, *gracias.*

Many thanks to Jane Camillin at Pitch for belief in this book and to their entire team for their diligence and guidance pulling it all together – Graham, Duncan, Dean, Andrea and others behind the scenes.

I will have missed others who encouraged me, and I apologise for any omissions. Like omissions, any mistakes herein are wholly mine.

During proofreading my dad, Bob, passed away. He'll be missed but always remembered and it's fitting he can live on in these pages, alongside so many greats who played a game he loved. Robert Reid, 1938–2024.

Bibliography & Sources

As some of the books below appear in different editions in different countries, the publishers are not listed.

A word on the TV footage for 1984 at St Andrews that I reference: it's the original TV highlights from the four days of the Open, and the commentary and camera angles do not always align with the Official Film (in fact, some angles materially differ).

Alliss, P., *Peter Alliss' Golf Heroes*, 2007

Alliss, P., *Supreme Champions of Golf*, 1986

Alliss, P., *The Open: The British Open Golf Championship since the War*, 1984

Ballesteros, S., *Seve: The Autobiography*, 2008

Ballesteros, S., Andrisani, J., *Natural Golf*, 1989

Ballesteros, S., Green, R., *Trouble-Shooting*, 1996

Beckett, A., *When the Lights Went Out: Britain in the Seventies*, 2010

Berger, J., *Ways of Seeing*, 2008

Berger, J., Dyer, G., *The Selected Essays of John Berger*, 2001

Boswell, T., *Strokes of Genius*, 1989

Bowden, K., Aultman, D., *The Methods of Golf's Masters: How They Played – and What You Can Learn from Them*, 2000

Brenan, G., *The Face of Spain*, 1987

Burns, J., *La Roja: A Journey Through Spanish Football*, 2012
Burns, J., *Spain: A Literary Companion*, 1995
Campbell, M., *The Scottish Golf Book*, 1999
Cannon, D., *Severiano Ballesteros*, 1986
Cercas, J., *Soldiers of Salamis*, 2004
Cercas, J., *The Anatomy of a Moment*, 2012
Chieger, B., Sullivan, P., *The Book of Golf Quotations*, 1987
Conan Doyle, A., *The Great Boer War*, 1900
Cook, K., *Tommy's Honor*, 2008
Corcoran, M., *Duel in the Sun: Tom Watson and Jack Nicklaus in the Battle of Turnberry*, 2002
Crawford, M.B., *Shop Class as Soulcraft: An Inquiry into the Value of Work*, 2010
Crawford, M.B., *Why We Drive*, 2020
Dabell, N., *How We Won the Ryder Cup: The Caddies' Stories*, 2011
Dabell, N., *Winning The Open: The Caddies' Stories*, 2011
Danto, A.C., *The Transfiguration of the Commonplace*, 1981
Danto, A.C., *What Art Is*, 2014
Davis, M., *Ben Hogan: The Man Behind the Mystique*, 2002
Davis, M., Alexander, J., *The Hogan Mystique*, 1994
Deford, F., *Over Time: My Life as a Sportswriter*, 2013
Doak, T., *The Anatomy of a Golf Course: The Art of Golf Architecture*, 2013
Doak, T., *Tom Doak's Little Red Book of Golf Architecture*, 2017
Doust, D., *Seve: The Young Champion*, 1982
Dyer, G., *The Ongoing Moment: A Book About Photographs*, 2012
Dyer, G., *White Sands: Experiences from the Outside World*, 2016
Eco, U., *On Beauty: A History of a Western Idea*, 2010

Evans, A., *From Old Tom to the Tiger: The Golf Majors, 1860-2010: The First 150 Years*, 2012

Facaros, D., Pauls, M., *Cadogan Guides Northern Spain*, 2012

Field, B., *Arnie, Seve, and a Fleck of Golf History: Heroes, Underdogs, Courses, and Championships*, 2014

Gallico, P., *Farewell to Sport*, 1988

Gombrich, E.H., *The Story of Art*, 2007

Green, R., *Seve: Golf's Flawed Genius*, 2008

Halberstam, D., *Everything They Had: Sports Writing from David Halberstam*, 2008

Hall, M., Allen, D., *Houdini Shots: The Ultimate Short-Game Survival Guide*, 2013

Heat-Moon, W. Least, *Blue Highways*, 1982

Heat-Moon, W. Least, *Here, There, Elsewhere: Stories from the Road*, 2013

Heat-Moon, W. Least, *Prairy Erth: (A Deep Map)*, 1999

Heat-Moon, W. Least, *Roads to Quoz: An American Mosey*, 2008

Hemingway, E., *Death in the Afternoon*, 2000

Hooper, J., *The New Spaniards*, 2006

Huber, J., *Four Days in July: Tom Watson, the 2009 Open Championship, and a Tournament for the Ages*, 2011

Hughes, R., *The Spectacle of Skill: Selected Writings of Robert Hughes*, 2016

Hughes, R., *Things I Didn't Know*, 2007

Hutchinson, H.G, *Golf (Badminton Library)*, 1987

Illustrated, S. (ed.), *Golf: Four Decades of Sports Illustrated's Finest Writing on the Game of Golf*, 1996

Innes, J. & G., *How To Play the Old Course (St Andrews and All About It)*, 1975

Jacobs, J., Bowden, K., *Practical Golf*, 1972

Jarman, C.M., *The Ryder Cup: The Definitive History of Playing Golf for Pride and Country*, 1999
Jimenez, J.R., Maurer, C., *The Complete Perfectionist: A Poetics of Work*, 2012
Johnson, S., *The Official U.S. Open Almanac*, 1995
Joy, D., Macfarlane Lowe, I., *St Andrews & The Open Championship: The Official History*, 1999
Kagge, E., *Silence: In the Age of Noise*, 2018
Kemp, M., *Art in History, 600BC to 2000AD: Ideas in Profile*, 2015
Kimmelman, M., *The Accidental Masterpiece: On the Art of Life and Vice Versa*, 2006
Kurlansky, M., *The Basque History of the World*, 2011
Llamazares, J., *Wolf Moon*, 2017
Llamazares, J., *Yellow Rain*, 2006
Lorca, F.G., Maurer, C., *In Search of Duende*, 2010
Macdonald, C.B., *Methods of Early Golf Architecture: The Selected Writings of C.B. Macdonald, George C. Thomas, Robert Hunter: Volume 2*, 2013
MacKenzie, A., *Methods of Early Golf Architecture: The Selected Writings of Alister MacKenzie, H.S. Colt, and A.W. Tillinghast: Volume 1*, 2013
Macpherson, Scott, *St Andrews: The Evolution of the Old Course*, 2007
Magris, C., *Journeying*, 2018
McCord, R., *The Quotable Golfer*, 2000
McCormack, M., *The World of Professional Golf 1977*, 1977
McCormack, M., *The World of Professional Golf 1980*, 1980
McCormack, M., *The World of Professional Golf 1981*, 1981
McCormack, M., *The World of Professional Golf 1983*, 1983
McCormack, M., *The World of Professional Golf 1984*, 1984
McCormack, M., *The World of Professional Golf 1985*, 1985

McPhee, J., *Draft No.4*, 2018
McPhee, J., *Levels of the Game*, 2014
McPhee, J., *The Patch*, 2018
Miller, J., *I Call the Shots*, 2004
Moriarity, J., *Playing Through: Modern Golf's Most Iconic Players and Moments*, 2016
Morris, J., *Spain*, 2008
Murphy, M., *Golf in the Kingdom*, 1994
Nelson, B., *How I Played the Game: An Autobiography*, 2006
Nicklaus, J., Bowden, K., *My Most Memorable Shots in the Majors*, 1988
Norwood, B., *Open Championship 1984*, 1984
Noteboom, C., *Roads to Santiago: Detours and Riddles in the Land and History of Spain*, 2014
Olman, M.W., Olman, J.M., *St Andrews and Golf*, 1995
Palmer, A., *A Golfer's Life*, 1999
Posnanski, J., *The Secret of Golf: The Story of Tom Watson and Jack Nicklaus*, 2015
Preston, P., *The Spanish Holocaust: Inquisition and Extermination in Twentieth-Century Spain*, 2013
Pritchett, V.S., *The Spanish Temper*, 2012
Pugh, P., Lord, H., *The Ryder Cup: A History of Golf's Greatest Match*, 2012
Raban, J., *The Oxford Book of the Sea*, 2001
Schaap, D., *Massacre at Winged Foot: The U.S. Open minute-by-minute*, 1974
Scruton, R., *Beauty: A Very Short Introduction*, 2011
Shaw, J., *Prestwick Golf Club: A History and Some Records*, 1938
Sheldon, P., Doust, D., *Seve*, 1986
Simpson, W., *The Art of Golf*, 1887
Solomon, D., *Jackson Pollock: A Biography*, 2001

Sommers, R., *Golf Anecdotes: From the Links of Scotland to Tiger Woods*, 2004
Sommers, R., *The US Open: Golf's Ultimate Challenge*, 1996
Spencer, R., *The Sporting News Selects 50 Greatest Golfers: A Celebration of the All-time Best*, 2002
Sommers, R., Brown, C., *Great Shots*, 1989
St John, L., *Seve: The Biography*, 1994
Tait, A., *Seve: A Biography of Severiano Ballesteros*, 2005
Tremlett, G., *Ghosts of Spain: Travels Through a Country's Hidden Past*, 2012
Trevino, L., Blair, S., *Super Mex*, 1983
Walker, T., *In Spain*, 1989
Watson, T., *Back to Basics*, 1994
Watson, T., Seitz, N., *Getting Up and Down: How to Save Strokes from Forty Yards*, 1984
Wheen, F., *How Mumbo-Jumbo Conquered the World: A Short History of Modern Delusions*, 2004
Wheen, F., *Strange Days Indeed: The 1970s – The Golden Days of Paranoia*, 2010
Wilson, M., Bowden, K., *The Best of Henry Longhurst*, 1979
Wind, H.W., *America's Gift to Golf: Herbert Warren Wind on the Masters*, 2011
Wind, H.W., *Following Through: Herbert Warren Wind on Golf*, 1995
Wind, H.W., *The Complete Golfer*, 1954
Wright, I., Connor, J., *Summers with Seve: My Life As Severiano Ballesteros' Caddie*, 1991

Print Media

The Herald, *The Daily Record*, *The Daily Express*, *The Times*, *The Daily Mail*, *The Telegraph*, *The Sun*, *The New York Times*, *The Washington Post*, *ABC Madrid*, *Le Monde*, *The Pittsburgh Post-Gazette*, *The Age*, *The Sunday Times*, *The Sunday Telegraph*, *Sports Illustrated*, *Golf Magazine*, *Golf Monthly*, *Golf World*, *Golf Illustrated*, *Golf Digest*, *Par Golf*, *The New Yorker*, *The Open Programme* (1978, 1980, 1982, 1983, 1984, 1985), *Stanford Magazine*, *The Associated Press*, *The Scotsman*, *The Courier*

Television, Film, Radio and Podcasts

McKellar Gold Podcast, *The Shotgun Start* podcast, *The Film Programme* (BBC Radio 4), *Spain: Living Abroad* (BBC Radio 3), *LA Review of Books* podcast, *Masters Tournament footage* (The Masters), *US Open footage* (ABC Television), *US Open footage* (USGA), *The Open Championship Official Films* (R&A), *Open Championship highlights 1984* (BBC), *Ryder Cup footage* (Ryder Cup), *Seve: The Definitive Story of a Golfing Genius* (Lace), *Seve – A Study of the Ballesteros Legend* (ITN), *Desert Island Discs* (BBC), *Winning with Seve: Nick de Paul interview* (Golfing World), *Goya: Crazy Like a Genius* (Oxford Film & Television), *Art of Spain: The Mystical North* (BBC), *Seve: The Legend* (BBC), *The Great Escape* (The Mirisch Company), *The Naked Pilgrim: The Road to Santiago* (Wag Entertainment), *The Sporting Greats Collection: Legends of Golf – Player, Nicklaus and Ballesteros* (Pitch)